THE SANE SOCIETY

P. 79 An Interesting approach to
Folk Psychology : the concept of
"social character"

BOOKS BY ERICH FROMM

Escape from Freedom

Man for Himself: An Inquiry into the Psychology of Ethics

Psychoanalysis and Religion

The Forgotten Language: An Introduction to
the Understanding of Dreams, Fairy Tales, and Myths

The Sane Society

The Art of Loving

Sigmund Freud's Mission

Zen Buddhism and Psychoanalysis
(with D. T. Suzuki and R. de Martino)

Marx's Concept of Man

The Dogma of Christ and Other Essays on Religion,
Psychology, and Culture

The Heart of Man

Beyond the Chains of Illusion

May Man Prevail

The Nature of Man
(with Ramon Xirau)

The Revolution of Hope

Humanist Socialism (ed.)

You Shall Be as Gods: A Radical Interpretation of the
Old Testament and Its Tradition

Social Character in a Mexican Village (with Michael Maccoby)

The Crisis of Psychoanalysis: Essays on Freud, Marx,
and Social Psychology

The Anatomy of Human Destructiveness

THE SANE
SOCIETY

ERICH
FROMM

AN OWL BOOK

HENRY HOLT AND COMPANY
NEW YORK

Library of Congress Cataloging-in-Publication Data
Fromm, Erich, 1900–
    The sane society / Erich Fromm. — 1st Owl book ed.
        p.   cm.
    "An Owl book."
    Reprint. Originally published: New York : Rinehart, 1955.
    ISBN 0-8050-1402-0
    1. Liberty. 2. Authoritarianism. 3. Capitalism. 4. Socialism.
5. Psychoanalysis—Social aspects. I. Title.
HM271.F75   1990
320.5'3—dc20   90-34662
                                                         CIP

Henry Holt books are available at special discounts
for bulk purchases for sales promotions, premiums,
fund-raising, or educational use. Special editions
or book excerpts can also be created to specification.

For details contact:
Special Sales Director
Henry Holt and Company, Inc.
115 West 18th Street
New York, New York 10011

First published in hardcover by Holt, Rinehart and Winston in 1955.

First Owl Book Edition—1990

Printed in the United States of America
Recognizing the importance of preserving
the written word, Henry Holt and Company, Inc.,
by policy, prints all of its first editions
on acid-free paper. ∞

1   3   5   7   9   10   8   6   4   2

ACKNOWLEDGMENTS

Grateful acknowledgment is made to the following publishers who have so generously granted permission for the use of excerpts from their publications:

FORTUNE, New York, N.Y., for permission to reprint selections from "The Transients," by William H. Whyte, Jr., which appeared in the May, June, July and August 1953 issues of *Fortune*, Copyright 1953 by Time Inc.

HARPER & BROTHERS, New York, N.Y., for permission to reprint selections from *Capitalism, Socialism and Democracy* by Joseph A. Schumpeter, Copyright, 1942, by Joseph A. Schumpeter, and from *All Things Common* by Claire Huchet Bishop, Copyright, 1950, by Harper & Brothers.

HARPER & BROTHERS, New York, N.Y. and CHATTO & WINDUS LTD., London, England, for permission to reprint Aldous Huxley's Introduction to *Brave New World*, Copyright, 1946, by Aldous Huxley.

THE LINCOLN ELECTRIC COMPANY, Cleveland, Ohio, for permission to reprint selections from *Incentive Management* by J. F. Lincoln.

THE MACMILLAN COMPANY, New York, N.Y. and A. & C. BLACK LTD., London, England, for permission to reprint selections from *The Philosophy of Civilization* by Albert Schweitzer.

Sane Society: Basic Concepts
of Humanistic
Psychoanalysis

FOREWORD

This book is a continuation of *Escape from Freedom*, written over fifteen years ago. In *Escape from Freedom* I tried to show that the totalitarian movements appealed to a deep-seated craving to escape from the freedom man had achieved in the modern world; that modern man, free *from* medieval ties, was not free *to* build a meaningful life based on reason and love, hence sought new security in submission to a leader, race or state.

In *The Sane Society* I try to show that life in twentieth-century Democracy constitutes in many ways another escape from freedom, and the analysis of this particular escape, centered around the concept of alienation, constitutes a good part of this book.

In another way too, is *The Sane Society* a continuation of *Escape from Freedom*, and to some extent, of *Man for Himself*. In both books I have treated specific psychological mechanism, as far as it seemed pertinent to the main topic. In *Escape from Freedom*, I dealt mainly with the problem of the authoritarian character (sadism, masochism, etc.). In *Man for Himself* I developed the idea of various character orientations, substituting for the Freudian scheme of libido development one of the evolution of character in interpersonal terms. In *The Sane Society* I have tried to develop more systematically the basic concepts of what I have called here "humanistic psychoanalysis." Quite naturally, older ideas expressed earlier could not be omitted; but I tried to treat them more briefly and to give more space to those aspects which are the result of my observations and thoughts in the last years.

I hope the reader of my previous books will have no difficulty in seeing the continuity of thought, as well as some changes, leading to the main thesis of humanistic psychoanalysis: that the basic passions of man are not rooted in his instinctive needs, but in the specific conditions of human existence, in the need to find a new relatedness to man and nature after having lost the primary relatedness of the pre-human stage. While in this respect my ideas differ essentially from those of Freud, they are nevertheless based on his fundamental findings, carried further under the influence of ideas and experiences of a generation standing on Freud's shoulders. But just because of the implicit and explicit criticism of Freud contained in these pages, I want to state very clearly that I see great dangers in the development of certain trends in psychoanalysis which, while criticizing certain errors in Freud's system, relinquish with the errors also the most valuable parts of Freud's teaching: his scientific method, his evolutionary concept, his concept of the unconscious as a truly irrational force rather than as a sum total of erroneous ideas. Furthermore, there is danger that psychoanalysis loses another fundamental trait of Freudian thinking, the courage to defy common sense and public opinion.

Eventually, *The Sane Society* proceeds from the purely critical analysis presented in *Escape from Freedom*, to concrete suggestions for the functioning of a Sane Society. The main point in this last part of the book is not so much the belief that each one of the recommended measures is necessarily "right," but that progress can only occur when changes are made simultaneously in the economic, socio-political and cultural spheres; that any progress restricted to *one* sphere is destructive to progress in *all* spheres.

I am deeply indebted to a number of friends who have been helpful to me by reading the manuscript and expressing constructive suggestions and criticism. Specifically I want to mention only one of them, George Fuchs, who died during the time I was working on this book. Originally we had planned to write the book together, but due to his prolonged illness, this plan could not be carried out. His help, however, was considerable. We had lengthy discussions, and he wrote me many letters and memos, especially with regard to problems of socialist theory, which helped to clarify and sometimes to revise my own ideas. I have mentioned his name in the text a few times, but my obligation to him goes much further than these specific references might indicate.

I want to express my thanks to Dr. G. R. Hargreaves, Chief of the Mental Health Section of the World Health Organization, for his help in securing the data on alcoholism, suicide and homicide.

E. F.

Normative Humanism   P14 +15

① -different than Sociological Relativism
② - an attempt to find a satisfactory
    answer to problem of human Existence

goal
③ - The Healthy mature person should
    attain
        a) freedom
        b) spontaneity
        c) a genuine (real?) expression of SELF

If Person fails to attain ③ because

of I) Family or Personal } → Neurosis
        Reasons

    II) Socially patterned reasons
            ↳ The Culture
                is defective.

TABLE OF CONTENTS

xi

TABLE OF CONTENTS *(cont'd)*

TABLE OF CONTENTS *(cont'd)*

And he shall judge among many people, and rebuke strong nations afar off; and they shall beat their swords into plowshares, and their spears into pruninghooks: nation shall not lift up a sword against nation, neither shall they learn war any more.

But they shall sit every man under his vine and under his fig tree; and none shall make them afraid: for the mouth of the Lord of hosts hath spoken it.

MICAH

There exists no more difficult art than living. For other arts and sciences, numerous teachers are to be found everywhere. Even young people believe that they have acquired these in such a way, that they can teach them to others: throughout the whole of life, one must continue to learn to live and, what will amaze you even more, throughout life one must learn to die.

SENECA

This world and yonder world are incessantly giving birth: every cause is a mother, its effect the child.

When the effect is born, it too becomes a cause and gives birth to wondrous effects.

These causes are generation on generation, but it needs a very well lighted eye to see the links in their chain.

RUMI

Things are in the saddle and ride mankind.

EMERSON

The human race had the wisdom to create science and art; why should it not be capable to create a world of justice, brotherliness and peace? The human race has produced Plato, Homer, Shakespeare, and Hugo, Michelangelo and Beethoven, Pascal and Newton, all these human heroes whose genius is only the contact with the fundamental truths, with the innermost essence of the universe. Why then should the same race not produce those leaders capable of leading it to those forms of communal life which are closest to the lives and the harmony of the universe?

LEON BLUM

THE SANE SOCIETY

ARE WE SANE?

Nothing is more common than the idea that we, the people living in the Western world of the twentieth century, are eminently sane. Even the fact that a great number of individuals in our midst suffer from more or less severe forms of mental illness produces little doubt with respect to the general standard of our mental health. We are sure that by introducing better methods of mental hygiene we shall improve *still further* the state of our mental health, and as far as individual mental disturbances are concerned, we look at them as strictly individual incidents, perhaps with some amazement that so many of these incidents should occur in a culture which is supposedly so sane.

Can we be so sure that we are not deceiving ourselves? Many an inmate of an insane asylum is convinced that everybody else is crazy, except himself. Many a severe neurotic believes that his compulsive rituals or his hysterical outbursts are normal reactions to somewhat abnormal circumstances. What about ourselves?

Let us, in good psychiatric fashion, look at the facts. In the last one hundred years we, in the Western world, have created a greater material wealth than any other society in the history

3

of the human race. Yet we have managed to kill off millions of our population in an arrangement which we call "war." Aside from smaller wars, we had larger ones in 1870, 1914 and 1939. During these wars, every participant firmly believed that he was fighting in his self-defense, for his honor, or that he was backed up by God. The groups with whom one is at war are, often from one day to the next, looked upon as cruel, irrational fiends, whom one must defeat to save the world from evil. But a few years after the mutual slaughter is over, the enemies of yesterday are our friends, the friends of yesterday our enemies, and again in full seriousness we begin to paint them with appropriate colors of black and white. At this moment, in the year 1955, we are prepared for a mass slaughter which would, if it came to pass, surpass any slaughter the human race has arranged so far. One of the greatest discoveries in the field of natural science is prepared for this purpose. Everybody is looking with a mixture of confidence and apprehension to the "statesmen" of the various peoples, ready to heap all praise on them if they "succeed in avoiding a war," and ignoring the fact that it is only these very statesmen who ever cause a war, usually not even through their bad intentions, but by their unreasonable mismanagement of the affairs entrusted to them.

In these outbursts of destructiveness and paranoid suspicion, however, we are not behaving differently from what the civilized part of mankind has done in the last three thousand years of history. According to Victor Cherbulliez, from 1500 B.C. to 1860 A.D. no less than about eight thousand peace treaties were signed, each one supposed to secure permanent peace, and each one lasting on an average two years! [1]

[1] From H. B. Stevens, *The Recovery of Culture*, Harper and Brothers, New York, 1949, p. 221.

Our direction of economic affairs is scarcely more encouraging. We live in an economic system in which a particularly good crop is often an economic disaster, and we restrict some of our agricultural productivity in order to "stabilize the market," although there are millions of people who do not have the very things we restrict, and who need them badly. Right now our economic system is functioning very well, because, among other reasons, we spend billions of dollars per year to produce armaments. Economists look with some apprehension to the time when we stop producing armaments, and the idea that the state should produce houses and other useful and needed things instead of weapons, easily provokes accusations of endangering freedom and individual initiative.

We have a literacy above 90 per cent of the population. We have radio, television, movies, a newspaper a day for everybody. But instead of giving us the best of past and present literature and music, these media of communication, supplemented by advertising, fill the minds of men with the cheapest trash, lacking in any sense of reality, with sadistic phantasies which a halfway cultured person would be embarrassed to entertain even once in a while. But while the mind of everybody, young and old, is thus poisoned, we go on blissfully to see to it that no "immorality" occurs on the screen. Any suggestion that the government should finance the production of movies and radio programs which would enlighten and improve the minds of our people would be met again with indignation and accusations in the name of freedom and idealism.

We have reduced the average working hours to about half what they were one hundred years ago. We today have more free time available than our forefathers dared to dream of. But what has happened? We do not know how to use the newly gained free

5

time; we try to kill the time we have saved, and are glad when another day is over.

Why should I continue with a picture which is known to everybody? Certainly, if an individual acted in this fashion, serious doubts would be raised as to his sanity; should he, however, claim that there is nothing wrong, and that he is acting perfectly reasonably, then the diagnosis would not even be doubtful any more.

Yet many psychiatrists and psychologists refuse to entertain the idea that society as a whole may be lacking in sanity. They hold that the problem of mental health in a society is only that of the number of "unadjusted" individuals, and not that of a possible unadjustment of the culture itself. This book deals with the latter problem; not with individual pathology, but with the *pathology of normalcy,* particularly with the pathology of contemporary Western society. But before entering into the intricate discussion of the concept of social pathology, let us look at some data, revealing and suggestive in themselves, which make reference to the incidence of *individual* pathology in Western culture.

What is the incidence of mental illness in the various countries of the Western world? It is a most amazing fact that there are no data which answer this question. While there are exact comparative statistical data on material resources, employment, birth and death rates, there is no adequate information about mental illness. At the most we have some exact data for a number of countries, like the United States and Sweden, but they only refer to admissions of patients to mental institutions, and they are not helpful in making estimates of comparative frequency of mental illness. These figures tell us just as much about improved psychiatric care and institutional facilities as they tell us about increase in incidence of mental illness.[1] The fact that more than half of all hospital beds in the United States are used for mental patients on whom we spend an annual sum of over a billion dollars may not be an indication of any increase in mental illness, but only of an increasing care. Some other figures, however, are more indicative of the occurrence of the more severe mental disturbances. If 17.7 per cent of all rejections of draftees in the last war were for reasons of mental illness, this fact certainly bespeaks a high degree of mental disturbance, even if we have no comparative figures referring to the past, or to other countries.

The only comparative data which can give us a rough indication of mental health, are those for suicide, homicide and alcoholism. No doubt the problem of suicide is a most complex one, and no single factor can be assumed to be *the* cause. But even without entering at this point into a discussion of suicide, I consider it a safe assumption that a high suicide rate in a given population is expressive of a lack of mental stability and mental health. That it is not a consequence of material poverty is clearly evidenced by all figures. The poorest countries have the lowest incidence of suicide, and the increasing material prosperity in Europe was accompanied by an increasing number of suicides.[2] As to alcoholism, there is no doubt that it, too, is a symptom of mental and emotional instability.

The motives for homicide are probably less indicative of pathology than those for suicide. However, though countries with a high homicide rate show a low suicide rate, their combined rates bring us to an interesting conclusion. If we classify both homicide and suicide as "destructive acts," our tables demonstrate that

[1] cf. H. Goldhamer and A. Marshall, *Psychosis and Civilization*, Free Press, Glencoe, 1953.

[2] cf. Maurice Halbwachs, *Les Causes du Suicide*, Félix Alcan, Paris, 1930, pp. 109 and 112.

their combined rate is not constant, but fluctuating between the extremes of 35.76 and 4.24. This contradicts Freud's assumption of the comparative constancy of destructiveness which underlies his theory of the death instinct. It disproves the implication that destructiveness maintains an invariable rate, differing only in directions toward the self or the outside world.

The following tables show the incidence of suicide, homicide and alcoholism for some of the most important European and North American countries.

TABLE I.[1]

(Per 100,000 of adult population)

COUNTRY	SUICIDE	HOMICIDE
Denmark	35.09	0.67
Switzerland	33.72	1.42
Finland	23.35	6.45
Sweden	19.74	1.01
United States	15.52	8.50
France	14.83	1.53
Portugal	14.24	2.79
England and Wales	13.43	0.63
Australia	13.03	1.57
Canada	11.40	1.67
Scotland	8.06	0.52
Norway	7.84	0.38
Spain	7.71	2.88
Italy	7.67	7.38
Northern Ireland	4.82	0.13
Ireland (Republic)	3.70	0.54

[1] The information in the first and second tables is derived from 1. World Health Organization (1951) *Annual epidemiological and vital statistics, 1939–46. Part I. Vital statistics and causes of death*, Geneva, pp. 38–71, (the figures from this source have been converted for greater accuracy from total to adult population), and 2. World Health Organization, (1952) *Epidem. vital Statist. Rep.* 5, 377. That of the third table, from the Report on the First Session of the Alcoholism Subcommittee, of the Expert Committee on Mental Health, World Health Organization, Geneva, 1951.

TABLE II.

COUNTRY	DESTRUCTIVE ACTS Homicide and Suicide combined
Denmark	35.76
Switzerland	35.14
Finland	29.80
United States	24.02
Sweden	20.75
Portugal	17.03
France	16.36
Italy	15.05
Australia	14.60
England and Wales	14.06
Canada	13.07
Spain	10.59
Scotland	8.58
Norway	8.22
Northern Ireland	4.95
Ireland (Republic)	4.24

(Both the above tables show the figures for 1946)

TABLE III.

COUNTRY	ESTIMATED NUMBER OF ALCOHOLICS With or without complications (Per 100,000 of adult population)
United States	3,952 (1948)
France	2,850 (1945)
Sweden	2,580 (1946)
Switzerland	2,385 (1947)
Denmark	1,950 (1948)
Norway	1,560 (1947)
Finland	1,430 (1947)
Australia	1,340 (1947)
England and Wales	1,100 (1948)
Italy	500 (1942)

9

A quick glance at these tables shows a remarkable phenomenon: Denmark, Switzerland, Finland, Sweden and the United States are the countries with the highest suicide rate, and the highest combined suicide and homicide rate, while Spain, Italy, Northern Ireland and the Republic of Ireland are those with the lowest suicide and homicide rate. The figures for alcoholism show that the same countries—the United States, Switzerland, Sweden and Denmark—which have the highest suicide rate, have also the highest alcoholism rate, with the main difference that the United States are leading in this group, and that France has the second place, instead of the sixth place it has with regard to suicide.

These figures are startling and challenging indeed. Even if we should doubt whether the high frequency of suicide alone indicates a lack of mental health in a population, the fact that suicide and alcoholism figures largely coincide, seems to make it plain that we deal here with symptoms of mental unbalance.

We find then that the countries in Europe which are among the most democratic, peaceful and prosperous ones, and the United States, the most prosperous country in the world, show the most severe symptoms of mental disturbance. The aim of the whole socio-economic development of the Western world is that of the materially comfortable life, relatively equal distribution of wealth, stable democracy and peace, and the very countries which have come closest to this aim show the most severe signs of mental unbalance! It is true that these figures in themselves do not *prove* anything, but at least they are startling. Even before we enter into a more thorough discussion of the whole problem, these data raise a question as to whether there is not something fundamentally wrong with our way of life and with the aims toward which we are striving.

Could it be that the middle-class life of prosperity, while satisfying our material needs leaves us with a feeling of intense boredom, and that suicide and alcoholism are pathological ways of escape from this boredom? Could it be that these figures are a drastic illustration for the truth of the statement that "man lives not by bread alone," and that they show that modern civilization fails to satisfy profound needs in man? If so, what are these needs?

The following chapters are an attempt to answer this question, and to arrive at a critical evaluation of the effect contemporary Western culture has on the mental health and sanity of the people living under our system. However, before we enter into the specific discussion of these questions, it seems that we should take up the general problem of the pathology of normalcy, which is the premise underlying the whole trend of thought expressed in this book.

2

CAN A SOCIETY BE SICK?—
THE PATHOLOGY OF NORMALCY [1]

To speak of a whole society as lacking in mental health implies a controversial assumption contrary to the position of *sociological relativism* held by most social scientists today. They postulate that each society is normal inasmuch as it functions, and that pathology can be defined only in terms of the individual's lack of adjustment to the ways of life in his society.

To speak of a "sane society" implies a premise different from sociological relativism. It makes sense only if we assume that there can be a society which is *not* sane, and this assumption, in turn, implies that there are universal criteria for mental health which are valid for the human race as such, and according to which the state of health of each society can be judged. This position of *normative humanism* is based on a few fundamental premises.

The species "man," can be defined not only in anatomical and physiological terms; its members share basic *psychic* qualities, the laws which govern their mental and emotional functioning, and the aims for a satisfactory solution of the problem of human

---

[1] In this chapter I have drawn on my paper, "Individual and Social Origins of Neurosis," *Am. Soc. Rev.* IX, 4, 1944, p. 380 ff.

His pt. of view: Normative Humanism

existence. It is true that our knowledge of man is still so incomplete that we cannot yet give a satisfactory definition of man in a psychological sense. It is the task of the "science of man" to arrive eventually at a correct description of what deserves to be called human nature. What has often been called "human nature" is but one of its many manifestations—and often a pathological one—and the function of such mistaken definition usually has been to defend a particular type of society as being the necessary outcome of man's mental constitution.

Against such reactionary use of the concept of human nature, the Liberals, since the eighteenth century, have stressed the malleability of human nature and the decisive influence of environmental factors. True and important as such emphasis is, it has led many social scientists to an assumption that man's mental constitution is a blank piece of paper, on which society and culture write their text, and which has no intrinsic quality of its own. This assumption is just as untenable and just as destructive of social progress as the opposite view was. The real problem is to infer the *core* common to the whole human race from the innumerable *manifestations* of human nature, the normal as well as the pathological ones, as we can observe them in different individuals and cultures. The task is furthermore to recognize the laws inherent in human nature and the inherent goals for its development and unfolding.

This concept of human nature is different from the way the term "human nature" is used conventionally. Just as man transforms the world around him, so he transforms himself in the process of history. He is his own creation, as it were. But just as he can only transform and modify the natural materials around him according to their nature, so he can only transform and modify himself according to his own nature. What man *does* in the process of history is to develop this potential, and to transform it according to its own possibilities. The point of view taken here is neither a "biological" nor a "sociological" one if that would mean separating these two aspects from each other. It is rather one transcending such dichotomy by the assumption that the main passions and drives in man result from the *total existence* of man, that they are definite and ascertainable, some of them conducive to health and happiness, others to sickness and unhappiness. Any given social order does not *create* these fundamental strivings but it determines which of the limited number of potential passions are to become manifest or dominant. Man as he appears in any given culture is always a manifestation of human nature, a manifestation, however, which in its specific outcome is determined by the social arrangements under which he lives. Just as the infant is born with all human potentialities which are to develop under favorable social and cultural conditions, so the human race, in the process of history, develops into what it potentially is.

The approach of *normative humanism* is based on the assumption that, as in any other problem, there are right and wrong, satisfactory and unsatisfactory solutions to the problem of human existence. Mental health is achieved if man develops into full maturity according to the characteristics and laws of human nature. Mental illness consists in the failure of such development. From this premise the criterion of mental health is not one of individual adjustment to a given social order, but a universal one, valid for all men, of giving a satisfactory answer to the problem of human existence.

What is so deceptive about the state of mind of the members of a society is the "consensual validation" of their concepts. It is naïvely assumed that the fact that the majority of people share certain ideas or feelings proves the validity of these ideas and feelings. Nothing is further from the truth. Consensual validation as such has no bearing whatsoever on reason or mental health. Just as there is a *"folie à deux"* there is a *"folie à millions."* The fact that millions of people share the same vices does not make these vices virtues, the fact that they share so many errors does not make the errors to be truths, and the fact that millions of people share the same forms of mental pathology does not make these people sane.

There is, however, an important difference between individual and social mental illness, which suggests a differentiation between two concepts: that of *defect*, and that of *neurosis*. If a person fails to attain freedom, spontaneity, a genuine expression of self, he may be considered to have a severe defect, provided we assume that freedom and spontaneity are the objective goals to be attained by every human being. If such a goal is not attained by the majority of members of any given society, we deal with the phenomenon of *socially patterned* defect. The individual shares it with many others; he is not aware of it as a defect, and his security is not threatened by the experience of being different, of being an outcast, as it were. What he may have lost in richness and in a genuine feeling of happiness, is made up by the security of fitting in with the rest of mankind—*as he knows them.* As a matter of fact, his very defect may have been raised to a virtue by his culture, and thus may give him an enhanced feeling of achievement.

An illustration is the feeling of guilt and anxiety which Calvin's doctrines aroused in men. It may be said that the person who is overwhelmed by a feeling of his own powerlessness and unworthiness, by unceasing doubt as to whether he is saved or condemned to eternal punishment, who is hardly capable of genuine joy, suffers from a severe defect. Yet this very defect was culturally patterned; it was looked upon as particularly valuable, and the individual was thus protected from the neurosis which he would have acquired in a culture where the same defect gave him a feeling of profound inadequacy and isolation.

Spinoza formulated the problem of the socially patterned defect very clearly. He says: "Many people are seized by one and the same affect with great consistency. All his senses are so strongly affected by one object that he believes this object to be present even if it is not. If this happens while the person is awake, the person is believed to be insane. . . . But if the *greedy* person thinks only of money and possessions, the *ambitious* one only of fame, one does not think of them as being insane, but only as annoying; generally one has contempt for them. But *factually* greediness, ambition, and so forth are forms of insanity, although usually one does not think of them as 'illness.' " [1]

These words were written a few hundred years ago; they still hold true, although the defects have been culturally patterned to *such* an extent now that they are not even generally thought any more to be annoying or contemptible. Today we come across a person who acts and feels like an automaton; who never experiences anything which is really his; who experiences himself entirely as the person he thinks he is supposed to be; whose artificial smile has replaced genuine laughter; whose meaningless chatter has replaced communicative speech; whose dulled despair has taken the place of genuine pain. Two statements can be made about this person. One is that he suffers from a defect of spontaneity and individuality which may seem incurable. At the same time, it may be said that he does not differ essentially from millions of others who are in the same position. For most of them, the culture provides patterns which enable them *to live with a defect without becoming ill*. It is as if each culture provided the remedy against the outbreak of manifest neurotic symptoms which would result from the defect produced by it.

[1] cf. Spinoza, *Ethics*, IV Prop. 44 Schol.

Little ability here to enjoy Solitude

Suppose that in our Western culture movies, radios, television, sports events and newspapers ceased to function for only four weeks. With these main avenues of escape closed, what would be the consequences for people thrown back upon their own resources? I have no doubt that even in this short time thousands of nervous breakdowns would occur, and many more thousands of people would be thrown into a state of acute anxiety, not different from the picture which is diagnosed clinically as "neurosis." [1] If the opiate against the socially patterned defect were withdrawn, the manifest illness would make its appearance.

For a minority, the pattern provided by the culture does not work. They are often those whose individual defect is more severe than that of the average person, so that the culturally offered remedies are not sufficient to prevent the outbreak of manifest illness. (A case in point is the person whose aim in life is to attain power and fame. While this aim is, in itself, a pathological one, there is nevertheless a difference between the person who uses his powers to attain this aim realistically, and the more severely sick one who has so little emerged from his infantile grandiosity that he does not do anything toward the attainment of his goal but waits for a miracle to happen and, thus feeling more and more powerless, ends up in a feeling of futility and bitterness.) But there are also those whose character structure, and hence whose conflicts, differ from those of the majority, so that the remedies which are effective for most of their fellow men are of no help to them. Among this group we sometimes find

[1] I have made the following experiment with various classes of undergraduate college students: they were told to imagine that they were to stay for three days alone in their rooms, without a radio, or escapist literature, although provided with "good" literature, normal food and all other physical comforts. They were asked to imagine what their reaction to this experience would be. The response of about 90 per cent in each group ranged from a feeling of acute panic, to that of an exceedingly trying experience, which they might overcome by sleeping long, doing all kinds of little chores, eagerly awaiting the end of this period. Only a small minority felt that they would be at ease and enjoy the time when they were with themselves.

people of greater integrity and sensitivity than the majority, who for this very reason are incapable of accepting the cultural opiate, while at the same time they are not strong and healthy enough to live soundly "against the stream."

The foregoing discussion on the difference between neurosis and the socially patterned defect may give the impression that if society only provides the remedies against the outbreak of manifest symptoms, all goes well, and it can continue to function smoothly, however great the defects created by it. History shows us, however, that this is not the case.

It is true indeed, that man, in contrast to the animal, shows an almost infinite malleability; just as he can eat almost anything, live under practically any kind of climate and adjust himself to it, there is hardly any psychic condition which he cannot endure, and under which he cannot carry on. He can live free, and as a slave. Rich and in luxury, and under conditions of half-starvation. He can live as a warrior, and peaceably; as an exploiter and robber, and as a member of a co-operating and loving fellowship. There is hardly a psychic state in which man cannot live, and hardly anything which cannot be done with him, and for which he cannot be used. All these considerations seem to justify the assumption that there is no such thing as a nature common to all men, and that would mean in fact that there is no such thing as a species "man," except in a physiological and anatomical sense.

Yet, in spite of all this evidence, the history of man shows that we have omitted one fact. Despots and ruling cliques can succeed in dominating and exploiting their fellow man, but they cannot prevent *reactions* to this inhuman treatment. Their subjects become frightened, suspicious, lonely and, if not due to external reasons, their systems collapse at some point because fears, suspicions and loneliness eventually incapacitate the majority to function effectively and intelligently. Whole nations, or

The Human reacts to The "socially patterned defect" (eventually!)

social groups within them, can be subjugated and exploited for a long time, but *they react.* They react with apathy or such impairment of intelligence, initiative and skills that they gradually fail to perform the functions which should serve their rulers. Or they react by the accumulation of such hate and destructiveness as to bring about an end to themselves, their rulers and their system. Again their reaction may create such independence and longing for freedom that a better society is built upon their creative impulses. Which reaction occurs, depends on many factors: on economic and political ones, and on the spiritual climate in which people live. But whatever the reactions are, the statement that man can live under almost any condition is only half true; it must be supplemented by the other statement, that if he lives under conditions which are contrary to his nature and to the basic requirements for human growth and sanity, he cannot help reacting; he must either deteriorate and perish, or bring about conditions which are more in accordance with his needs.

Summary

That human nature and society can have conflicting demands, and hence that a whole society can be sick, is an assumption which was made very explicitly by Freud, most extensively in his *Civilization and Its Discontent.*

He starts out with the premise of a human nature common to the human race, throughout all cultures and ages, and of certain ascertainable needs and strivings inherent in that nature. He believes that culture and civilization develop in an ever-increasing contrast to the needs of man, and thus he arrives at the concept of the "social neurosis." "If the evolution of civilization," he writes, "has such a far-reaching similarity with the development of an individual, and if the same methods are employed in both, would not the diagnosis be justified that many systems of civilization—or epochs of it—possibly even the whole of humanity—have become 'neurotic' under the pressure of the civilizing trends?

To analytic dissection of these neuroses, therapeutic recommendations might follow which could claim a great practical interest. I would not say that such an attempt to apply psychoanalysis to civilized society would be fanciful or doomed to fruitlessness. But it behooves us to be very careful, not to forget that after all we are dealing only with analogies, and that it is dangerous, not only with men but also with concepts, to drag them out of the region where they originated and have matured. The diagnosis of *collective neuroses*, moreover, will be confronted by a special difficulty. In the neurosis of an individual we can use as a starting point the contrast presented to us between the patient and his environment which we assume to be 'normal.' No such background as this would be available for any society similarly affected; it would have to be supplied in some other way. And with regard to any therapeutic application of our knowledge, what would be the use of the most acute analysis of social neuroses, since no one possesses the power to compel the community to adopt the therapy? In spite of all these difficulties, we may expect that one day someone will venture upon this *research into the pathology of civilized communities.*" [1]

This book *does* venture upon this research. It is based on the idea that a sane society is that which corresponds to the needs of man—not necessarily to what he *feels* to be his needs, because even the most pathological aims can be felt subjectively as that which the person wants most; but to what his needs are *objectively*, as they can be ascertained by the study of man. It is our first task then, to ascertain what is the nature of man, and what are the needs which stem from this nature. We then must proceed to examine the role of society in the evolution of man and to study

[1] S. Freud, *Civilization and Its Discontents*, translated from the German by J. Riviere, The Hogarth Press, Ltd., London, 1953, pp. 141–142. (Italics mine.)

its furthering role for the development of men as well as the recurrent *conflicts between human nature and society*—and the consequences of these conflicts, particularly as far as modern society is concerned.

3

THE HUMAN SITUATION—
THE KEY TO HUMANISTIC
PSYCHOANALYSIS

THE HUMAN SITUATION

Man, in respect to his body and his physiological functions, belongs to the animal kingdom. The functioning of the animal is determined by instincts, by specific action patterns which are in turn determined by inherited neurological structures. The higher an animal is in the scale of development, the more flexibility of action pattern and the less completeness of structural adjustment do we find at birth. In the higher primates we even find considerable intelligence; that is, use of thought for the accomplishment of desired goals, thus enabling the animal to go far beyond the instinctively prescribed action pattern. But great as the development within the animal kingdom is, certain basic elements of existence remain the same.

The animal "is lived" through biological laws of nature; it is part of nature and never transcends it. It has no conscience of a moral nature, and no awareness of itself and of its existence; it has no reason, if by reason we mean the ability to penetrate the surface grasped by the senses and to understand the essence behind that surface; therefore the animal has no concept of the truth, even though it may have an idea of what is useful.

Animal existence is one of harmony between the animal and nature; not, of course, in the sense that the natural conditions do not often threaten the animal and force it to a bitter fight for survival, but in the sense that the animal is equipped by nature to cope with the very conditions it is to meet, just as the seed of a plant is equipped by nature to make use of the conditions of soil, climate, etcetera, to which it has become adapted in the evolutionary process.

At a certain point of animal evolution, there occurred a unique break, comparable to the first emergence of matter, to the first emergence of life, and to the first emergence of animal existence. This new event happens when in the evolutionary process, action ceases to be essentially determined by instinct; when the adaptation of nature loses its coercive character; when action is no longer fixed by hereditarily given mechanisms. When the animal transcends nature, when it transcends the purely passive role of the creature, when it becomes, biologically speaking, the most helpless animal, *man is born*. At this point, the animal has emancipated itself from nature by erect posture, the brain has grown far beyond what it was in the highest animal. This birth of man may have lasted for hundreds of thousands of years, but what matters is that a new species arose, transcending nature, that *life became aware of itself*.

Self-awareness, reason and imagination disrupt the "harmony" which characterizes animal existence. Their emergence has made man into an anomaly, into the freak of the universe. He is part of nature, subject to her physical laws and unable to change them, yet he transcends the rest of nature. He is set apart while being a part; he is homeless, yet chained to the home he shares with all creatures. Cast into this world at an accidental place and time, he is forced out of it, again accidentally. Being aware of himself, he

— Self Awareness
adds new
dimension

— Reason + Imagination
make possible varied ways
of looking at his problems
+ creation to those
solutions to those
problems

realizes his powerlessness and the limitations of his existence. He visualizes his own end: death. Never is he free from the dichotomy of his existence: he cannot rid himself of his mind, even if he should want to; he cannot rid himself of his body as long as he is alive—and his body makes him want to be alive.

Reason, man's blessing, is also his curse; it forces him to cope everlastingly with the task of solving an insoluble dichotomy. Human existence is different in this respect from that of all other organisms; it is in a state of constant and unavoidable disequilibrium. Man's life cannot "be lived" by repeating the pattern of his species; *he* must live. Man is the only animal that can be *bored*, that can feel evicted from paradise. Man is the only animal who finds his own existence a problem which he has to solve and from which he cannot escape. He cannot go back to the prehuman state of harmony with nature; he must proceed to develop his reason until he becomes the master of nature, and of himself.

But man's birth ontogenetically as well as phylogenetically is essentially a *negative* event. He lacks the instinctive adaptation to nature, he lacks physical strength, he is the most helpless of all animals at birth, and in need of protection for a much longer period of time than any of them. While he has lost the unity with nature, he has not been given the means to lead a new existence outside of nature. His reason is most rudimentary, he has no knowledge of nature's processes, nor tools to replace the lost instincts; he lives divided into small groups, with no knowledge of himself or of others; indeed, the biblical Paradise myth expresses the situation with perfect clarity. Man, who lives in the Garden of Eden, in complete harmony with nature but without awareness of himself, begins his history by the first act of freedom, disobedience to a command. Concomitantly, he becomes aware of himself, of his separateness, of his helplessness; he is expelled from Paradise, and two angels with fiery swords prevent his return.

24

Man's evolution is based on the fact that he has lost his original home, nature—and that he can never return to it, can never become an animal again. There is only one way he can take: to emerge fully from his natural home, to find a new home—one which he creates, by making the world a human one and by becoming truly human himself.

When man is born, the human race as well as the individual, he is thrown out of a situation which was definite, as definite as the instincts, into a situation which is indefinite, uncertain and open. There is certainty only about the past, and about the future as far as it is death—which actually is return to the past, the inorganic state of matter.

The problem of man's existence, then, is unique in the whole of nature; he has fallen out of nature, as it were, and is still in it; he is partly divine, partly animal; partly infinite, partly finite. *The necessity to find ever-new solutions for the contradictions in his existence, to find ever-higher forms of unity with nature, his fellowmen and himself, is the source of all psychic forces which motivate man, of all his passions, affects and anxieties.* [Quot.]

The animal is content if its physiological needs—its hunger, its thirst and its sexual needs—are satisfied. Inasmuch as man is *also* animal, these needs are likewise imperative and must be satisfied. *But inasmuch as man is human, the satisfaction of these instinctual needs is not sufficient to make him happy; they are not even sufficient to make him sane. The archimedic point of the specifically human dynamism lies in this uniqueness of the human situation; the understanding of man's psyche must be based on the analysis of man's needs stemming from the conditions of his existence.*

The problem, then, which the human race as well as each individual has to solve is that of being born. Physical birth, if we think of the individual, is by no means as decisive and singular an act as it appears to be. It is, indeed, an important change from intrauterine into extrauterine life; but in many respects the infant after birth is not different from the infant before birth; it cannot perceive things outside, cannot feed itself; it is completely dependent on the mother, and would perish without her help. Actually, the process of birth continues. The child begins to recognize outside objects, to react affectively, to grasp things and to co-ordinate his movements, to walk. But birth continues. The child learns to speak, it learns to know the use and function of things, it learns to relate itself to others, to avoid punishment and gain praise and liking. Slowly, the growing person learns to love, to develop reason, to look at the world objectively. He begins to develop his powers; to acquire a sense of identity, to overcome the seduction of his senses for the sake of an integrated life. Birth then, in the conventional meaning of the word, is only the beginning of birth in the broader sense. The whole life of the individual is nothing but the process of giving birth to himself; indeed, we should be fully born, when we die—although it is the tragic fate of most individuals to die before they are born.

From all we know about the evolution of the human race, the birth of man is to be understood in the same sense as the birth of the individual. When man had transcended a certain threshold of minimum instinctive adaptation, he ceased to be an animal; but he was as helpless and unequipped for human existence as the individual infant is at birth. The birth of man began with the first members of the species homo sapiens, and human history is nothing but the whole process of this birth. It has taken man hundreds of thousands of years to take the first steps into human life; he went through a narcissistic phase of magic omnipotent orientation, through totemism, nature worship, until he arrived at the beginnings of the formation of conscience, objectivity, brotherly love. In the last four thousand years of his history, he has developed visions of the fully born and fully awakened man, visions expressed in not too different ways by the great teachers of man in Egypt, China, India, Palestine, Greece and Mexico.

The fact that man's birth is primarily a negative act, that of being thrown out of the original oneness with nature, that he cannot return to where he came from, implies that the process of birth is by no means an easy one. Each step into his new human existence is frightening. It always means to give up a secure state, which was relatively known, for one which is new, which one has not yet mastered. Undoubtedly, if the infant could think at the moment of the severance of the umbilical cord, he would experience the fear of dying. A loving fate protects us from this first panic. But at any new step, at any new stage of our birth, we are afraid again. We are never free from two conflicting tendencies: one to emerge from the womb, from the animal form of existence into a more human existence, from bondage to freedom; another, to return to the womb, to nature, to certainty and security. In the history of the individual, and of the race, the progressive tendency has proven to be stronger, yet the phenomena of mental illness and the regression of the human race to positions apparently relinquished generations ago, show the intense struggle which accompanies each new act of birth.[1]

MAN'S NEEDS—AS THEY STEM FROM THE CONDITIONS OF HIS EXISTENCE

Man's life is determined by the inescapable alternative between regression and progression, between return to animal exist-

---

[1] It is in this polarity that I see the true kernel in Freud's hypothesis of the existence of a life and death instinct; the difference to Freud's theory is, that the forward-going and the retrogressive impulse have not the same biologically determined strength, but that normally, the forward-going life instinct is stronger and increases in relative strength the more it grows.

The Sane Society

ence and arrival at human existence. Any attempt to return is painful, it inevitably leads to suffering and mental sickness, to death either physiologically or mentally (insanity). Every step forward is frightening and painful too, until a certain point has been reached where fear and doubt have only minor proportions. Aside from the physiologically nourished cravings (hunger, thirst, sex), all essential human cravings are determined by this polarity. Man has to solve a problem, he can never rest in the given situation of a passive adaptation to nature. Even the most complete satisfaction of all his instinctive needs does not solve his *human* problem; his most intensive passions and needs are not those rooted in his body, but those rooted in the very peculiarity of his existence.

There lies also the key to humanistic psychoanalysis. Freud, searching for the basic force which motivates human passions and desires believed he had found it in the libido. But powerful as the sexual drive and all its derivations are, they are by no means the most powerful forces within man and their frustration is not the cause of mental disturbance. The most powerful forces motivating man's behavior stem from the condition of his existence, the "human situation."

looks like Maslow

Man cannot live statically because his inner contradictions drive him to seek for an equilibrium, for a new harmony instead of the lost animal harmony with nature. After he has satisfied his animal needs, he is driven by his human needs. While his body tells him what to eat and what to avoid—his conscience ought to tell him which needs to cultivate and satisfy, and which needs to let wither and starve out. But hunger and appetite are functions of the body with which man is born—conscience, while potentially present, requires the guidance of men and principles which develop only during the growth of culture.

28

All passions and strivings of man are attempts to find an answer to his existence or, as we may also say, they are an attempt to avoid insanity. (It may be said in passing that the real problem of mental life is not why some people become insane, but rather why most avoid insanity.) Both the mentally healthy and the neurotic are driven by the need to find an answer, the only difference being that one answer corresponds more to the total needs of man, and hence is more conducive to the unfolding of his powers and to his happiness than the other. All cultures provide for a patterned system in which certain solutions are predominant, hence certain strivings and satisfactions. Whether we deal with primitive religions, with theistic or non-theistic religions, they are all attempts to give an answer to man's existential problem. The finest, as well as the most barbaric cultures have the same function—the difference is only whether the answer given is better or worse. The deviate from the cultural pattern is just as much in search of an answer as his more well-adjusted brother. His answer may be better or worse than the one given by his culture—it is always another answer to the same fundamental question raised by human existence. In this sense all cultures are religious and every neurosis is a private form of religion, provided we mean by religion an attempt to answer the problem of human existence. Indeed, the tremendous energy in the forces producing mental illness, as well as those behind art and religion could never be understood as an outcome of frustrated or sublimated physiological needs; they are attempts to solve the problem of being born human. All men are idealists and cannot help being idealists, provided we mean by idealism the striving for the satisfaction of needs which are specifically human and transcend the physiological needs of the organism. The difference is only that one idealism is a good and adequate solution, the other a bad and destructive one. The decision as to what is good and bad has to be made on the basis of our knowledge of man's nature and the laws which govern its growth.

What are these needs and passions stemming from the existence of man?

A. RELATEDNESS VS. NARCISSISM

Man is torn away from the primary union with nature, which characterizes animal existence. Having at the same time reason and imagination, he is aware of his aloneness and separateness; of his powerlessness and ignorance; of the accidentalness of his birth and of his death. He could not face this state of being for a second if he could not find new ties with his fellow man which replace the old ones, regulated by instincts. Even if all his physiological needs were satisfied, he would experience his state of aloneness and individuation as a prison from which he had to break out in order to retain his sanity. In fact, the insane person is the one who has completely failed to establish any kind of union, and is imprisoned, even if he is not behind barred windows. The necessity to unite with other living beings, to be related to them, is an imperative need on the fulfillment of which man's sanity depends. This need is behind all phenomena which constitute the whole gamut of intimate human relations, of all passions which are called love in the broadest sense of the word.

There are several ways in which this union can be sought and achieved. Man can attempt to become one with the world by *submission* to a person, to a group, to an institution, to God. In this way he transcends the separateness of his individual existence by becoming part of somebody or something bigger than himself, and experiences his identity in connection with the power to which he has submitted. Another possibility of overcoming separateness lies in the opposite direction: man can try to unite himself with the world by having *power* over it, by making others a part of himself, and thus transcending his individual existence by domination. The common element in both submission and domination is the symbiotic nature of relatedness. Both persons involved have lost their integrity and freedom; they live on each other and from each other, satisfying their craving for closeness, yet suffering from the lack of inner strength and self-reliance which would require freedom and independence, and furthermore constantly threatened by the conscious or unconscious hostility which is bound to arise from the symbiotic relationship.[1] The realization of the submissive (masochistic) or the domineering (sadistic) passion never leads to satisfaction. They have a self-propelling dynamism, and because no amount of submission, or domination (or possession, or fame) is enough to give a sense of identity and union, more and more of it is sought. The ultimate result of these passions is defeat. It cannot be otherwise; while these passions aim at the establishment of a sense of union, they destroy the sense of integrity. The person driven by any one of these passions actually becomes dependent on others; instead of developing his own individual being, he is dependent on those to whom he submits, or whom he dominates.

There is only one passion which satisfies man's need to unite himself with the world, and to acquire at the same time a sense of integrity and individuality, and this is *love. Love is union* with somebody, or something, outside oneself, *under the condition of retaining the separateness and integrity of one's own self.* It is an experience of sharing, of communion, which permits the full unfolding of one's own inner activity. The experience of love does away with the necessity of illusions. There is no need to inflate the image of the other person, or of myself, since the reality of

[1] cf. the more detailed analysis of the symbiotic relatedness in E. Fromm, *Escape from Freedom,* Rinehart & Company, Inc., New York, 1941, p. 141 ff.

active sharing and loving permits me to transcend my individual-
ized existence, and at the same time to experience myself as the
bearer of the active powers which constitute the act of loving.
What matters is the particular *quality* of loving, not the object.
Love is in the experience of human solidarity with our fellow
creatures, it is in the erotic love of man and woman, in the love
of the mother for the child, and also in the love for oneself, as a
human being; it is in the mystical experience of union. In the act
of loving, I am one with All, and yet I am myself, a unique,
separate, limited, mortal human being. Indeed out of the very
polarity between separateness and union, love is born and reborn.

Love is one aspect of what I have called the productive orientation: the active and creative relatedness of man to his fellow man,
to himself and to nature. In the realm of *thought*, this productive
orientation is expressed in the proper grasp of the world by reason. In the realm of *action*, the productive orientation is expressed
in productive work, the prototype of which is art and craftsmanship. In the realm of *feeling*, the productive orientation is expressed
in love, which is the experience of union with another person,
with all men, and with nature, under the condition of retaining
one's sense of integrity and independence. In the experience of
love the paradox happens that two people become one, and remain
two at the same time. Love in this sense is never restricted to one
person. If I can love only one person, and nobody else, if my love
for one person makes me more alienated and distant from my
fellow man, I may be attached to this person in any number of
ways, yet I do not love. If I can say, "I love you," I say, "I love
in you all of humanity, all that is alive; I love in you also myself." Self-love, in this sense, is the opposite of selfishness. The
latter is actually a greedy concern with oneself which springs
from and compensates for the lack of genuine love for oneself.

32

Love, paradoxically, makes me more independent because it makes me stronger and happier—yet it makes me one with the loved person to the extent that individuality seems to be extinguished for the moment. In loving I experience "I am you," you—the loved person, you—the stranger, you—everything alive. In the experience of love lies the only answer to being human, lies sanity.

Productive love always implies a syndrome of attitudes; that of *care, responsibility, respect* and *knowledge*.[1] If I love, I care—that is, I am actively concerned with the other person's growth and happiness; I am not a spectator. I am responsible, that is, I respond to his needs, to those he can express and more so to those he cannot or does not express. I respect him, that is (according to the original meaning of *re-spicere*) I look at him as he is, objectively and not distorted by my wishes and fears. I know him, I have penetrated through his surface to the core of his being and related myself to him from my core, from the center, as against the periphery, of my being.[2]

Productive love when directed toward equals may be called *brotherly love*. In *motherly love* (Hebrew: *rachamim*, from *rechem* = womb) the relationship between the two persons involved is one of inequality; the child is helpless and dependent on the mother. In order to grow, it must become more and more independent, until he does not need mother any more. Thus the mother-child relationship is paradoxical and, in a sense, tragic. It requires the most intense love on the mother's side, and yet this very love must help the child to grow away from the mother, and to become fully independent. It is easy for any mother to

---

[1] cf. for a more detailed discussion of these concepts my *Man for Himself*, Rinehart & Company, Inc., New York, 1947, p. 96 ff.

[2] The identity between "to love" and "to know" is contained in the Hebrew *jadoa* and in the German *meinen* and *minnen*.

love her child before this process of separation has begun—but it is the task in which most fail, to love the child and at the same time to let it go—and to *want* to let it go.

In *erotic love* (Gr. *eros;* Hebrew: *ahawa,* from the root "to glow"), another drive is involved: that for fusion and union with another person. While brotherly love refers to all men and motherly love to the child and all those who are in need of our help, erotic love is directed to one person, normally of the opposite sex, with whom fusion and oneness is desired. Erotic love begins with separateness, and ends in oneness. Motherly love begins with oneness, and leads to separateness. If the need for fusion were realized in motherly love, it would mean destruction of the child as an independent being, since the child needs to emerge from his mother, rather than to remain tied to her. If erotic love lacks brotherly love and is *only* motivated by the wish for fusion, it is sexual desire without love, or the perversion of love as we find it in the sadistic and masochistic forms of "love."

One understands fully man's need to be related only if one considers the outcome of the failure of any kind of relatedness, if one appreciates the meaning of *narcissism.* The only reality the infant can experience is his own body and his needs, physiological needs and the need for warmth and affection. He has not yet the experience of "I" as separate from "thou." He is still in a state of oneness with the world, but a oneness before the awakening of his sense of individuality and reality. The world outside exists only as so much food, or so much warmth to be used for the satisfaction of his own needs, but not as something or somebody who is recognized realistically and objectively. This orientation has been named by Freud that of "primary narcissism." In normal development, this state of narcissism is slowly overcome by a growing awareness of reality outside, and by a correspondingly growing sense of "I" as differentiated from "thou." This change occurs at first on the level of sensory perception, when things and people are perceived as different and specific entities, a recognition which lays the foundation for the possibility of speech; to name things pre-supposes recognizing them as individual and separate entities.[1] It takes much longer until the narcissistic state is overcome emotionally; for the child up to the age of seven or eight years, other people still exist mainly as means for the satisfaction of his needs. They are exchangeable inasmuch as they fulfill the function of satisfying these needs, and it is only around the ages of between eight and nine years that another person is experienced in such a way that the child can begin to love, that is to say, in H. S. Sullivan's formulation, to feel that the needs of another person are as important as his own.[2][3]

Primary narcissism is a normal phenomenon, conforming with the normal physiological and mental development of the child. But narcissism exists also in later stages of life ("secondary narcissism," according to Freud), if the growing child fails to develop the capacity for love, or loses it again. Narcissism is the essence of all severe psychic pathology. For the narcissistically involved person, there is only one reality, that of his own thought

[1] cf. Jean Piaget's discussion of this point in *The Child's Conception of the World*, Harcourt, Brace & Company, Inc., New York, p. 151.

[2] cf. H. S. Sullivan, *The Interpersonal Theory of Psychiatry*, Norton Co., New York, 1953, p. 49 ff.

[3] This love is usually felt at first toward the child's contemporaries, and not toward the parents. The pleasing idea that children "love" their parents before they love anybody else must be considered as one of the many illusions which stem from wishful thinking. For the child, at this age, father and mother are more objects of dependency or fear than of love, which by its very nature is based on equality and independence. Love for parents, if we differentiate it from affectionate but passive attachment, incestuous fixation, conventional or fearful submission, develops—if at all—at a later age rather than in childhood, although its beginnings can be found—under fortunate circumstances—at an earlier age. (The same point has been made, somewhat more sharply, by H. S. Sullivan in his *Interpersonal Theory of Psychiatry*.) Many parents, however, are not willing to accept this reality and react to it by resenting the child's first real love attachments either overtly or in the even more effective form of making fun of them. Their conscious or unconscious jealousy is one of the most powerful obstacles to the child's development of the capacity to love.

processes, feelings and needs. The world outside is not experienced or perceived *objectively, i.e.,* as existing in its own terms, conditions and needs. The most extreme form of narcissism is to be seen in all forms of insanity. The insane person has lost contact with the world; he has withdrawn into himself; he cannot experience reality, either physical or human reality *as it is,* but only as formed and determined by his own inner processes. He either does *not* react to the world outside, or if he does, reacts not in terms of *its* reality, but only in terms of his own processes of thought and feeling. Narcissism is the opposite pole to objectivity, reason and love.

The fact that utter failure to relate oneself to the world is insanity, points to the other fact: that some form of relatedness is the condition for any kind of sane living. But among the various forms of relatedness, only the productive one, love, fulfills the condition of allowing one to retain one's freedom and integrity while being, at the same time, united with one's fellow man.

B. TRANSCENDENCE—CREATIVENESS VS. DESTRUCTIVENESS

Another aspect of the human situation, closely connected with the need for relatedness, is man's situation as a *creature,* and his need to transcend this very state of the passive creature. Man is thrown into this world without his knowledge, consent or will, and he is removed from it again without his consent or will. In this respect he is not different from the animal, from the plants, or from inorganic matter. But being endowed with reason and imagination, he cannot be content with the passive role of the creature, with the role of dice cast out of a cup. He is driven by the urge to transcend the role of the creature, the accidentalness and passivity of his existence, by becoming a "creator."

Man can create life. This is the miraculous quality which he indeed shares with all living beings, but with the difference that he alone is aware of being created and of being a creator. Man can create life, or rather, woman can create life, by giving birth to a child, and by caring for the child until it is sufficiently grown to take care of his own needs. Man—man and woman—can create by planting seeds, by producing material objects, by creating art, by creating ideas, by loving one another. In the act of creation man transcends himself as a creature, raises himself beyond the passivity and accidentalness of his existence into the realm of purposefulness and freedom. In man's need for transcendence lies one of the roots for love, as well as for art, religion and material production.

To create presupposes activity and care. It presupposes love for that which one creates. How then does man solve the problem of transcending himself, if he is not capable of creating, if he cannot love? *There is another answer to this need for transcendence: if I cannot create life, I can destroy it. To destroy life makes me also transcend it.* Indeed, that man can destroy life is just as miraculous a feat as that he can create it, for life is *the* miracle, the inexplicable. In the act of destruction, man sets himself above life; he transcends himself as a creature. Thus, the ultimate choice for man, inasmuch as he is driven to transcend himself, is to create or to destroy, to love or to hate. The enormous power of the will for destruction which we see in the history of man, and which we have witnessed so frightfully in our own time, is rooted in the nature of man, just as the drive to create is rooted in it. To say that man is capable of developing his primary potentiality for love and reason does not imply the naive belief in man's goodness. Destructiveness is a secondary potentiality, rooted in the very existence of man, and having the same intensity and power as any passion can have.[1] But—and this is the essential point of my argument—it is only the *alternative* to creativeness. Creation and destruction, love and hate, are not two instincts which exist independently. They are both answers to the same need for transcendence, and the will to destroy must rise when the will to create cannot be satisfied. However, the satisfaction of the need to create leads to happiness; destructiveness to suffering, most of all, for the destroyer himself.

C. ROOTEDNESS—BROTHERLINESS VS. INCEST

Man's birth as man means the beginning of his emergence from his natural home, the beginning of the severance of his natural ties. Yet, this very severance is frightening; if man loses his natural roots, where is he and who is he? He would stand alone, without a home; without roots; he could not bear the isolation and helplessness of this position. He would become insane. He can dispense with the *natural* roots only insofar as he finds new *human* roots and only after he has found them can he feel at home again in this world. Is it surprising, then, to find a deep craving in man not to sever the natural ties, to fight against being torn away from nature, from mother, blood and soil?

The most elementary of the natural ties is the tie of the child to the mother. The child begins life in the mother's womb, and exists there for a much longer time than is the case with most animals; even after birth, the child remains physically helpless, and completely dependent on the mother; this period of helplessness and dependence again is much more protracted than with any animal. In the first years of life no full separation between child and mother has occurred. The satisfaction of all his physio-

---

[1] The formulation given here does not contradict the one given in *Man for Himself*, loc. cit., where I wrote that: "destructiveness is the outcome of unlived life." In the concept of transcendence presented here, I try to show more specifically what aspect of unlived life leads to destructiveness.

logical needs, of his vital need for warmth and affection depend on her; she has not only given birth to him, but she continues to give life to him. Her care is not dependent on anything the child does for her, on any obligation which the child has to fulfill; it is unconditional. She cares because the new creature is her child. The child, in these decisive first years of his life, has the experience of his mother as the fountain of life, as an all-enveloping, protective, nourishing power. Mother is food; she is love; she is warmth; she is earth. To be loved by her means to be alive, to be rooted, to be at home.

Just as birth means to leave the enveloping protection of the womb, growing up means to leave the protective orbit of the mother. Yet even in the mature adult, the longing for this situation as it once existed never ceases completely, in spite of the fact that there is, indeed, a great difference between the adult and the child. The adult has the means to stand on his own feet, to take care of himself, to be responsible for himself and even for others, while the child is not yet capable of doing all this. But considering the increased perplexities of life, the fragmentary nature of our knowledge, the accidentalness of adult existence, the unavoidable errors we make, the situation of the adult is by no means as different from that of the child as it is generally assumed. Every adult is in need of help, of warmth, of protection, in many ways differing and yet in many ways similar to the needs of the child. Is it surprising to find in the average adult a deep longing for the security and rootedness which the relationship to his mother once gave him? Is it not to be expected that he cannot give up this intense longing unless he finds other ways of being rooted?

In psychopathology we find ample evidence for this phenomenon of the refusal to leave the all-enveloping orbit of the mother. In the most extreme form we find the craving to return to the mother's womb. A person completely obsessed by this desire may offer the picture of schizophrenia. He feels and acts like the foetus in the mother's womb, incapable of assuming even the most elementary functions of a small child. In many of the more severe neuroses we find the same craving, but as a repressed desire, manifested only in dreams, symptoms and neurotic behavior, which results from the conflict between the deep desire to stay in the mother's womb and the adult part of the personality which tends to live a normal life. In dreams this craving appears in symbols like being in a dark cave, in a one-man submarine, diving into deep water, etc. In the behavior of such a person, we find a fear of life, and a deep fascination for death (death, in phantasy, being the return to the womb, to mother earth).

The less severe form of the fixation to mother is to be found in those cases where a person has permitted himself to be born, as it were, but where he is afraid to take the next step of birth, to be weaned from mother's breasts. People who have become stuck at this stage of birth, have a deep craving to be mothered, nursed, protected by a motherly figure; they are the eternally dependent ones, who are frightened and insecure when motherly protection is withdrawn, but optimistic and active when a loving mother or mother-substitute is provided, either realistically or in phantasy.

These pathological phenomena in individual life have their parallel in the evolution of the human race. The clearest expression of this lies in the fact of the universality of the incest tabu, which we find even in the most primitive societies. The incest tabu is the necessary condition for all human development, not because of its sexual, but because of its affective aspect. Man, in order to be born, in order to progress, has to sever the umbilical cord; he has to overcome the deep craving to remain tied to mother. The incestuous desire has its strength not from the sexual attraction to mother, but from the deep-seated craving to remain in, or to return to the all-enveloping womb, or to the all-nourishing breasts. The incest tabu is nothing else but the two cherubim with fiery swords, guarding the entrance to paradise and preventing man from returning to the pre-individual existence of oneness with nature.

The problem of incest, however, is not restricted to fixation to the mother. The tie to her is only the most elementary form of all natural ties of blood which give man a sense of rootedness and belonging. The ties of blood are extended to those who are blood relatives, whatever the system is according to which such relationships are established. The *family* and the *clan*, and later on the state, nation or church, assume the same function which the individual mother had originally for the child. The individual leans on them, feels rooted in them, has his sense of identity as a part of them, and not as an individual apart from them. The person who does not belong to the same clan is considered as alien and dangerous—as not sharing in the same human qualities which only the own clan possesses.

The fixation to the mother was recognized by Freud as the crucial problem of human development, both of the race and of the individual. In accordance with his system, he explained the intensity of the fixation to the mother as derived from the little boy's *sexual* attraction to her, as the expression of the incestuous striving inherent in man's nature. He assumed that the fixation's perpetuation in later life resulted from the continuing sexual desire. By relating this assumption to his observations of the son's opposition to the father, he reconciled assumption and observation into a most ingenious explanation, that of the "Oedipus complex." He explained hostility to the father as a result of sexual rivalry with him.

But while Freud saw the tremendous importance of the fixation to the mother, he emasculated his discovery by the peculiar interpretation he gave to it. He projects into the little boy the sexual feeling of the adult man; the little boy having, as Freud recognized, sexual desires, was supposed to be sexually attracted to the woman closest to him, and only by the superior power of the rival in this triangle, is he forced to give up his desire, without ever recovering fully from this frustration. Freud's theory is a curiously rationalistic interpretation of the observable facts. In putting the emphasis on the *sexual* aspect of the incestuous desire, Freud explains the boy's desire as something rational in itself and evades the real problem: the depth and intensity of the *irrational affective* tie to the mother, the wish to return into her orbit, to remain a part of her, the fear of emerging fully from her. In Freud's explanation the incestuous wish cannot be fulfilled because of the presence of the father-rival, while in reality the incestuous wish is in contrast to all requirements of adult life.

Thus, the theory of the Oedipus complex is at the same time the acknowledgment *and* the denial of the crucial phenomenon: man's longing for mother's love. In giving the incestuous striving paramount significance, the importance of the tie with mother is recognized; by explaining it as sexual the emotional—and true —meaning of the tie is denied.

Whenever fixation to the mother is also sexual—and this undoubtedly happens—it is because the affective fixation is so strong that it also influences the sexual desire, but not because the sexual desire is at the root of the fixation. On the contrary, sexual desire as such is notoriously fickle with regard to its objects, and generally sexual desire is precisely the force which helps the adolescent in his *separation* from mother, and not the one which binds him to her. Where we find that the intense attachment to mother has changed this normal function of the sexual drive, two possibilities must be considered. One is that the sexual desire for mother is a defense against the desire to return to the womb; the latter leads to insanity or death, while the sexual desire is at least compatible with life. One is saved from the fear of the threatening womb by the nearer-to-life phantasy of entering the vagina with the appropriate organ.[1] The other possibility to be considered is that the phantasy of sexual intercourse with the mother does not have the quality of adult male sexuality, that of voluntary, pleasurable activity, but that of passivity, of being conquered and possessed by the mother, even in the sexual sphere. Aside from these two possibilities which are indicative of more severe pathology, we find instances of sexual incestuous wishes which are stimulated by a seductive mother and, although expressive of mother fixation, less indicative of severe pathology.

That Freud himself distorted his great discovery may have been due to an unsolved problem in the relationship to his own mother, but it was certainly largely influenced by the strictly patriarchal attitude which was so characteristic of Freud's time, and which he shared so completely. The mother was dethroned from her paramount place as the object of love—and her place was given to the father, who was believed to be the most important figure in the child's affections. It sounds almost unbelievable today, when the patriarchal bias has lost much of its strength, to read the following statement written by Freud: "I could not point to any need in childhood as strong as that for a *father's protection*." [2] Similarly, he wrote in 1908, referring to the death of his father, that the father's death is "the most important event, the most poignant loss, in a man's life." [3] Thus Freud gives the father the place which in reality is that of the mother, and degrades the mother into the

---

[1] This sequence is expressed, for instance, in dreams in which the dreamer finds himself in a cave, with the fear of being suffocated, then having intercourse with his mother with a feeling of relief.

[2] S. Freud, *Civilization and Its Discontent*, translated by J. Riviere, The Hogarth Press Ltd., London, 1953, p. 21. (My italics, E. F.)

[3] Quoted from E. Jones, *The Life and Work of Sigmund Freud*, Basic Books, Inc., New York, 1953, Vol. I, p. 324.

object of sexual lust. The goddess is transformed into the prostitute, the father elevated to the central figure of the universe.[1]

There was another genius, living a generation before Freud, who saw the central role of the tie to the mother in the development of man: Johann Jacob Bachofen.[2] Because he was not narrowed down by the rationalistic, sexual interpretation of the fixation to the mother, he could see the facts more profoundly and more objectively. In his theory of the matriarchal society he assumed that mankind went through a stage, preceding that of the patriarchate, where the ties to the mother, as well as those to blood and soil, were the paramount form of relatedness, both individually and socially. In this form of social organization, as was pointed out above, the mother was the central figure in the family, in social life and in religion. Even though many of Bachofen's historical constructions are not tenable, there can be no doubt that he uncovered a form of social organization and a psychological structure which had been ignored by psychologists and anthropologists because, from their patriarchal orientation, the idea of a society ruled by women rather than by men was just absurd. Yet, there is a great deal of evidence that Greece and India, before the invasion from the north, had cultures of a matriarchal structure. The great number and the significance of mother goddesses points in the same direction. (Venus of Willendorf, Mother Goddess at Mohengo-Daro, Isis, Istar, Rhea, Cybele, Hathor, the Serpent Goddess at Nippur, the Akkadian Water Goddess Ai, Demeter and the Indian Goddess Kali, the giver and destroyer of life, are only a few examples.) Even in many contemporary primitive societies, we can see remnants of the matriarchal structure in matrilineal forms of consanguinity, or matrilocal forms of mar-

[1] In this elimination of the mother figure, Freud does for psychology what Luther did for religion. Properly speaking, Freud is the psychologist of Protestantism.
[2] cf. J. J. Bachofen, *Mutterrecht und Ur Religion*, ed. R. Marx, A. Kroener Verl. Stuttgart, 1954.

riage; more significantly we can find many examples of the matriarchal kind of relatedness to mother, blood and soil, even where the social forms are not matriarchal any more.

While Freud saw in the incestuous fixation only a negative, pathogenic element, Bachofen saw clearly both the negative and the positive aspects of the attachment to the mother figure. *The positive aspect is a sense of affirmation of life, freedom, and equality which pervades the matriarchal structure.* Inasmuch as men are childen of nature, and children of mothers, they are all equal, have the same rights and claims, and the only value that counts is that of life. To put it differently, the mother loves her children not because one is better than the other, not because one fulfills her expectations more than the other, but because they are her children, and in that quality they are all alike and have the same right to love and care. The *negative* aspect of the matriarchal structure was also clearly seen by Bachofen: *by being bound to nature, to blood and soil, man is blocked from developing his individuality and his reason.* He remains a child and incapable of progress.[1]

Bachofen gave an equally broad and profound interpretation of the role of the father, again pointing out both the positive and negative aspects of the fatherly function. Paraphrasing Bachofen's ideas and somewhat enlarging on them, I would say that man, not equipped to create children (I am speaking here, of course, of the *experience* of pregnancy and birth, and not of the purely rational knowledge that the male sperm is necessary for

---

[1] It is interesting to note how these two aspects of the matriarchal structure have been seized upon by two opposite philosophies in the last hundred years. The Marxist school embraced Bachofen's theories with great enthusiasm because of the element of equality and freedom inherent in the matriarchal structure (cf. Friedrich Engels *The Origin of the Family, Private Property and the State*). After many years in which Bachofen's theories had hardly found any attention, the Nazi philosophers seized upon them and showed equal enthusiasm, but for the opposite reasons. They were attracted by the very irrationality of the bonds of blood and soil which is the other aspect of the matriarchal structure as presented by Bachofen.

the creation of a child), not charged with the task of nursing and taking care of them, is more remote from nature than woman. Because he is less rooted in nature, he is forced to develop his reason, to build up a man-made world of ideas, principles and man-made things which replace nature as a ground of existence and security. The relationship of the child to the father does not have the same intensity as that to the mother, because the father never has the all-enveloping, all-protective, all-loving role which the mother has for the first years of the child's life. On the contrary, in all patriarchal societies, the relationship of the son to the father is one of submission on the one hand, but of rebellion on the other, and this contains in itself a permanent element of dissolution. The submission to the father is different from the fixation to the mother. The latter is a continuation of the natural tie, of the fixation to nature. The former is man-made, artificial, based on power and law, and therefore less compelling and forceful than the tie to the mother. While the mother represents nature and unconditioned love, the father represents abstraction, conscience, duty, law and hierarchy. The father's love for the son is not like the unconditioned love of the mother for her children *because they are her children,* but it is the love for the son whom he likes best because he lives up most to his expectations, and is best equipped to become the heir to the father's property and worldly functions.

From this follows an important difference between motherly and fatherly love; in the relationship to mother, there is little the child can do to regulate or control it. Motherly love is like an act of grace; if it is there, it is a blessing—if it is not there it cannot be created. Here lies the reason why individuals who have not overcome the fixation to mother often try to procure motherly love in a neurotic, magical way by making themselves helpless, sick or by regressing emotionally to the stage of an infant. The magic idea is: if I make myself into a helpless child, mother is bound to appear and to take care of me. The relationship to father, on the other hand, can be controlled. He wants the son to grow up, to take responsibility, to think, to build; or/and to be obedient, to serve father, to be like him. Whether father's expectations are more on development or on obedience, the son has a chance to acquire father's love, to produce father's affection by doing the desired things. To sum up: *the positive aspects of the patriarchal complex are reason, discipline, conscience and individualism; the negative aspects are hierarchy, oppression, inequality, submission.*[1]

Patriarchy

Positive

Negative

It is of special significance to note the close connection between the fatherly and motherly figures and *moral* principles. Freud, in his concept of the super-ego, relates only the father figure to the development of conscience. He assumed that the little boy, frightened by the castration threat of the rival father, incorporates the male parent—or rather his commands and prohibitions—into the formation of a conscience.[2] But there is not only a *fatherly* but also a *motherly conscience*; there is a voice which tells us to do our duty, and a voice which tells us to love and to forgive—others as well as ourselves. It is true that both types of conscience are originally influenced by the fatherly and motherly figures, but in the process of maturing, the conscience becomes more and more independent from these original father and mother figures; *we become*, as it were, *our own father and our own mother*, and we become also our own child. The father within ourselves tells us "this you ought to do" and "that you ought not to do." If we have

See Kohlberg + Gilligan

---

[1] These negative aspects are nowhere more clearly expressed than in the figure of Creon in Aeschylus' *Antigone*.

[2] In *Man for Himself* I have discussed the relativistic character of Freud's Super-Ego concept, and differentiated between an authoritarian conscience, and humanistic conscience, which is the voice recalling us to ourselves. cf. *Man for Himself, loc. cit.*, Ch. IV, 2.

done the wrong thing, he scolds us, and if we have done the right thing, he praises us. But while the father in us speaks in this manner, the mother in us speaks in a very different language. It is as if she were saying "your father is quite right in scolding you, but do not take him too seriously; whatever you have done, you are my child, I love you, and I forgive you; nothing you have done can interfere with your claim to life and happiness." Father's and mother's voices speak a different language; in fact, they seem to say opposite things. Yet the contradiction between the principle of duty and the principle of love, of fatherly and motherly conscience is a contradiction inherent in human existence, and both sides of the contradiction must be accepted. The conscience which follows only the commands of duty is as distorted as a conscience which follows only the commands of love. The inner father's and the inner mother's voices speak not only with regard to man's attitude toward himself, but also toward all his fellow men. He may judge his fellow man with his fatherly conscience, but he must at the same time hear in himself the voice of the mother, who feels love for all fellow creatures, for all that is alive, and who forgives all transgressions.[1]

Before I continue the discussion of man's basic needs, I want to give a brief description of the various phases of rootedness as they can be observed in the history of mankind, even though this exposition interrupts somewhat the main line of thought of this chapter.

While the infant is rooted in mother, man in his historical in-

---

[1] It is interesting to study the respective weight of the fatherly and motherly principle in the concept of God in the Jewish and Christian religions. The God who sends the flood because everybody is wicked except Noah, represents the fatherly conscience. The God who speaks to Jonah, feeling compassion "with that great city wherein are more than six score thousand persons that cannot discern between their right hand and their left hand and also much cattle" speaks with the voice of the all-forgiving mother. The same polarity between the fatherly and motherly function of God can be clearly seen in the further development of the Jewish, as well as of the Christian religions, especially in mysticism.

fancy (which is still by far the largest part of history in terms of time) remains rooted in nature. Though having emerged from nature the natural world remains his home; here are still his roots. He tries to find security regressing to and identifying himself with nature, the world of plants and animals. This attempt to hold on to nature can be clearly seen in many primitive myths and religious rituals. When man worships trees and animals as his idols, he worships particularizations of nature; they are the protecting, powerful forces whose worship is the worship of nature itself. In relating himself to them, the individual finds his sense of identity and belonging, as part of nature. The same holds true for the relationship to the *soil* on which one lives. The tribe often is not only unified by the common blood, but also by the common soil, and this very combination of blood and soil gives it its strength as the real home and frame of orientation for the individual.

In this phase of human evolution man still feels himself as part of the natural world, that of animals and plants. Only when he has taken the decisive step to emerge fully from nature does he try to create a definite demarcation line between himself and the animal world. An illustration of this idea can be found in the belief of the Winnebago Indians, that in the beginning the creatures did not yet have any permanent form. All were a kind of neutral being which could transform itself into either man or animal. At a certain period they decided to evolve definitely into animal or into man. Since that time, animals have remained animals, and man has remained man.[1] The same idea is expressed in the Aztec belief that the world, before the era in which we live now, was only populated by animals, until with Quetzalcoatl the era of human beings emerged; the same feeling is expressed in the

[1] This example is taken from Paul Radin, *Gott und Mensch in der Primitiven Welt*, Rhein Verlag, Zürich, 1953, p. 30.

belief still to be found among some Mexican Indians that a certain animal corresponds to one particular person; or in the belief of the Maoris that a certain tree (planted at birth) corresponds to one individual. It is expressed in the many rituals in which man identifies himself with an animal by garbing himself as one or in the selection of an animal totem.

This passive relationship to nature corresponded to man's economic activities. He started out as a food gatherer and hunter, and were it not for primitive tools and the use of fire he could be said to differ but little from the animal. In the process of history his skills grew, and his relationship to nature is transformed from a passive into an active one. He develops animal husbandry, learns to cultivate the land, achieves an ever-increasing skill in art and craftsmanship, exchanges his products for those of foreign countries and thus becomes a traveller and trader.

His gods change correspondingly. As long as he feels largely identified with nature, his gods are part of nature. When his skills as an artisan grow, he builds idols out of stone or wood, or gold. When he has evolved still further, and gained a greater feeling of his own strength, his gods have the shape of human beings. At first—and this seems to correspond to an agricultural stage—God appears to him in the form of the all-protecting and all-nourishing "Great Mother." Eventually he begins to worship fatherly gods, representing reason, principles, laws. This last and decisive turn away from rootedness in nature and from dependence on a loving mother seems to have begun with the emergence of the great rational and patriarchal religions. In Egypt, with the religious revolution of Ikhnaton in the fourteenth century B.C.; in Palestine with the formation of the Mosaic religion around the same time; in India and Greece with the arrival of the Northern invaders not much later. Many rituals expressed this new idea. In the sacrifice of animals, the animal in man is sacrificed to God. In the biblical food taboo, which forbids eating the blood of the animal (because "the blood is its life"), a strict demarcation line is put between man and animal. In the concept of God—who represents the unifying principle of all life, who is invisible and unlimited—the opposite pole to the natural, finite, diversified world, to the world of things, has been established. Man, created in God's likeness, shares God's qualities; he emerges from nature and strives to be fully born, to be fully awake.[1] This process reached a further stage in the middle of the first millennium in China, with Confucius and Lao-tse; in India with Buddha; in Greece with the philosophers of the Greek enlightenment and in Palestine with the biblical prophets, and then a new peak with Christianity and Stoicism within the Roman Empire, with Quetzalcoatl in Mexico [2] and another half millennium later with Mohammed in Africa.

Our Western culture is built on two foundations: the Jewish and the Greek cultures. Considering the Jewish tradition, the foundations of which are laid down in the Old Testament, we find that it constitutes a relatively pure form of patriarchal culture, built upon the power of the father in the family, of the priest and king in society, and of a fatherly God in Heaven. However, in spite of this extreme form of patriarchalism, one can still recognize the older matriarchal elements as they existed in the earth and nature-bound (telluric) religions, which were defeated by the rational, patriarchal religions during the second millennium B.C.

In the story of Creation we find man still in a primitive unity with the soil, without the necessity to work, and without con-

[1] While revising this manuscript, I find in Alfred Weber's *Der Dritte oder der Vierte Mensch*, R. Piper Co., München, 1953, pp. 9 ff., a scheme of historical development which has some similarities to the one in my text. He assumes a "chthonic period" from 4000 to 1200 B.C. which was characterized by the fixation to earth in agricultural peoples.

[2] I follow in this unorthodox dating the writings and personal communications of Laurette Séjourné, cf. her "El Mensaje de Quetzalcoatl," *Cuadernos Americanos*, V, 1954.

sciousness of himself. The woman is the more intelligent, active and daring of the two, and only after the "fall" the patriarchal God announces the principle that man shall rule over woman. The entire Old Testament is an elaboration of the patriarchal principle in various ways, by the establishment of a hierarchical pattern of a theocratic state, and a strictly patriarchal family organization. In the family structure as described by the Old Testament, we find always the figure of the *favorite* son: Abel as against Cain; Jacob as against Esau; Joseph against his brothers; and in a broader sense, the people of Israel as the favorite son of God. Instead of the equality of all children in the eyes of the mother, we find the favorite, who is most like the father, and most liked by the father as his successor and as the heir to his property. In the fight for the position of the favorite son, and thus for the inheritance, the brothers turn into enemies, equality gives way to hierarchy.

The Old Testament postulates not only a strict tabu of incest, but also a prohibition of the fixation to the soil. *Human history* is described as beginning with the expulsion of man from paradise, from the soil in which he was rooted, and with which he felt one. *Jewish* history is described as beginning with the command to Abraham to leave the country in which he was born, and to go "to a country which thou knowest not." From Palestine, the tribe wanders to Egypt; from there, again it returns to Palestine. But the new settlement is not final either. The teachings of the prophets are directed against the new incestuous involvement with the soil and nature as it was manifest in Canaanitic idolatry. They proclaimed the principle that a people who has regressed from the principles of reason and justice to those of the incestuous tie to the soil, will be driven away from its soil and will wander in the world homeless and soilless until it has fully developed the principles of reason, until it has overcome the in-

cestuous tie to the soil and nature; only then can the people return to their homeland, only then will the soil be a blessing, a
human home freed from the curse of incest. The concept of the
Messianic time is that of the complete victory over the incestuous
ties, and the full establishment of the spiritual reality of moral
and intellectual conscience, not only among the Jews, but among
all peoples of the earth.

The crowning and central concept of the patriarchal development of the Old Testament lies, of course, in the concept of God.
He represents the unifying principle behind the manifoldness of
phenomena. Man is created in the likeness of God; hence all men
are equal—equal in their common spiritual qualities, in their common reason, and in their capacity for brotherly love.

Early Christianity is a further development of this spirit,
not so much in the emphasis on the idea of love which we find
expressed in many parts of the Old Testament, but by its emphasis
on the supernational character of religion. As the prophets
challenged the validity of the existence of their own state, because it did not live up to the demands of conscience, so the
early Christians challenged the moral legitimacy of the Roman
Empire, because it violated the principles of love and justice.

While the Jewish-Christian tradition emphasized the *moral*
aspect, Greek thought found its most creative expression in the
intellectual aspect of the patriarchal spirit. In Greece, as in
Palestine, we find a patriarchal world which, in both its social
and religious aspects, had victoriously emerged from an earlier
matriarchal structure. Just as Eve was not born from a woman
but made from Adam's rib, so Athene was not a child of a woman,
but came from Zeus's head. The remainder of an older matriarchal world can still be seen, as Bachofen has shown, in the
figures of goddesses which are subordinate to the patriarchal
Olympic world. The Greeks laid the foundation for the intel-

lectual development of the Western world. They laid down the "first principles" of scientific thought, were the first to build "theory" as a foundation of science, to develop a systematic philosophy as it had not existed in any culture before. They created a theory of the state and of society based on their experience of the Greek polis, to be continued in Rome, on the social basis of a vast unified empire.

On account of the incapacity of the Roman Empire to continue a progressive social and political evolution, the development came to a standstill around the fourth century, but not before a new powerful institution had been built, the Catholic Church. While earlier Christianity had been a spiritually revolutionary movement of the poor and disinherited, who questioned the moral legitimacy of the existing state, the faith of a minority which accepted persecution and death as God's witnesses, it was to change in an incredibly short time into the official religion of the Roman State. While the Roman Empire's social structure was slowly freezing into a feudal order that was to survive in Europe for a thousand years, the Catholic religion's social structure began to change, too. The prophetic attitude that encouraged the questioning and criticizing of secular power's violation of the principles of love and justice receded in importance. The new attitude called for indiscriminating support of the Church's power as an institution. Such psychological satisfaction was given to the masses, that they accepted their dependency and poverty with resignation, making little effort to improve their social condition.[1]

[1] The change in the social role and function of Christianity was connected with profound changes in its spirit; the church became a hierarchical organization. The emphasis shifted increasingly from expectation of Christ's second coming and the establishment of a new order of love and justice, to the fact of the original coming—and the apostolic message of man's salvation from his inherent sinfulness. Connected with this was another change. The original concept of Christ was contained in the adoptionist dogma which said that God had adopted the man Jesus as

Change from Matriarchal to Patriarchal

The most important change from the standpoint of this discussion is that of a shifting of emphasis from a purely patriarchal
to a blending between matriarchal and patriarchal elements. The
Jewish God of the Old Testament had been a strictly patriarchal
god; in the Catholic development, the idea of the all-loving and
all-forgiving mother is re-introduced. The Catholic Church herself—the all-embracing mother—and the Virgin Mother, sym-
bolize the maternal spirit of forgiveness and love, while God,
the father, represented in the hierarchichal principle the authority
to which man had to submit without complaining or rebelling.
No doubt this blending of fatherly and motherly elements was
one of the main factors to which the church owed its tremendous
attraction and influence over the minds of the people. The masses,
oppressed by patriarchal authorities, could turn to the loving
mother who would comfort them and intercede for them.

The historical function of the church was by no means only
that of helping to establish a feudal order. Its most important
achievement, greatly helped by the Arabs and Jews, was to
transmit the essential elements of Jewish and Greek thought to
the primitive culture of Europe. It is as if Western history had
stood still for about a thousand years to wait for the moment
when Northern Europe had been brought to the point of development at which the Mediterranean world had arrived at the
beginning of the dark ages. When the spiritual heritage of Athens
and Jerusalem had been transmitted to, and had saturated the
Northern European peoples, the frozen social structure began to

---

his son, that is to say, that a man, a suffering and poor one, had become a god. In
this dogma the revolutionary hopes and longings of the poor and downtrodden had
found a religious expression. One year after Christianity was declared the official religion of the Roman Empire, the dogma was officially accepted that God and Jesus
were identical, of the same essence, and that God had only manifested himself in
the flesh of a man. In this new view, the revolutionary idea of the elevation of man
to God had been substituted by God's act of love to come down to man, as it were,
and thus save him from his corruption. (cf. E. Fromm, *Die Entwicklung des Christus
Dogmas*, Psychoanalytischer Verlag, Vienna, 1931.)

thaw and an explosive social and spiritual development began again.

The Catholic theology in the thirteenth and fourteenth centuries, the ideas of the Italian Renaissance, "discovering the individual and nature," the concepts of humanism and of natural law and the Reformation are the foundations of the new development. The most drastic and most far-reaching effect on European and world development was that of the Reformation. Protestantism and Calvinism went back to the purely patriarchal spirit of the Old Testament and eliminated the mother element from the religious concept. Man was not any more enveloped by the motherly love of the church and the Virgin; he was alone, facing a severe and strict God whose mercy he could obtain only by an act of complete surrender. The princes and the state became all-powerful, sanctioned by the demands of God. The emancipation from feudal bonds led to the increased feeling of isolation and powerlessness, but at the same time the positive aspect of the paternal principle asserted itself in the renaissance of rational thought and individualism.[1]

The renaissance of the patriarchal spirit since the sixteenth century, especially in Protestant countries, shows both the *positive* and *negative* aspect of patriarchism. The negative aspect manifested itself in a new submission to the state and temporal power, to the ever-increasing importance of man-made laws and secular hierarchies. The positive aspect showed itself in the increasing spirit of rationality and objectivity and in the growth of individual and social conscience. The flowering of science in our day is one of the most impressive manifestations of rational thought the human race has ever produced. But the *matriarchal complex*, in both its positive and negative aspects, has by no means

[1] cf. the thorough and brilliant analysis of these problems in M. N. Roy, *Reason, Romanticism and Revolution*, Renaissance Publishing Co., Calcutta, 1952.

Positive

disappeared from the modern Western scene. Its positive aspect, the idea of human equality, of the sacredness of life, of all men's right to share in the fruits of nature, found expression in the ideas of natural law, humanism, enlightenment philosophy and the objectives of democratic socialism. Common to all these ideas is the concept that all men are children of Mother Earth and have a right to be nourished by her, and to enjoy happiness without having to prove this right by the achievement of any particular status. The brotherhood of all men implies that they are all the sons of the same mother, who have an inalienable right to love and happiness. In this concept, the incestuous tie to the mother is eliminated. By the mastery over nature as it manifests itself in industrial production, man frees himself from his fixation to the bonds of blood and soil, he humanizes nature and naturalizes himself.

But side by side with the development of the positive aspects of the matriarchal complex we find, in the European development, the persistence of, or even further, regression to its negative aspects—the fixation to blood and soil. Man—freed from the traditional bonds of the medieval community, afraid of the new freedom which transformed him into an isolated atom—escaped into a new idolatry of blood and soil, of which nationalism and racism are the two most evident expressions. Along with the progressive development, which is a blending of the positive aspect of both patriarchal and matriarchal spirit, went the development of the negative aspects of both principles: the worship of the state, blended with the idolatry of the race or nation. Fascism, Nazism and Stalinism, are the most drastic manifestations of this blend of state and clan worship, both principles embodied in the figure of a "Fuehrer."

But the new totalitarianisms are by no means the only manifestations of incestuous fixation in our time. The breakdown of the Catholic supernational world of the Middle Ages would have led to a higher form of "catholicism," that is, of human universalism overcoming clan worship, had the development followed the intentions of the spiritual leaders of humanist thought since the Renaissance. But while science and technique created the conditions for such development, the Western world fell back into new forms of clan idolatry, that very orientation which the prophets of the Old Testament and early Christianity tried to uproot. Nationalism, originally a progressive movement, replaced the bonds of feudalism and absolutism. The average man today obtains his sense of identity from his belonging to a nation, rather than from his being a "son of man." His objectivity, that is, his reason, is warped by this fixation. He judges the "stranger" with different criteria than the members of his own clan. His feelings toward the stranger are equally warped. Those who are not "familiar" by bonds of blood and soil (expressed by common language, customs, food, songs, etc.) are looked upon with suspicion, and paranoid delusions about them can spring up at the slightest provocation. This incestuous fixation not only poisons the relationship of the individual to the stranger, but to the members of his own clan and to himself. The person who has not freed himself from the ties to blood and soil is not yet fully born as a human being; his capacity for love and reason are crippled; he does not experience himself nor his fellow man in their—and his own—human reality.

Nationalism is our form of incest, is our idolatry, is our insanity. "Patriotism" is its cult. It should hardly be necessary to say, that by "patriotism" I mean that attitude which puts the own nation above humanity, above the principles of truth and justice; not the loving interest in one's own nation, which is the concern with the nation's spiritual as much as with its material welfare—never with its power over other nations. Just as love for one individual which excludes the love for others is not love, love for one's country which is not part of one's love for humanity is not love, but idolatrous worship.[1]

The idolatrous character of national feeling can be seen in the reaction to the violations of clan symbols, a reaction which is very different from that to the violation of religious or moral symbols. Let us picture a man who takes the flag of his country to a street of one of the cities of the Western world, and tramples on it in view of other people. He would be lucky not to be lynched. Almost everybody would feel a sense of furious indignation, which hardly permits of any objective thought. The man who desecrated the flag would have done something unspeakable; he would have committed a crime which is not *one* crime among others, but *the* crime, the one unforgivable and unpardonable. Not quite as drastic, but nevertheless qualitatively the same would be the reaction to a man who says, "I do not love my country," or, in the case of war, "I do not care for my country's victory." Such a sentence is a real sacrilege, and a man saying it becomes a monster, an outlaw in the feelings of his fellow men.

In order to understand the particular quality of the feeling aroused, we may compare this reaction to one which would occur if a man got up and said, "I am in favor of killing all Negroes, or all Jews; I am in favor of starting a war in order to conquer new territory." Indeed, most people would feel that this was an unethical, inhuman opinion. But the crucial point is that the particular feeling of an uncontrollable deep-seated indignation and rage would not occur. Such an opinion is just "bad," but it is not a sacrilege, it is not an attack against "the sacred." Even if a man should speak disparagingly of God, he would hardly arouse the same feeling of indignation as against *the* crime, against the

---

[1] cf. to the problem of nationalism the comprehensive and profound study by R. Rocker, "Nationalism and Culture," *Rocker Publ. Comm.*, Los Angeles, 1937.

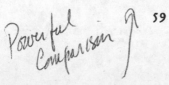
Powerful Comparison

sacrilege which is the violation of the symbols of the country. It is easy to rationalize the reaction to a violation of the national symbols by saying that a man who does not respect his country shows a lack of human solidarity and of social feeling; but is this not true also of the man who advocates war, or the killing of innocent people, or who exploits others for his own advantage? Undoubtedly, lack of concern for one's own country is an expression of a lack of social responsibility and of human solidarity, as are the other acts mentioned here, but the reaction to the violation of the flag is fundamentally different from the reaction to the denial of social responsibility in all other aspects. The one object is "sacred," a symbol of clan worship; the others are not.

After the great European Revolutions of the seventeenth and eighteenth centuries failed to transform "freedom from" into "freedom to," nationalism and state worship became the symptoms of a regression to incestuous fixation. Only when man succeeds in developing his reason and love further than he has done so far, only when he can build a world based on human solidarity and justice, only when he can feel rooted in the experience of universal brotherliness, will he have found a new, human form of rootedness, will he have transformed his world into a truly human home.

D. SENSE OF IDENTITY—INDIVIDUALITY VS. HERD CONFORMITY

Man may be defined as the animal that can say "I," that can be aware of himself as a separate entity. The animal being within nature, and not transcending it, has no awareness of himself, has no need for a sense of identity. Man, being torn away from nature, being endowed with reason and imagination, needs to form a concept of himself, needs to say and to feel: "I am I." Because he is not *lived*, but *lives*, because he has lost the original

unity with nature, has to make decisions, is aware of himself and
of his neighbor as different persons, he must be able to sense
himself as the subject of his actions. As with the need for relatedness, rootedness, and transcendence, this need for a sense of identity
is so vital and imperative that man could not remain sane if he did
not find some way of satisfying it. Man's sense of identity develops in the process of emerging from the "primary bonds"
which tie him to mother and nature. The infant, still feeling
one with mother, cannot yet say "I," nor has he any need for it.
Only after he has conceived of the outer world as being separate
and different from himself does he come to the awareness of himself as a distinct being, and one of the last words he learns to
use is "I," in reference to himself.

In the development of *the human race* the degree to which
man is aware of himself as a separate self depends on the extent
to which he has emerged from the clan and the extent to which
the process of individuation has developed. The member of a
primitive clan might express his sense of identity in the formula
"I am we"; he cannot yet conceive of himself as an "individual,"
existing apart from his group. In the medieval world, the individual was identified with his social role in the feudal hierarchy.
The peasant was not a man who happened to be a peasant, the
feudal lord not a man who happened to be a feudal lord. *He was*
a peasant or a lord, and this sense of his unalterable station was
an essential part of his sense of identity. When the feudal system
broke down, this sense of identity was shaken and the acute
question "who am I?" arose—or more precisely, "How do I know
that I am I?" This is the question which was raised, in a philosophical form, by Descartes. He answered the quest for identity
by saying, "I doubt—hence I think, I think—hence I am." This
answer put all the emphasis on the experience of "I" as the
subject of any *thinking* activity, and failed to see that the "I"

is experienced also in the process of feeling and creative action.

The development of Western culture went in the direction of creating the basis for the full experience of individuality. By making the individual free politically and economically, by teaching him to think for himself and freeing him from an authoritarian pressure, one hoped to enable him to feel "I" in the sense that he was the center and active subject of his powers and experienced himself as such. But only a minority achieved the new experience of "I." For the majority, individualism was not much more than a façade behind which was hidden the failure to acquire an individual sense of identity.

Many substitutes for a truly individual sense of identity were sought for, and found. Nation, religion, class and occupation serve to furnish a sense of identity. "I am an American," "I am a Protestant," "I am a businessman," are the formulae which help a man experience a sense of identity after the original clan identity has disappeared and before a truly individual sense of identity has been acquired. These different identifications are, in contemporary society, usually employed together. They are in a broad sense status identifications, and they are more efficient if blended with older feudal remnants, as in European countries. In the United States, in which so little is left of feudal relics, and in which there is so much social mobility, these status identifications are naturally less efficient, and the sense of identity is shifted more and more to the experience of conformity.

Inasmuch as I am not different, inasmuch as I am like the others, and recognized by them as "a regular fellow," I can sense myself as "I." I am—"as you desire me"—as Pirandello put it in the title of one of his plays. Instead of the pre-individualistic clan identity, a new herd identity develops, in which the sense of identity rests on the sense of an unquestionable belonging to the crowd. That this uniformity and conformity are often not recognized as such, and are covered by the illusion of individuality, does not alter the facts.

The problem of the sense of identity is not, as it is usually understood, merely a philosophical problem, or a problem only concerning our mind and thought. The need to feel a sense of identity stems from the very condition of human existence, and it is the source of the most intense strivings. Since I cannot remain sane without the sense of "I," I am driven to do almost anything to acquire this sense. Behind the intense passion for status and conformity is this very need, and it is sometimes even stronger than the need for physical survival. What could be more obvious than the fact that people are willing to risk their lives, to give up their love, to surrender their freedom, to sacrifice their own thoughts, for the sake of being one of the herd, of conforming, and thus of acquiring a sense of identity, even though it is an illusory one.

E.   THE NEED FOR A FRAME OF ORIENTATION AND
     DEVOTION—REASON VS. IRRATIONALITY

The fact that man has reason and imagination leads not only to the necessity for having a sense of his own identity, but also for orienting himself in the world intellectually. This need can be compared with the process of physical orientation which develops in the first years of life, and which is completed when the child can walk by himself, touch and handle things, knowing what they are. But when the ability to walk and to speak has been acquired, only the first step in the direction of orientation has been taken. Man finds himself surrounded by many puzzling phenomena and, having reason, he has to make sense of them, has to put them in some context which he can understand and which permits him to deal with them in his thoughts. The further his reason develops, the more adequate becomes his system of orientation, that is, the more it approximates reality. But even if man's frame of orientation is utterly illusory, it satisfies his need for some picture which is meaningful to him. Whether he believes in the power of a totem animal, in a rain god, or in the superiority and destiny of his race, his need for some frame of orientation is satisfied. Quite obviously, the picture of the world which he has depends on the development of his reason and of his knowledge. Although biologically the brain capacity of the human race has remained the same for thousands of generations, it takes a long evolutionary process to arrive at *objectivity*, that is, to acquire the faculty to see the world, nature, other persons and oneself as they are, and not distorted by desires and fears. The more man develops this objectivity, the more he is in touch with reality, the more he matures, the better can he create a human world in which he is at home. Reason is man's faculty for *grasping* the world by thought, in contradiction to intelligence, which is man's ability to *manipulate* the world with the help of thought. Reason is man's instrument for arriving at the truth, intelligence is man's instrument for manipulating the world more successfully; the former is essentially human, the latter belongs to the animal part of man.

Reason is a faculty which must be practiced, in order to develop, and it is indivisible. By this I mean that the faculty for objectivity refers to the knowledge of nature as well as to the knowledge of man, of society and of oneself. If one lives in illusions about one sector of life, one's capacity for reason is restricted or damaged, and thus the use of reason is inhibited with regard to all other sectors. Reason in this respect is like love. Just as love is an orientation which refers to all objects and is incompatible with the restriction to one object, so is reason a human faculty which must embrace the whole of the world with which man is confronted.

a) some frame necessary
b) rational frame most helpful.

The need for a frame of orientation exists on two levels; the first and the more fundamental need is to have *some* frame of orientation, regardless of whether it is true or false. Unless man has such a subjectively satisfactory frame of orientation, he cannot live sanely. On the second level the need is to be in touch with reality by reason, to grasp the world objectively. But the necessity to develop his reason is not as immediate as that to develop some frame of orientation, since what is at stake for man in the latter case is his happiness and serenity, and not his sanity. This becomes very clear if we study the function of *rationalization*. However unreasonable or immoral an action may be, man has an insuperable urge to rationalize it, that is, to prove to himself and to others that his action is determined by reason, common sense, or at least conventional morality. He has little difficulty in acting irrationally, but it is almost impossible for him not to give his action the appearance of reasonable motivation.

If man were only a disembodied intellect, his aim would be achieved by a comprehensive thought system. But since he is an entity endowed with a body as well as a mind, he has to react to the dichotomy of his existence not only in thinking but in the total process of living, in his feelings and actions. Hence any satisfying system of orientation contains not only intellectual elements but elements of feeling and sensing which are expressed in the relationship to an object of devotion.

The answers given to man's need for a system of orientation and an object of devotion differ widely both in content and in form. There are primitive systems such an animism and totemism in which natural objects or ancestors represent answers to man's quest for meaning. There are non-theistic systems like Buddhism, which are usually called religions although in their original form there is no concept of God. There are purely philosophical systems, like Stoicism, and there are the monotheistic religious systems which give an answer to man's quest for meaning in reference to the concept of God.

But whatever their contents, they all respond to man's need to have not only some thought system, but also an object of devotion which gives meaning to his existence and to his position in the world. Only the analysis of the various forms of religion can show which answers are better and which are worse solutions to man's quest for meaning and devotion, "better" or "worse" always considered from the standpoint of man's nature and his development.[1]

[1] cf. for a more extensive discussion of this problem, my *Psychoanalysis and Religion*, Yale University Press, 1950. The discussion of the need for an object of devotion and for rituals is continued in Chapter VIII, 4, of this book.

▪ 4 ▪

MENTAL HEALTH AND SOCIETY

The concept of mental health depends on our concept of the nature of man. In the previous chapter the attempt was made to show that the needs and passions of man stem from the peculiar condition of his existence. Those needs which he shares with the animal—hunger, thirst, need for sleep and sexual satisfaction— are important, being rooted in the inner chemistry of the body, and they can become all powerful when they remain unsatisfied. *Maslow* (This holds true, of course, more of the need for food and sleep than of sex, which if not satisfied never assumes the power of the other needs, at least not for physiological reasons.) But even their complete satisfaction is not a sufficient condition for sanity and mental health. These depend on the satisfaction of those needs *Sanity + Mental Health* and passions which are specifically human, and which stem from the conditions of the human situation: the need for relatedness, transcendence, rootedness, the need for a sense of identity and the need for a frame of orientation and devotion. The great passions of man, his lust for power, his vanity, his search for truth, his passion for love and brotherliness, his destructiveness as well as his creativeness, every powerful desire which motivates man's actions, is rooted in this specific human source, not in the

Unsuccessful but creative attempt to paint a big picture Explanation of Neuroses + Psychosis.

various stages of his libido as Freud's construction postulated.

Man's solution to his physiological needs is, psychologically speaking, utterly simple; the difficulty here is a purely sociological and economic one. Man's solution to his human needs is exceedingly complex, it depends on many factors and last, not least, on the way his society is organized and how this organization determines the human relations within it.

The basic psychic needs stemming from the peculiarities of human existence must be satisfied in one form or other, unless man is to become insane, just as his physiological needs must be satisfied lest he die. But *the way* in which the psychic needs can be satisfied are manifold, and the difference between various ways of satisfaction is tantamount to the difference between various degrees of mental health. If one of the basic necessities has found no fulfillment, insanity is the result; if it is satisfied but in an unsatisfactory way—considering the nature of human existence— neurosis (either manifest or in the form of a socially patterned defect) is the consequence. Man has to relate himself to others; but if he does it in a symbiotic or alienated way, he loses his independence and integrity; he is weak, suffers, becomes hostile, or apathetic; only if he can relate himself to others in a loving way does he feel one with them and at the same time preserve his integrity. Only by productive work does he relate himself to nature, becoming one with her, and yet not submerging in her. As long as man remains rooted incestuously in nature, mother, clan, he is blocked from developing his individuality, his reason; he remains the helpless prey of nature, and yet he can never feel one with her. Only if he develops his reason and his love, if he can experience the natural and the social world in a human way, can he feel at home, secure in himself, and the master of his life. It is hardly necessary to point out that of two possible forms of transcendence, destructiveness is conducive

Relatedness

Individuality

Transcendence

68

to suffering, creativeness to happiness. It is also easy to see that only a sense of identity based on the experience of his own powers can give strength, while all forms of identity experience based on the group, leave man dependent, hence weak. Eventually, only to the extent to which he grasps reality, can he make this world *his;* if he lives in illusions, he never changes the conditions which necessitate these illusions.

Summing up, it can be said that the concept of mental health follows from the very conditions of human existence, and it is the same for man in all ages and all cultures. *Mental health is characterized by the ability to love and to create, by the emergence from incestuous ties to clan and soil, by a sense of identity based on one's experience of self as the subject and agent of one's powers, by the grasp of reality inside and outside of ourselves, that is, by the development of objectivity and reason.*

This concept of mental health coincides essentially with the norms postulated by the great spiritual teachers of the human race. This coincidence appears to some modern psychologists to be a proof that our psychological premises are not "scientific" but philosophic or religious "ideals." They find it difficult, apparently, to draw the conclusion that the great teachings of all cultures were based on rational insight into the nature of man, on the conditions for his full development. This latter conclusion seems also to be more in line with the fact that in the most diverse places of this globe, at different periods of history, the "awakened ones" have preached the same norms, with none, or with little influence from one upon the other. Ikhnaton, Moses, Kung Futse, Lao-tse, Buddha, Isaiah, Socrates, Jesus have postulated the same norms for human life, with only small and insignificant differences.

There is one particular difficulty which many psychiatrists and psychologists have to overcome in order to accept the ideas of *humanistic psychoanalysis*. They still think in the philosophic premises of the nineteenth-century materialism which assumed that all important psychic phenomena must be rooted in (and caused by) corresponding *physiological*, somatic processes. Thus Freud, whose basic philosophical orientation was molded by this type of materialism, believed that he had found this physiological substratum of human passion in the "libido." In the theory presented here, there are no corresponding *physiological* substrata to the needs for relatedness, transcendence, etc. The substratum is not a physical one, but the total human personality in its interaction with the world, nature and man; *it is the human practice of life as it results from the conditions of human existence*. Our philosophic premise is not that of the nineteenth-century materialism, but one which takes the action of man and his interaction with his fellow man and with nature as the basic empirical datum for the study of man.

Our concept of mental health leads into a theoretical difficulty if we consider the concept of human evolution. There is reason to assume that the history of man, hundreds of thousands of years ago, starts out with a truly "primitive" culture, where man's reason has not developed beyond the most rudimentary beginnings, where his frame of orientation has little relation to reality and truth. Should we speak of this primitive man as lacking in mental health, when he is simply lacking in qualities which only further evolution could give him? Indeed, one answer could be given to this question which would open up an easy solution; this answer lies in the obvious analogy between the evolution of the human race, and the evolution of the individual. If an adult had the attitude and orientation of a one-month-old child, we certainly would classify him as severely sick, probably as schizophrenic. For the one-month-old baby, however, the same attitude is normal and healthy, because it corresponds to the stage of his psychic development. The mental sickness of the adult, then, can be characterized, as Freud has shown, as a fixation or regression to an orientation which belongs to a former evolutionary state, and which is not adequate any more, considering the state of development the person should have reached. In the same way one could say that the human race, like the infant, starts out with a primitive orientation, and one would call healthy all forms of human orientation, which correspond to the adequate state of human evolution; while one would call "sick" those "fixations" or "regressions" which represent earlier states of development after the human race has already passed through them. Attractive as such a solution is, it does not take into account one fact. The one-month-old child has not yet the organic basis for a mature attitude. He could under no circumstances think, feel or act like a mature adult. Man, on the contrary, for hundreds of thousands of years, has had all the organic equipment for maturity; his brain, bodily co-ordination, physical strength have not changed in all that time. His evolution depended entirely on his ability to transmit knowledge to future generations, and thus to accumulate it. Human evolution is the result of cultural development, and not of an organic change. The infant of the most primitive culture, put into a highly developed culture, would develop like all other children in this culture, because the only factor determining his development is the cultural factor. In other words, while the one-month-old child could never have the spiritual maturity of an adult—whatever the cultural conditions are—any man from the primitive stage on, could have the perfection of man at the peak of his evolution provided he were given the cultural conditions for such maturity. It follows that to speak of primitive, incestuous, unreasonable man, as being in a normal evolutionary phase is different from making the same statement about the infant. Yet, on the other hand, the development of culture is a necessary condition for human development. Thus, there does not seem to be a completely satisfactory answer to the problem; from one standpoint we may speak of a lack in mental health; from another standpoint we may speak of an early phase in development. But the difficulty is great only if we deal with the problem in its most general form; as soon as we come to the more concrete problems of our time, we find the problem much less complicated. We have reached a state of individuation in which only the fully developed mature personality can make fruitful use of freedom; if the individual has not developed his reason and his capacity for love, he is incapable of bearing the burden of freedom and individuality, and tries to escape into artificial ties which give him a sense of belonging and rootedness. Any regression today from freedom into artificial rootedness in state or race is a sign of mental illness, since such regression does not correspond to the state of evolution already reached and results in unquestionably pathological phenomena.

Regardless of whether we speak of "mental health" or of the "mature development" of the human race, the concept of mental health or of maturity is an objective one, arrived at by the examination of the "human situation" and the human necessities and needs stemming from it. It follows, as I pointed out in Chapter II, that mental health cannot be defined in terms of the "adjustment" of the individual to his society, but, on the contrary, *that it must be defined in terms of the adjustment of society to the needs of man*, of its role in furthering or hindering the development of mental health. Whether or not the individual is healthy, is primarily not an individual matter, but depends on the structure of his society. A healthy society furthers man's capacity to love his fellow men, to work creatively, to develop his reason and objectivity, to have a sense of self which is based on the experience of his own productive powers. An unhealthy

72

society is one which creates mutual hostility, distrust, which transforms man into an instrument of use and exploitation for others, which deprives him of a sense of self, except inasmuch as he submits to others or becomes an automaton. Society can have both functions; it can further man's healthy development, and it can hinder it; in fact most societies do both, and the question is only to what degree and in what directions their positive and negative influence is exercised.

This view that mental health is to be determined *objectively* and that society has both a furthering *and* a distorting influence on man, contradicts not only the relativistic view, discussed above, but two other views which I want to discuss now. One, decidedly the most popular one today, wants to make us believe that contemporary Western society and more especially, the "American way of life" corresponds to the deepest needs of human nature and that adjustment to this way of life means mental health and maturity. Social psychology, instead of being a tool for the criticism of society, thus becomes the apologist for the status quo. The concept of "maturity" and "mental health" in this view, corresponds to the desirable attitude of a worker or employee in industry or business. To give one example for this adjustment concept, I take a definition by Dr. Strecker, on emotional maturity. "I define maturity," he says, "as the ability to stick to a job, the capacity to give more on any job than is asked for, reliability, persistence to carry out a plan regardless of the difficulties, the ability to work with other people under organization and authority, the ability to make decisions, a will to life, flexibility, independence, and tolerance." [1] It is quite clear that what Strecker here describes as maturity are the virtues of a good worker, employee or soldier in the big social organizations of our time; they are the qualities

[1] E. A. Strecker, *Their Mothers' Sons*, J. B. Lippincott Company, Philadelphia and New York, 1951, p. 211.

which are usually mentioned in advertisements for a junior executive. To him, and many others who think like him, maturity is the same as adjustment to our society, without ever raising the question whether this adjustment is to a healthy or a pathological way of conducting one's life.

Hobbes + Freud

In contrast to this view is the one which runs from Hobbes to Freud, and which assumes a basic and unalterable *contradiction between human nature and society*, a contradiction which follows from the alleged asocial nature of man. For Freud, man is driven by two biologically rooted impulses: the craving for sexual pleasure, and for destruction. The aim of his sexual desire is complete sexual freedom, that is, unlimited sexual access to all women he might find desirable. "Man discovered by experience that sexual (genital) love afforded him his greatest gratification, so that it became in effect the prototype of all happiness to him." He thus must have been impelled "to seek his happiness further along the path of sexual relations, to make genital erotism the central point of his life." [1]

The other aim of the natural sexual desire is the incestuous desire for the mother which, by its very nature, creates conflict with and hostility against the father. Freud expressed the importance of this aspect of sexuality by stating that the prohibition against incest is "perhaps the most maiming wound ever inflicted throughout the ages on the erotic life of man." [2]

Quite in line with the ideas of Rousseau, Freud maintains that primitive man has yet to cope with no, or exceedingly few restrictions to the satisfaction of those basic desires. He can give vent to his aggression, and there are few limitations to the satisfaction of his sexual impulses. "In actual fact, primitive man . . . knew nothing of any restrictions on his instincts. . . .

[1] *Civilization and Its Discontents, loc. cit.,* p. 69.
[2] *Ibid.,* p. 74.

Civilized man has exchanged some part of his chances of happiness for a measure of 'security.' " [1]

While Freud follows Rousseau in the idea of the "happy savage," he follows Hobbes in his assumption of the basic hostility between men. "*Homo homini lupus;* who has the courage to dispute it in the face of all the evidence in his own life and in history?" [2] Freud asks. Man's aggressiveness, Freud thinks, has two sources: one, the innate striving for destruction (death instinct) and the other the frustration of his instinctual desires, imposed upon him by civilization. While man may channel part of his aggression against himself, through the Super-Ego, and while a minority can sublimate their sexual desire into brotherly love, aggressiveness remains ineradicable. Men will always compete with, and attack each other, if not for material things, then for the "prerogatives in sexual relationships, which must arouse the strongest rancour and most violent enmity among men and women who are otherwise equal. Let us suppose this were also to be removed by instituting complete liberty in sexual life, so that the family, the germ-cell of culture, ceased to exist; one could not, it is true, foresee the new paths on which cultural development might then proceed, but one thing one would be bound to expect, and that is that the ineffaceable feature of human nature would follow wherever it led." [3] Since for Freud love is in its essence sexual desire, he is compelled to assume a contradiction between love and social cohesion. Love, according to him, is by its very nature egotistical and antisocial, and the sense of solidarity and brotherly love are not primary feelings rooted in man's nature, but aim-inhibited sexual desires.

On the basis of his concept of man, that of his inherent wish

[1] *Ibid.*, pp. 91, 92.
[2] *Ibid.*, p. 85.
[3] *Ibid.*, p. 89.

for unlimited sexual satisfaction, and of his destructiveness, Freud must arrive at a picture of the necessary *conflict* between civilization and mental health and happiness. Primitive man is healthy and happy because he is not frustrated in his basic instincts, but he lacks the blessings of culture. Civilized man is more secure, enjoys art and science, but he is bound to be neurotic because of the continued frustration of his instincts, enforced by civilization.

For Freud, social life and civilization are essentially in contrast to the needs of human nature as he sees it, and man is confronted with the tragic alternative between happiness based on the unrestricted satisfaction of his instincts, and security and cultural achievements based on instinctual frustration, hence conducive to neurosis and all other forms of mental sickness. Civilization, to Freud, is the product of instinctual frustration and thus the cause of mental illness.

Freud's concept of human nature as being essentially competitive (and asocial) is the same as we find it in most authors who believe that the characteristics of man in modern Capitalism are his natural characteristics. Freud's theory of the Oedipus complex is based on the assumption of the "natural" antagonism and competitiveness between father and sons for the love of the mother. This competition is said to be unavoidable because of the natural incestuous strivings in the sons. Freud only follows the same trend of thought in his assumption that the instincts of each man make him desire to have the prerogative in sexual relationships, and thus create violent enmity among themselves. We cannot fail to see that Freud's whole theory of sex is conceived on the anthropological premise that competition and mutual hostility are inherent in human nature.

Darwin gave expression to this principle in the sphere of *biology* with his theory of a competitive "struggle for survival." Economists like Ricardo and the Manchester school translated it into

Each has very different ramifications for mental health

the sphere of *economy*. Later, Freud, under the influence of the same anthropological premises, was to claim it for the sphere of *sexual desires*. His basic concept is that of a "homo sexualis" as that of the economists was that of the "homo economicus." Both the "economic" man and the "sexual" man are convenient fabrications whose alleged nature—isolated, asocial, greedy and competitive—makes Capitalism appear as the system which corresponds perfectly to human nature, and places it beyond the reach of criticism.

Both positions, the "adjustment view" and the Hobbes-Freudian view of the necessary conflict between human nature and society, imply the defense of contemporary society and they both are one-sided distortions. Furthermore, they both ignore the fact that society is not only in conflict with the *asocial* aspects of man, partly produced by itself, but often also with his most valuable human qualities, which it suppresses rather than furthers.

An objective examination of the relation between society and human nature must consider both the furthering and the inhibiting impact of society on man, taking into account the nature of man and the needs stemming from it. Since most authors have emphasized the positive influence of modern society on man, I shall in this book pay less attention to this aspect and more to the somewhat neglected pathogenic function of modern society.

[Handwritten notes:]

Summary
3 Views
The "individual"
① (this) Man + Society can live together in a constructive + productive relationship

② Adjustment Theory: The "Best" Society has evolved (Here + Now) + Individual must adjust to it.

③ Hobbes + Freud — Man + Society in necessary conflict

▪ 5 ▪

MAN IN CAPITALISTIC SOCIETY

THE SOCIAL CHARACTER

Mental health cannot be discussed meaningfully as an abstract quality of abstract people. If we are to discuss now the state of mental health in contemporary Western man, and if we are to consider what factors in his mode of life make for in-sanity and what others are conducive to sanity, we have to study the influence of the specific conditions of our mode of production and of our social and political organization on the nature of man; we have to arrive at a picture of the personality of the average man living and working under these conditions. Only if we can arrive at such a picture of the *"social character,"* tentative and incomplete as it may be, do we have a basis on which to judge the mental health and sanity of modern man.

What is meant by social character? I refer in this concept to *the nucleus of the character structure which is shared by most members of the same culture* in contradistinction to the *individual character in which people belonging to the same culture differ from each other.* The concept of social character is not a statistical concept in the sense that it is simply the sum total of character traits to be found in the majority of people in a given culture.

social character / what is shared by most members of a culture.

78

It can be understood only in reference to the *function* of the social character which we shall now proceed to discuss.[1]

Each society is structuralized and operates in certain ways which are necessitated by a number of objective conditions. These conditions include methods of production and distribution which in turn depend on raw materials, industrial techniques, climate, size of population, and political and geographical factors, cultural traditions and influences to which society is exposed. There is no "society" in general, but only specific social structures which operate in different and ascertainable ways. Although these social structures do change in the course of historical development, they are relatively fixed at any given historical period, and society can exist only by operating within the framework of its particular structure. The members of the society and/or the various classes or status groups within it have to behave in such a way as to be able to function in the sense required by the social system. It is the function of the social character to shape the energies of the members of society in such a way that their behavior is not a matter of conscious decision as to whether or not to follow the social pattern, but one of *wanting to act as they have to act* and at the same time finding gratification in acting according to the requirements of the culture. In other words, it is the social character's function *to mold and channel human energy within a given society for the purpose of the continued functioning of this society.*

Modern, industrial society, for instance, could not have attained its ends had it not harnessed the energy of free men for work in an

---

[1] In the following pages I have drawn on my paper, "Psychoanalytic Characterology and Its Application to the Understanding of Culture," in *Culture and Personality,* ed. by G. S. Sargent and M. Smith, Viking Fund, 1949, pp. 1–12. The concept of the social character was developed originally in my "Die psychoanalytische Charakterologie in ihrer Anwendurg für die Soziologie" in *Zeitschrift für Sozialforschung,* I, Hirschfeld, Leipzig, 1931.

 a statement of Folk Psychology

unprecedented degree. Man had to be molded into a person who was eager to spend most of his energy for the purpose of work, who acquired discipline, particularly orderliness and punctuality, to a degree unknown in most other cultures. It would not have sufficed if each individual had to make up his mind consciously every day that he wanted to work, to be on time, etcetera, since any such conscious deliberation would lead to many more exceptions than the smooth functioning of society can afford. Nor would threat and force have sufficed as a motive, since the highly differentiated tasks in modern industrial society can in the long run only be the work of free men and not of forced labor. The *necessity* for work, for punctuality and orderliness had to be transformed into an inner *drive* for these aims. This means that society had to produce a social character in which these strivings were inherent.

The *genesis* of the social character cannot be understood by referring to one single cause but by understanding the interaction of sociological and ideological factors. Inasmuch as economic factors are less easily changeable, they have a certain predominance in this interplay. This does not mean that the drive for material gain is the only or even the most powerful motivating force in man. It does mean that the individual and society are primarily concerned with the task of survival, and that only when survival is secured can they proceed to the satisfaction of other imperative human needs. The task of survival implies that man has to produce, that is, he has to secure the minimum of food and shelter necessary for survival, and the tools needed for even the most rudimentary processes of production. The method of production in turn determines the social relations existing in a given society. It determines the mode and practice of life. However, religious, political and philosophical ideas are not purely secondary projective systems. While they are rooted in the social

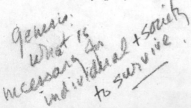

80

character, they in turn also determine, systematize and stabilize the social character.

Let me state again, in speaking of the socio-economic structure of society as molding man's character, we speak only of one pole in the interconnection between social organization and man. The other pole to be considered is man's nature, molding in turn the social conditions in which he lives. The social process can be understood only if we start out with the knowledge of the reality of man, his psychic properties as well as his physiological ones, and if we examine the interaction between the nature of man and the nature of the external conditions under which he lives and which he has to master if he is to survive.

While it is true that man can adapt himself to almost any conditions, he is not a blank sheet of paper on which culture writes its text. Needs like the striving for happiness, harmony, love and freedom are inherent in his nature. They are also dynamic factors in the historical process which, if frustrated, tend to arouse psychic reactions, ultimately creating the very conditions suited to the original strivings. As long as the objective conditions of the society and the culture remain stable, the social character has a predominantly stabilizing function. If the external conditions change in such a way that they do not fit any more with the traditional social character, a *lag* arises which often changes the function of character into an element of disintegration instead of stabilization, into dynamite instead of a social mortar, as it were.

Provided this concept of the genesis and function of the social character is correct, we are confronted with a puzzling problem. Is not the assumption that the character structure is molded by the role which the individual has to play in his culture contradicted by the assumption that a person's character is molded in his childhood? Can both views pretend to be true in view of the fact that the child in his early years of life has comparatively little contact with society as such? This question is not as difficult to answer as it may seem at first glance. We must differentiate between the factors which are responsible for the particular *contents* of the social character and the *methods* by which the social character is produced. The structure of society and the function of the individual in the social structure may be considered to determine the content of the social character. The family on the other hand may be considered to be the *psychic agency of society*, the institution which has the function of transmitting the requirements of society to the growing child. The family fulfills this function in two ways. First, and this is the most important factor, by the influence the character of the parents has on the character formation of the growing child. Since the character of most parents is an expression of the social character, they transmit in this way the essential features of the socially desirable character structure to the child. The parents' love and happiness are communicated to the child as well as their anxiety or hostility. In addition to the character of the parents, the methods of childhood training which are customary in a culture also have the function of molding the character of the child in a socially desirable direction. There are various methods and techniques of child training which can fulfill the same end, and on the other hand there can be methods which seem identical but which nevertheless are different because of the character structure of those who practice these methods. By focusing on methods of child training, we can never explain the social character. Methods of child training are significant only as a mechanism of *transmission*, and they can be understood correctly only if we understand first what kinds of personalities are desirable and necessary in any given culture.[1]

---

[1] In the assumption that methods of child training in themselves are the cause for the particular formation of a culture lies the weakness of the approach by Kardiner.

The problem, then, of the socio-economic conditions in modern industrial society which create the personality of modern Western man and are responsible for the disturbances in his mental health require an understanding of those elements specific to the capitalistic mode of production, of an "acquisitive society" in an industrial age. Sketchy and elementary as such a description by a noneconomist must necessarily be, I hope it is neverthless sufficient to form the basis for the following analysis of the social character of man in present-day Western society.

THE STRUCTURE OF CAPITALISM AND THE CHARACTER OF MAN

A History of Capitalism

A. SEVENTEENTH- AND EIGHTEENTH-CENTURY CAPITALISM

The economic system which has become dominant in the West since the seventeenth and eighteenth centuries is Capitalism. In spite of great changes which have occurred within this system, there are certain features which have endured throughout its history and, with reference to these common features, it is legitimate to use the concept of Capitalism for the economic system existing throughout this whole period.

Common features

Briefly, these common features are: 1—the existence of politically and legally free men; 2—the fact that free men (workers and employees) sell their labor to the owner of capital on the labor market, by contract; 3—the existence of the commodity market as a mechanism by which prices are determined and the exchange of the social product is regulated; 4—the principle that each individual acts with the aim of seeking a profit for himself, and

---

Gorer and others, whose work is based in this respect on the orthodox Freudian premises.

yet that, by the competitive action of many, the greatest advantage is supposed to accrue for all.

While these features are common to Capitalism throughout the last few centuries, the changes within this period are as important as are the similarities. While we are most concerned in our analysis with the impact of the contemporary socio-economic structure on man, we shall at least briefly discuss the features of seventeenth- and eighteenth-century Capitalism, and those of nineteenth-century Capitalism which are different from the development of society and man in the twentieth century.

Speaking of the seventeenth and eighteenth centuries, two aspects must be mentioned which characterize this early period of Capitalism. First, that technique and industry were in the beginning compared with the development in the nineteenth and twentieth centuries, and second that at the same time the practices and ideas of medieval culture still had a considerable influence on the economic practices of this period. Thus it was supposed to be un-Christian and unethical for one merchant to try to lure customers from another by force of lower prices or any other inducements. In the fifth edition of the *Complete English Tradesman* (1745), it is stated that since the death of the author, Defoe, in 1731, "this underselling practice is grown to such a shameful height, that particular persons publicly advertise that they undersell the rest of the trade." [1] The *Complete English Tradesman*, fifth edition, cites a concrete case in which an "overgrown tradesman" who had more money than his competitors, and thus was not forced to use credit, bought his wares directly from the producer, transported them himself, instead of through a middleman, and sold them directly to the retailer, thus enabling the latter to sell the material for one penny cheaper per yard. The

---

[1] I follow here the description and quote illustrations given by W. Sombart, *Der Bourgeois*, München and Leipzig, 1923, p. 201 ff.

84

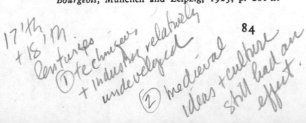

comment of the Complete Tradesman is that the result of this whole method is only to enrich this "covetous man," and to enable another man to buy his cloth a little cheaper, "a very small advantage" which is in no relation to the damage done the other businessmen.[1] We find similar prohibitions against underselling in ordinances in Germany and France throughout the whole eighteenth century.

It is well known how skeptical people were in that period toward new machines, inasmuch as they threatened to take away work from man. Colbert called them "the enemy of labour," and Montesquieu says, "Esprit de Loi" (XXIII, 15,) that machines which diminish the numbers of workers are "pernicious." The various attitudes just mentioned are based on principles which had determined the life of man for many centuries. Most important of all was the principle that society and economy exist for man, and not man for them. No economic progress was supposed to be healthy if it hurt any group within the society; needless to say this concept was closely related to traditionalist thoughts in so much as the traditional social balance was to be preserved, and any disturbance was believed to be harmful.

B. NINETEENTH-CENTURY CAPITALISM

In the nineteenth century the traditionalistic attitude of the eighteenth changes, first slowly and then rapidly. The living human being, with his desires and woes, loses more and more his central place in the system, and this place is occupied by business and production. Man ceases to be "the measure of all things" in the economic sphere. The most characteristic element of nineteenth-century Capitalism was first of all, ruthless exploitation of the worker; it was believed to be a natural or a social law that hundreds of thousands of workers were living at the point of

[1] *Ibid.*, p. 206.

starvation. The owner of capital was supposed to be morally right if, in the pursuit of profit, he exploited to the maximum the labor he hired. There was hardly any sense of human solidarity between the owner of capital and his workers. The law of the economic jungle was supreme. All the restrictive ideas of previous centuries were left behind. One seeks out the customer, tries to undersell one's competitor, and the competitive fight against equals is as ruthless and unrestricted as the exploitation of the worker. With the use of the steam engine, division of labor grows, and so does the size of enterprises. The capitalistic principle that each one seeks his own profit and thus contributes to the happiness of all becomes the guiding principle of human behavior.

The market as the prime regulator is freed from all traditional restrictive elements and comes fully into its own in the nineteenth century. While everybody believes himself to act according to his own interest, he is actually determined by the anonymous laws of the market and of the economic machine. The individual capitalist expands his enterprise not primarily because he *wants* to, but because he *has* to, because—as Carnegie said in his autobiography—postponement of further expansion would mean regression. Actually as a business grows, one has to continue making it bigger, whether one wants to or not. In this function of the economic law which operates behind the back of man and forces him to do things without giving him the freedom to decide, we see the beginning of a constellation which comes to its fruition only in the twentieth century.

In our time it is not only the law of the market which has its own life and rules over man, but also the development of science and technique. For a number of reasons, the problems and organization of science today are such that a scientist does not choose his problems; the problems force themselves upon the scientist. He solves one problem, and the result is not that he is more

86

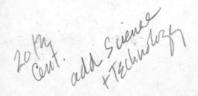

secure or certain, but that ten other new problems open up in place of the single solved one. They force him to solve them; he has to go ahead at an ever-quickening pace. The same holds true for industrial techniques. The pace of science forces the pace of technique. Theoretical physics forces atomic energy on us; the successful production of the fission bomb forces upon us the manufacture of the hydrogen bomb. *We* do not choose our problems, we do not choose our products; we are pushed, we are forced —by what? By a system which has no purpose and goal transcending it, and which makes man its appendix.

We shall say a great deal more about this aspect of man's powerlessness in the analysis of contemporary Capitalism. At this point, however, we ought to dwell a little longer on the importance of the modern market as the central mechanism of distributing the social product, since the market is the basis for the formation of human relations in capitalistic society.

If the wealth of society corresponded to the actual needs of all its members, there would be no problem of distributing it; each member could take from the social product as much as he likes, or needs, and there would be no need of regulation, except in the purely *technical* sense of distribution. But aside from primitive societies, this condition has never existed up to now in human history. The needs were always greater than the sum total of the social product, and therefore a regulation had to be made on how to distribute it, how many and who should have the optimal satisfaction of their needs, and which classes had to be satisfied with less than they wanted. In most highly developed societies of the past, this decision was made essentially by force. Certain classes had the power to appropriate the best of the social product for themselves, and to assign to other classes the heavier and dirtier work and a smaller share of the product. Force was often implemented by social and religious tradition, which constituted such

87

a strong psychic force within people that it often made the threat
of physical force unnecessary.

The modern market is a self-regulating mechanism of distribution, which makes it unnecessary to divide the social product
according to an intended or traditional plan, and thus does away
with the necessity of the use of force within society. Of course,
the absence of force is more apparent than real. The worker who
has to accept the wage rate offered him on the labor market
is forced to accept the market condition because he could not
survive otherwise. Thus the "freedom" of the individual is largely
illusory. He is aware of the fact that there is no *outer* force which
compels him to enter into certain contracts; he is less aware of the
laws of the market which operate behind his back, as it were;
hence he believes that he is free, when he actually is not. But
 while this is so, the capitalist method of distribution by the market
mechanism is better than any other method devised so far in a
class society, because it is a basis for the relative political freedom of the individual, which characterizes capitalistic democracy.

The economic functioning of the market rests upon *competi-*
tion of many individuals who want to sell their commodities on
the commodity market, as they want to sell their labor or services
on the labor and personality market. This economic necessity
for competition led, especially in the second half of the nineteenth
century, to an increasingly competitive attitude, characterologically speaking. Man was driven by the desire to surpass his competitor, thus reversing completely the attitude characteristic of
the feudal age—that each one had in the social order his traditional
place with which he should be satisfied. As opposed to the social
stability in the medieval system, an unheard of social mobility
developed, in which everybody was struggling for the best places,
even though only a few were chosen to attain them. In this

scramble for success, the social and moral rules of human solidarity broke down; the importance of life was in being first in a competitive race.

Another factor which constitutes the capitalistic mode of production is that in this system the aim of all economic activity is *profit*. Now around this "profit motive" of Capitalism, a great deal of calculated and uncalculated confusion has been created. We have been told—and rightly so—that all economic activity is meaningful only if it results in a profit, that is to say, if we gain more than we have spent in the act of production. To make a living, even the pre-capitalist artisan had to spend on raw material and his apprentice's wage less than the price he charged for his product. In any society that supports industry, simple or complex, the value of the salable product must exceed the cost of production in order to provide capital needed for the replacement of machinery or other instruments for the development and increase of production. But the question of the profitableness of production is not the issue. Our problem is that our motive for production is not social usefulness, not satisfaction in the work process, but the profit derived from investment. The usefulness of his product to the consumer need not interest the individual capitalist at all. This does not mean that the capitalist, psychologically speaking, is driven by an insatiable greed for money. This may or may not be so, but it is not essential for the capitalistic mode of production. In fact, greed was much more frequently the capitalist's motive in an earlier phase than it is now, when ownership and management are largely separated, and when the aim of obtaining higher profits is subordinate to the wish for the ever-growing expansion and smooth running of an enterprise.

Income can, under the present system, be quite apart from personal effort or service. The owner of capital can earn without working. The essential human function of exchange of effort for income can become the abstracted manipulation of money for more money. This is most obvious in the case of the absentee owner of an industrial enterprise. It does not make any difference whether he owns the whole enterprise, or only a share of it. In each case he makes a profit from his capital and from the work of others without having to make any effort himself. There have been many pious justifications for this state of affairs. It has been said that the profits were a payment for the risk he takes in his investment, or for his self-depriving effort to save, which enabled him to accumulate the capital he can invest. But it is hardly necessary to prove that these marginal factors do not alter the elementary fact that Capitalism permits the making of profits without personal effort and productive function. But even as far as those who do work and perform services, their income is not in any reasonable correlation to the effort they make. A schoolteacher's earnings are but a fraction of those of a physician, in spite of the fact that her social function is of equal importance and her personal effort hardly less. The miner earns a fraction of the income of the manager of the mine, though his personal effort is greater if we consider the dangers and discomforts connected with his work.

What characterizes income distribution in Capitalism is the lack of balanced proportion between an individual's effort and work and the social recognition accorded them—financial compensation. This disproportion would, in a poorer society than ours, result in greater extremes of luxury and poverty than our standards of morals would tolerate. I am not stressing, however, the material effects of this disproportion, but its moral and psychological effects. One lies in the underevaluation of work, of human effort and skill. The other lies in the fact that as long as my gain is limited by the effort I make, my desire is limited. If, on the other hand, my income is not in proportion to my effort, there

argues that it increases materialistic desires

are no limitations to my desires, since their fulfillment is a matter of opportunities offered by certain market situations, and not dependent on my own capacities.[1]

Nineteenth-century Capitalism was truly *private* Capitalism. Individuals saw and seized new opportunities, acted economically, sensed new methods, acquired property, both for production and consumption—and enjoyed their property. This pleasure in property, aside from competitiveness and profit seeking, is one of the fundamental aspects of the character of the middle and upper classes of the ninteenth century. It is all the more important to note this trait because with regard to the pleasure in property and in saving, man today is so markedly different from his grandfathers. The mania for saving and for possession, in fact, has become the characteristic feature of the most backward class, the lower middle class, and is much more readily found in Europe than in America. We have here one of the examples where a trait of the social character which was once that of the most advanced class became, in the process of economic development, obsolete as it were, and is retained by the very groups which have developed the least.

Characterologically, the pleasure in possession and property has been described by Freud as an important aspect of the "anal character." From a different theoretical premise, I have described the same clinical picture in terms of the "hoarding orientation." Like all other character orientations, the hoarding one has positive and negative aspects, and whether the positive or the negative aspects are dominant depends on the relative strength of the productive

---

[1] We find here the same difference that exists with regard to physical desires in contrast to those which are not rooted in bodily needs; my desire to eat, for instance, is self-regulated by my physiological organization, and only in pathological cases is this desire not regulated by a physiological saturation point. Ambition, lust for power, and so on, which are not rooted in physiological needs of the organism have no such self-regulating mechanisms, and that is the reason why they are ever increasing and so dangerous.

orientation within the individual or social character. The positive aspects of this orientation, as I have described them in "Man for Himself" are: to be practical, economical, careful, reserved, cautious, tenacious, imperturbable, orderly, methodical and loyal. The corresponding negative aspects are, to be unimaginative, stingy, suspicious, cold, anxious, stubborn, indolent, pedantic, obsessional and possessive.[1] It can be easily seen that in the eighteenth and nineteenth centuries, when the hoarding orientation was geared to the necessities of economic progress, the positive characteristics were predominant, while in the twentieth century when these traits are the obsolete feature of an obsolete class, the negative aspects are almost exclusively present.

The breakdown of the traditional principle of human solidarity led to new forms of exploitation. In feudal society the lord was supposed to have the divine right to demand services and things from those subject to his domination, but at the same time he was bound by custom and was obligated to be responsible for his subjects, to protect them, and to provide them with at least the minimum—the traditional standard of living. Feudal exploitation took place in a system of mutual human obligations, and thus was governed by certain restrictions. Exploitation as it developed in the nineteenth century was essentially different. The worker, or rather his labor, was a commodity to be bought by the owner of capital, not essentially different from any other commodity on the market, and it was used to its fullest capacity by the buyer. Since it had been bought for its proper price on the labor market, there was no sense of reciprocity, or of any obligation on the part of the owner of capital, beyond that of paying the wages. If hundreds of thousands of workers were without work and on the point of starvation, that was their bad luck, the result of their inferior talents, or simply a social and natural law, which could not be

[1] cf. *Man for Himself*, p. 114.

92

changed. Exploitation was not personal any more, but it had become anonymous, as it were. It was the law of the market that condemned a man to work for starvation wages, rather than the intention or greed of any one individual. Nobody was responsible or guilty, nobody could change conditions either. One was dealing with the iron laws of society, or so it seemed.

In the twentieth century, such capitalistic exploitation as was customary in the nineteenth century has largely disappeared. This must not, however, becloud the insight into the fact that twentieth-century as well as nineteenth-century Capitalism is based on the principle that is to be found in all class societies: *the use of man by man.*

Since the modern capitalist "employs" labor, the social and political form of this exploitation has changed; what has not changed is that the owner of capital uses other men for the purpose of his own profit. The basic concept of *use* has nothing to do with cruel, or not cruel, ways of human treatment, but with the fundamental fact that one man serves another for purposes which are not his own but those of the employer. The concept of use of man by man has nothing to do even with the question whether one man uses another, or uses himself. The fact remains the same, that a man, a living human being, ceases to be an end in himself, and becomes the means for the economic interests of another man, or himself, or of an impersonal giant, the economic machine.

There are two obvious objections to the foregoing statements. One is that modern man is free to accept or to decline a contract, and therefore he is a voluntary participant in his social relation to the employer, and not a "thing." But this objection ignores the fact that in the first place he has no choice but to accept the existing conditions, and secondly, that even if he were not forced to accept these conditions, he would still be "employed," that is, made use of for purposes not his own, but of the capital whose profit he serves.

The other objection is that all social life, even in its most primitive form, requires a certain amount of social co-operation, and even discipline, and that certainly in the more complex form of industrial production, a person has to fulfill certain necessary and specialized functions. While this statement is quite true, it ignores the basic difference: in a society where no person has power over another, each person fulfills his functions on the basis of co-operation and mutuality. No one can command another person, except insofar as a relationship is based on mutual co-operation, on love, friendship or natural ties. Actually we find this present in many situations in our society today: the normal co-operation of husband and wife in their family life is to a large extent not any more determined by the power of the husband to command his wife, as it existed in older forms of patriarchal society, but on the principle of co-operation and mutuality. The same holds true for the relationship of friends, inasmuch as they perform certain services for each other and co-operate with each other. In these relationships no one would dare to think of *commanding* the other person; the only reason for expecting his help lies in the mutual feeling of love, friendship or simply human solidarity. The help of another person is secured by my active effort, as a human being, to elicit his love, friendship and sympathy. In the relationship of the employer to the employee, this is not the case. The employer has bought the services of the worker, and however human his treatment may be, he still commands him, not on a basis of mutuality, but on the basis of having bought his working time for so many hours a day.

The use of man by man is expressive of the *system of values underlying* the capitalistic system. *Capital, the dead past, employs labor—the living vitality and power of the present.* In the capitalistic hierarchy of values, capital stands higher than labor, amassed things higher than the manifestations of life. Capital employs labor, and not labor capital. The person who owns capital commands the person who "only" owns his life, human skill, vitality and creative productivity. "Things" are higher than man. The conflict between capital and labor is much more than the conflict between two classes, more than their fight for a greater share of the social product. It is the conflict between two principles of value: *that between the world of things, and their amassment, and the world of life and its productivity.*[1]

Closely related to the problem of exploitation and use, although even more complicated, is the problem of *authority* in nineteenth-century man. Any social system in which one group of the population is commanded by another, especially if the latter is a minority, must be based on a strong sense of *authority,* a sense which is increased in a strongly patriarchal society where the male sex is supposed to be superior to and in control of the female sex. Since the problem of authority is so crucial for our understanding of human relations in any kind of society, and since the attitude of authority has changed fundamentally from the nineteenth to the twentieth century, I want to begin the discussion of this problem by referring to a differentiation of authority which I made in "Escape from Freedom," and which still seems to me valid enough to be quoted as a basis for the following discussion: Authority is not a quality one person 'has,' in the sense that he has property or physical qualities. Authority refers to an interpersonal relation in which one person looks upon another as somebody superior to him. But there is a fundamental difference between a kind of

---

[1] cf. R. M. Tawney's discussion of the same point in *The Acquisitive Society,* Harcourt Brace & Company, New York, 1920, p. 99.

superiority-inferiority relation which can be called *rational* authority and one which may be described as *inhibiting*, or irrational authority.

An example will show what I have in mind. The relationship between teacher and student and that between slave owner and slave are both based on the superiority of the one over the other. The interests of teacher and pupil lie in the same direction. The teacher is satisfied if he succeeds in furthering the pupil; if he has failed to do so, the failure is his and the pupil's. The slave owner, on the other hand, wants to exploit the slave as much as possible; the more he gets out of him, the more he is satisfied. At the same time, the slave seeks to defend as best he can his claims for a minimum of happiness. These interests are definitely antagonistic, as what is of advantage to the one is detrimental to the other. The superiority has a different function in both cases: in the first, it is the condition for helping of the person subjected to the authority; in the second, it is the condition for his exploitation.

The dynamics of authority in these two types are different too: the more the student learns, the less wide is the gap between him and the teacher. He becomes more and more like the teacher himself. In other words, *the rational authority relationship tends to dissolve itself*. But when the superiority serves as a basis for exploitation, the distance becomes intensified through its long duration.

The psychological situation is different in each of these authority situations. In the first, elements of love, admiration, or gratitude are prevalent. The authority is at the same time an example with which one wants to identify one's self partially or totally. In the second situation, resentment or hostility will arise against the exploiter, subordination to whom is against one's own interests. But often, as in the case of a slave, his hatred would only

slave
represses

lead to conflicts which would subject the slave to suffering without a chance of winning. Therefore, the tendency will usually be to repress the feeling of hatred and sometimes even to replace it by a feeling of blind admiration. This has two functions: (1) to remove the painful and dangerous feeling of hatred, and (2) to soften the feeling of humiliation. If the person who rules over me is so wonderful or perfect, then I should not be ashamed of obeying him. I cannot be his equal because he is so much stronger, wiser, better, and so on, than I am. As a result, in the inhibiting kind of authority, the element either of hatred or of irrational overestimation and admiration of the authority will tend to *increase*. In the rational kind of authority, the strength of the emotional ties will tend to *decrease* in direct proportion to the degree in which the person subjected to the authority becomes stronger and thereby more similar to the authority.

?

The difference between rational and inhibiting authority is only a relative one. Even in the relationship between slave and master there are elements of advantage for the slave. He gets a minimum of food and protection which at least enables him to work for his master. On the other hand, it is only in an ideal relationship between teacher and student that we find a complete lack of antagonism of interests. There are many gradations between these two extreme cases, as in the relationship of a factory worker with his boss, or a farmer's son with his father, or a 'hausfrau' with her husband. Nevertheless, although in reality the two types of authority are blended, they are essentially different, and an analysis of a concrete authority situation must always determine the specific weight of each kind of authority.

They blend

The nineteenth-century social character is a good example of a mixture between rational and irrational authority. The character of society was essentially a hierarchical one, though no longer like the hierarchical character of feudal society based on divine law and tradition, but rather on the ownership of capital; those who owned it could buy, and thus command the labor of those who did not, and the latter had to obey, under penalty of starvation. There was a certain blending between the new and the old hierarchical pattern. The state, especially in the monarchial form, cultivated the old virtues of obedience and submission, to apply them to new contents and values. Obedience, in the nineteenth-century middle class, was still one of the fundamental virtues and disobedience one of the elementary vices.

At the same time, however, rational authority had developed side by side with irrational authority. Since the Reformation and the Renaissance man had begun to rely on his own reason as a guide to action and value judgment. He felt proud to have convictions which were his, and he respected the authority of scientists, philosophers, historians, who helped him to form his own judgments and to be sure of his own convictions. The decision between true and false, right and wrong, was of the utmost importance and, indeed, both the moral and the intellectual conscience assumed a paramount place in the character structure of nineteenth-century man. He may not have applied the rules of his conscience to men of a different color or even of a different social class, yet to some extent he was determined by his sense of right and wrong, and at least by the repression of the awareness of wrongdoing, if he did not succeed in avoiding wrong action.

Closely related to this sense of intellectual and moral conscience is another trait characteristic of the nineteenth century: the sense of pride and mastery. If we look today at the pictures of nineteenth-century life, the man with the beard, the tall silk hat and walking cane, we are easily struck by the ridiculous and negative aspect of nineteenth-century male pride—a man's vanity and naïve belief in himself as the highest accomplishment of nature and of history; but, especially if we consider the absence of this trait in our own time, we can see the positive aspects of this pride. Man had the feeling of having put himself into the saddle, so to speak, of having freed himself from domination by natural forces, and for the first time in history having become their master. He had freed himself from the shackles of medieval superstition, had even succeeded in the hundred years between 1814 and 1914 in creating one of the most peaceful periods history has ever known. He felt himself to be an individual, subject only to the laws of reason, following only his own decisions.

Summing up then, we may say that the social character of the nineteenth century was essentially competitive, hoarding, exploitative, authoritarian, aggressive, individualistic. Anticipating our later discussion, we may already emphasize here the great difference between nineteenth- and twentieth-century Capitalism. Instead of the exploitative and hoarding orientation we find the receptive and marketing orientation. Instead of competitiveness we find an increasing tendency toward "teamwork"; instead of a striving for ever-increasing profit, a wish for a steady and secure income; instead of exploitation, a tendency to share and spread wealth, and to manipulate others—and oneself; instead of rational and irrational but *overt* authority, we find *anonymous* authority —the authority of public opinion and the market; [1] instead of the individual conscience, the need to adjust and be approved of; instead of the sense of pride and mastery, an ever-increasing though mainly unconscious sense of powerlessness. [2]

If we look back at the pathological problems of nineteenth-

[1] However, as Russia and Germany show, the escape from freedom can also in the twentieth century take the form of complete submission to overt, irrational authority.

[2] It must be added that the foregoing description holds true mainly for the nineteenth-century middle class. The worker and farmer were different in many essential aspects. It is one of the elements in the development of the twentieth century that the character differences between the various social classes, especially those living in cities, have almost completely disappeared.

century man, they are, of course, closely related to the peculiarities of his social character. The exploitative and hoarding attitude caused human suffering and lack of respect for the dignity of man; it caused Europe to exploit Africa and Asia and her own working class ruthlessly and without regard for human values. The other pathogenic phenomenon of the nineteenth century, the role of irrational authority and the need to submit to it, led to the repression of thoughts and feelings which were tabooed by society. The most obvious symptom was the repression of sex and all that was natural in the body, movements, dress, architectural style, and so on. This repression resulted, as Freud thought, in various forms of neurotic pathology.

The reform movements of the nineteenth century and the beginning of the twentieth, which tried to cure social pathology, started from these main symptoms. All forms of Socialism from Anarchism to Marxism emphasized the necessity for abolishing exploitation and transforming the workingman into an independent, free and respected human being; they believed that if economic suffering were abolished, and if the workingman were free from the domination of the capitalist, all the positive achievements of the nineteenth century would come to their full fruition, while the vices would disappear. In the very same way Freud believed that if sexual repression were considerably diminished, neuroses and all forms of mental sickness would be diminished in consequence (even though in his later life his original optimism became more and more reduced). The liberals believed that complete freedom from irrational authorities would usher in a new millenium. The prescriptions for the care of human ills given by the liberals, the socialists and the psychoanalysts, different as they were from each other, nevertheless fit into the pathology and symptomatology characteristic of the nineteenth century. What was more natural than to expect that by abolishing exploitation and economic suffering, or by doing away with sexual repression and irrational authority, man would enter into an era of greater freedom, happiness, and progress than he had had in the nineteenth century?

Half a century has passed, and the main demands of the nineteenth-century reformers have been fulfilled. Speaking of the economically most progressive country, the United States, the economic exploitation of the masses has disappeared to a degree which would have sounded fantastic in Marx's time. The working class, instead of falling behind in the economic development of the whole society, has an increasing share in the national wealth, and it is a perfectly valid assumption that provided no major catastrophe occurs, there will, in about one or two generations, be no more marked poverty in the United States. Closely related to the increasing abolishment of economic suffering is the fact that the human and political situation of the worker has changed drastically. Largely through his unions, he has become a social "partner" of management. He cannot be ordered around, fired, abused, as he was even thirty years ago. He certainly does not look up any more to the "boss" as if he were a higher and superior being. He neither worships him nor hates him, although he might envy him for the greater advances he has made in the attainment of the socially desirable aims. As far as submission to irrational authority goes, the picture has changed drastically since the nineteenth century, as far as parent-child relations are concerned. Children are no longer afraid of their parents. They are companions, and if anybody feels slightly uneasy, it is not the child but the parents who fear not being up-to-date. In industry as well as in the army, there is a spirit of "team work" and equality which would have seemed unbelievable fifty years ago. In addition to all that, sexual repression has diminished to a remarkable degree; after the First World War, a sexual revolution took place in which old inhibitions and principles were thrown overboard. The idea of not satisfying a sexual wish was supposed to be old-fashioned or unhealthy. Even though there was a certain reaction against this attitude, on the whole the nineteenth-century system of tabus and repressions has almost disappeared.

Looked upon from the standards of the nineteenth century, we have achieved almost everything which seemed to be necessary for a saner society, and indeed, many people who still think in terms of the past century are convinced that we continue to progress. Consequently they also believe that the only threat to further progress lies in authoritarian societies, like the Soviet Union which, with its ruthless economic exploitation of workers for the sake of quicker accumulation of capital and the ruthless political authority necessary for the continuation of exploitation, resembles in many ways the earlier phase of Capitalism. For those, however, who do not look at our present society with the eyes of the nineteenth century, it is obvious that the fulfillment of the nineteenth-century hopes has by no means led to the expected results. In fact, it seems that in spite of material prosperity, political and sexual freedom, the world in the middle of the twentieth century is mentally sicker than it was in the nineteenth century. Indeed, "we are not in danger of becoming slaves any more, but of becoming robots," as Adlai Stevenson said so succinctly.[1] There is no overt authority which intimidates us, but we are governed by the fear of the anonymous authority of conformity. We do not submit to anyone personally; we do not go through conflicts with authority, but we have also no convictions of our own, almost no individuality, almost no sense of self. Quite obviously, the diagnosis of our pathology cannot follow the lines of the nineteenth century. We have to recognize the specific pathological problems of our time in order to arrive at a vision of that which

[1] In his speech at Columbia University, 1954.

is necessary to save the Western world from an increasing insanity. This diagnosis will be attempted in the following section, dealing with the social character of Western man in the twentieth century.

C. TWENTIETH-CENTURY SOCIETY

1. *Social and Economic Changes*

Drastic changes in industrial technique, economy and social structure have occurred in Capitalism between the nineteenth and the middle of the twentieth centuries. The changes in the character of man are not less drastic and fundamental. While we have already mentioned certain changes from nineteenth- to twentieth-century Capitalism—changes in the form of exploitation, in the form of authority, in the role of possessiveness—the following discussion will deal with those economic and characterological features of contemporary Capitalism which are the most fundamental ones in our time, even though they may have their origins in the nineteenth century or even earlier.

To begin with a negative statement, in contemporary Western society, the feudal traits are disappearing more and more, and the pure form of capitalistic society thus becomes further apparent. However, the absence of feudal remnants is still much more marked in the United States than in Western Europe. Capitalism in the United States is not only more powerful and more advanced than in Europe, it is also the model toward which European Capitalism is developing. It is such a model not because Europe is trying to imitate it, but because it is the most progressive form of Capitalism, freed from feudal remnants and shackles. The feudal heritage has, aside from its obvious negative qualities, many human traits which, compared with the attitude produced by pure Capitalism, are exceedingly attractive. European criticism

America: "purer" form of Capitalism

of the United States is based essentially on the older human values of feudalism, inasmuch as they are still alive in Europe. It is a criticism of the present in the name of a past which is rapidly disappearing in Europe itself. The difference between Europe and the United States in this respect is only the difference between an older and a newer phase of Capitalism, between a Capitalism still blended with feudal remnants and a pure form of it.

The most obvious change from the nineteenth to the twentieth century is the technical change, the increased use of the steam engine, of the combustion motor, of electricity and the beginning of the use of atomic energy. The development is characterized by the increasing replacement of manual work by machine work, and beyond that, of human intelligence by machine intelligence. While in 1850 men supplied 15 per cent of the energy for work, animals 79 per cent and machines 6 per cent, the ratio in 1960 will be 3 per cent, 1 per cent and 96 per cent respectively.[1] In the middle of the twentieth century we find an increasing tendency to employ automatically regulated machines which have their own "brains," and which bring about a fundamental change in the whole process of production.

The technical change in the mode of production is caused by, and in its turn necessitates, an increasing concentration of capital. The decrease in number and importance of smaller firms is in direct proportion to the increase of big economic colossi. A few figures may help to make concrete the picture which, in its general outline, is very well known. Of 573 independent American corporations covering most stocks traded on the New York Stock Exchange in 1930, 130 companies controlled more than 80 per cent of the assets of all the companies represented. The 200 largest nonbanking corporations controlled "nearly half of all non-

[1] cf. Th. Carskadom and R. Modley, *U.S.A., Measure of a Nation*, The Macmillan Company, New York, 1949, p. 3.

banking corporate wealth, while the remaining half was owned by the more than 300,000 smaller companies." [1] It must further be remembered that the influence of one of these huge companies extends far beyond the assets under its direct control. "Smaller companies which sell to or buy from the larger companies are likely to be influenced by them to a vastly greater extent than by other smaller companies with which they might deal. In many cases the continued prosperity of the smaller company depends on the favor of the larger and almost inevitably the interests of the latter become the interests of the former. The influence of the larger company on prices is often greatly increased by its mere size, even though it does not begin to approach a monopoly. Its political influence may be tremendous. Therefore, if roughly half of the corporate wealth is controlled by two hundred large corporations and half by smaller companies it is fair to assume that very much more than half of industry is dominated by these great units. This concentration is made even more significant when it is recalled that as a result of it, approximately 2,000 individuals out of a population of one hundred and twenty-five million are in a position to control and direct half of industry." [2] This concentration of power has been growing since 1933, and has yet not come to a stop.

The number of self-employed entrepreneurs has decreased considerably. While in the beginning of the nineteenth century approximately four fifths of the occupied population were self-employed entrepreneurs, around 1870 only one third belonged to this group, and by 1940 this old middle class comprised only one fifth of the occupied population, that is to say, only 25 per cent of its relative strength a hundred years earlier. Twenty-seven

[1] cf. A. A. Berle, Jr., and G. C. Means, *The Modern Corporation and Private Property*, The Macmillan Company, New York, 1940, pp. 27, 28.

[2] *Ibid.*, pp. 32, 33.

No. of entrepreneurs still decreasing.

thousand giant firms, constituting only 1 per cent of all the firms in the United States, employ over 50 per cent of all people engaged in business today, while on the other hand 1,500,000 one-man enterprises (nonfarming) employ only 6 per cent of all people employed in business.[1]

As these figures already indicate, with the concentration of enterprises goes an enormous increase of employees in these big enterprises. While the old middle class, composed of farmers, independent businessmen and professionals, formerly constituted 85 per cent of the middle class, it is now only 44 per cent; the new middle classes have increased from 15 per cent to 56 per cent in the same period. This new middle class is composed of managers, who have risen from 2 per cent to 6 per cent; salaried professionals, from 4 per cent to 14 per cent; sales people from 7 per cent to 14 per cent, and office workers from 2 per cent to 22 per cent. Altogether the new middle class has risen from 6 per cent to 25 per cent of the total labor force between 1870 and 1940, while the wage workers have declined from 61 per cent to 55 per cent of the labor force within the same period. As Mills puts it very succinctly ". . . *fewer individuals manipulate things; more handle people and symbols.*" [2]

With the increase in the importance of the giant enterprises, another development of utmost importance has occurred: the increasing separation of management from ownership. This point is illustrated by revealing figures in the classic work of Berle and Means. Of 144 companies for which information could be obtained among the 200 largest companies (in 1930) only 20 had under 5,000 stockholders, while 71 had between 20,000 and 500,000 stockholders.[3] Only in small companies did the manage-

---

[1] These figures are quoted from C. W. Mills, *White Collar*, Oxford University Press, New York, 1951, p. 63 ff.

[2] *Loc. cit.*, p. 63.

[3] These and the following figures are quoted from Berle and Means.

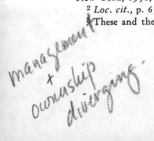

ment appear to hold an important stock interest, while in the large, and that is to say, the most important companies, there is an almost complete separation between stock ownership and management. In some of the largest railroad and utility companies, in 1929, the size of the largest holding by any one stockholder did not exceed 2.74 per cent, and this condition, according to Berle and Means, exists also in the industrial field. "When the industries are arranged in order of the average size of the management's holdings of stock . . . the proportion held by the officers and directors is seen to vary in almost exactly inverse ratio to the average size of the companies under consideration. With only two major exceptions, the larger the size of the company, the smaller was the proportion of the stock held by the management. In the railroads, with common stock averaging $52,000,000 per company, the holdings of the management amounted to 1.4% and in . . . miscellaneous mining and quarrying it amounted to 1.8%. Only where the companies are small did the management appear to hold important stock interest. The holdings of the latter amounted to less than 20%, except in industries with companies having an average capital under $1,000,-000, while but three industrial groups, each composed of companies averaging less than $200,000 showed directors and officers owning more than half the stock." [1] Taking the two tendencies, that of the relative increase of big enterprise and of the smallness of management holdings of big enterprises together, it is quite evident that the general trend is increasingly one in which the owner of capital is separate from the management. How the management controls the enterprise in spite of the fact that it does not own a considerable part, is a sociological and psychological problem which will be taken up later on.

Another fundamental change from nineteenth-century to con-

[1] Berle and Means, *loc. cit.*, p. 52.

*Domestic
Market*
↳

temporary Capitalism is the increase in significance of the domestic market. Our whole economic machine rests upon the principle of mass production and mass consumption. While in the nineteenth century the general tendency was to save, and not to indulge in expenses which could not be paid for immediately, the contemporary system is exactly the opposite. Everybody is coaxed into buying as much as he can, and before he has saved enough to pay for his purchases. The need for more consumption is strongly stimulated by advertising and all other methods of psychological pressure. This development goes hand in hand with the rise of the economic and social status of the working class. Especially in the United States, but also all over Europe, the working class has participated in the increased production of the whole economic system. The salary of the worker, and his social benefits, permit him a level of consumption which would have seemed fantastic one hundred years ago. His social and economic power has increased to the same degree and this not only with regard to salary and social benefits, but also to his human and social role in the factory.

Summary

Let us take another look at the most important elements in twentieth-century Capitalism: the disappearance of feudal traits, the revolutionary increase in industrial production, the increasing concentration of capital and bigness of business and government, the increasing number of people who manipulate figures and people, the separation of ownership from management, the rise of the working class economically and politically, the new methods of work in factory and office—and let us describe these changes from a slightly different aspect. The disappearance of feudal factors means the disappearance of irrational authority. Nobody is supposed to be higher than his neighbor by birth, God's will, natural law. Everybody is equal and free. Nobody may be exploited or commanded by virtue of a natural right. If one person is commanded by another, it is because the commanding one bought the labor or the services of the commanded one, on the labor market; he commands because they are both free and equal and thus could enter into a contractual relationship. However, with irrational authority—rational authority became obsolete, too. If the market and the contract regulates relationships, there is no need to know what is right and what is wrong and good and evil. All that is necessary is to know that things are *fair*—that the exchange is fair, and that things "work"—that they function.

Another decisive fact which the twentieth-century man experiences is the miracle of production. He commands forces thousands of times stronger than the ones nature had given him before; steam, oil, electricity, have become his servants and beasts of burden. He crosses the oceans, the continents—first in weeks, then in days, now in hours. He seemingly overcomes the law of gravity, and flies through the air; he converts deserts into fertile land, makes rain instead of praying for it. The miracle of production leads to the miracle of consumption. No more traditional barriers keep anyone from buying anything he takes a fancy to. He only needs to have the money. But more and more people have the money—not for the genuine pearls perhaps, but for the synthetic ones; for Fords which look like Cadillacs, for the cheap dresses which look like the expensive ones, for cigarettes which are the same for millionaires and for the workingman. Everything is within reach, can be bought, can be consumed. Where was there ever a society where this miracle happened?

Men work together. Thousands stream into the industrial plants and the offices—they come in cars, in subways, in buses, in trains —they work together, according to a rhythm measured by the experts, with methods worked out by the experts, not too fast, not too slow, but together; each a part of the whole. The evening stream flows back: they read the same newspaper, they listen to the radio, they see the movies, the same for those on the top and for those at the bottom of the ladder, for the intelligent and the stupid, for the educated and the uneducated. Produce, consume, enjoy together, in step, without asking questions. That is the rhythm of their lives.

What kind of men, then, does our society need? What is the "social character" suited to twentieth-century Capitalism?

It needs men who co-operate smoothly in large groups; who want to consume more and more, and whose tastes are standardized and can be easily influenced and anticipated.

It needs men who feel free and independent, not subject to any authority, or principle, or conscience—yet willing to be commanded, to do what is expected, to fit into the social machine without friction. How can man be guided without force, led without leaders, be prompted without any aim—except the one to be on the move, to function, to go ahead . . . ?

2. Characterological Changes

a. Quantification, Abstractification

In analyzing and describing the social character of contemporary man, one can choose any number of approaches, just as one does in describing the character structure of an individual. These approaches can differ either in the depth to which the analysis penetrates, or they can be centered around different aspects which are equally "deep," yet chosen according to the particular interest of the investigator.

In the following analysis I have chosen the concept of *alienation* as the central point from which I am going to develop the analysis of the contemporary social character. For one reason, because this concept seems to me to touch upon the deepest level of the modern personality; for another, because it is the most appropriate if one is concerned with the interaction between the contemporary socio-economic structure and the character structure of the average individual.[1]

We must introduce the discussion of alienation by speaking of one of the fundamental economic features of Capitalism, the process of *quantification* and *abstractification*.

The medieval artisan produced goods for a relatively small and known group of customers. His prices were determined by the need to make a profit which permitted him to live in a style traditionally commensurate with his social status. He knew from experience the costs of production, and even if he employed a few journeymen and apprentices, no elaborate system of bookkeeping or balance sheets was required for the operation of his business. The same held true for the production of the peasant, which required even less quantifying abstract methods. In contrast, the modern business enterprise rests upon its balance sheet. It cannot rest upon such concrete and direct observation as the artisan used to figure out his profits. Raw material, machinery, labor costs, as well as the product can be expressed in the same money value, and thus made comparable and fit to appear in the balance equation. All economic occurrences have to be strictly quantifiable, and only the balance sheets, the exact comparison of economic processes quantified in figures, tell the manager whether and to what degree he is engaged in a profitable, that is to say, a meaningful business activity.

This transformation of the concrete into the abstract has developed far beyond the balance sheet and the quantification of the economic occurrences in the sphere of production. The modern businessman not only deals with millions of dollars, but also with millions of customers, thousands of stockholders, and thousands

---

[1] As the reader familiar with the concept of the marketing orientation developed in *Man for Himself* will see, the phenomenon of alienation is the more general and underlies the more specific concept of the "marketing orientation."

of workers and employees; all these people become so many pieces in a gigantic machine which must be controlled, whose effects must be calculated; each man eventually can be expressed as an abstract entity, as a figure, and on this basis economic occurrences are calculated, trends are predicted, decisions are made.

Today, when only about 20 per cent of our working population is self-employed, the rest work for somebody else, and a man's life is dependent on someone who pays him a wage or a salary. But we should say "something," instead of "someone," because a worker is hired and fired by an institution, the managers of which are impersonal parts of the enterprise, rather than people in personal contact with the men they employ. Let us not forget another fact: in precapitalistic society, exchange was to a large extent one of goods and services; today, all work is rewarded with money. The close fabric of economic relations is regulated by money, the abstract expression of work—that is to say, we receive different quantities of the same for different qualities; and we give money for what we receive—again exchanging only different quantities for different qualities. Practically nobody, with the exception of the farm population, could live for even a few days without receiving and spending money, which stands for the abstract quality of concrete work.

Another aspect of capitalist production which results in increasing abstractification is the increasing division of labor. Division of labor as a whole exists in most known economic systems, and, even in most primitive communities, in the form of division of labor between the sexes. What is characteristic of capitalistic production is the degree to which this division has developed. While in the medieval economy there was a division of labor let us say between agricultural production and the work of the artisan, there was little such division within each sphere of production itself. The carpenter making a chair or table made the whole chair or the whole table, and even if some preparatory work was done by his apprentices, he was in control of the production, overseeing it in its entirety. In the modern industrial enterprise, the worker is not in touch with the whole product at any point. He is engaged in the performance of one specialized function, and while he might shift in the course of time from one function to another, he is still not related to the concrete product *as a whole*. He develops a specialized function, and the tendency is such, that the function of the modern industrial worker can be defined as working in a machinelike fashion in activities for which machine work has not yet been devised or which would be costlier than human work. The only person who is in touch with the whole product is the manager, but to him the product is an abstraction, whose essence is exchange value, while the worker, for whom it is concrete, never works on it as a whole.

Undoubtedly without quantification and abstractification modern mass production would be unthinkable. But in a society in which economic activities have become the main preoccupation of man, this process of quantification and abstractification has transcended the realm of economic production, and spread to the attitude of man to things, to people, and to himself.

In order to understand the abstractification process in modern man, we must first consider the ambiguous function of abstraction in general. It is obvious that abstractions in themselves are not a modern phenomenon. In fact, an increasing ability to form abstractions is characteristic of the cultural development of the human race. If I speak of "a table," I am using an abstraction; I am referring, not to a specific table in its full concreteness, but to the genus "table" which comprises all possible concrete tables. If I speak of "a man" I am not speaking of this or that person, in his concreteness and uniqueness, but of the genus "man," which comprises all individual persons. In other words, I make an abstraction. The development of philosophical or scientific thought is based on an increasing ability for such abstractification, and to give it up would mean to fall back into the most primitive way of thinking.

However, there are *two* ways of relating oneself to an object: one can relate oneself to it in its full concreteness; then the object appears with all its specific qualities, and there is no other object which is identical with it. And one can relate oneself to the object in an abstract way, that is, emphasizing only those qualities which it has in common with all other objects of the same genus, and thus accentuating some and ignoring other qualities. The full and productive relatedness to an object comprises this polarity of perceiving it in its uniqueness, and at the same time in its generality; in its concreteness, and at the same time in its abstractness.

In contemporary Western culture this polarity has given way to an almost exclusive reference to the abstract qualities of things and people, and to a neglect of relating oneself to their concreteness and uniqueness. Instead of forming abstract concepts where it is necessary and useful, everything, including ourselves, is being abstractified; the concrete reality of people and things to which we can relate with the reality of our own person, is replaced by abstractions, by ghosts that embody different quantities, but not different qualities.

It is quite customary to talk about a "three-million-dollar bridge," a "twenty-cent cigar," a "five-dollar watch," and this not only from the standpoint of the manufacturer or the consumer in the process of buying it, but as the essential point in the description. When one speaks of the "three-million-dollar bridge," one is not primarily concerned with its usefulness or beauty, that is, with its concrete qualities, but one speaks of it as of a commodity, the main quality of which is its exchange value, expressed in a quantity, that of money. This does not mean, of course, that one is not concerned also with the usefulness or beauty of the bridge, but it does mean that its concrete (use) value is *secondary* to its abstract (exchange) value in the way the object is experienced. The famous line by Gertrude Stein "a rose is a rose is a rose," is a protest against this abstract form of experience; for most people a rose is just *not* a rose, but a flower in a certain price range, to be bought on certain social occasions; even the most beautiful flower, provided it is a wild one, costing nothing, is not experienced in its beauty, compared to that of the rose, because it has no exchange value.

In other words, things are experienced as commodities, as embodiments of exchange value, not only while we are buying or selling, but in our attitude toward them when the economic transaction is finished. A thing, even after it has been bought, never quite loses its quality as a commodity in this sense; it is expendable, always retaining its exchange-value quality. A good illustration of this attitude is to be found in a report of the Executive Secretary of an important scientific organization as to how he spent a day in his office. The organization had just bought and moved into a building of their own. The Executive Secretary reports that during one of the first days after they had moved into the building, he got a call from a real estate agent, saying that some people were interested in buying the building and wanted to look at it. Although he knew that it was most unlikely that the organization would want to sell the building a few days after they had moved in, he could not resist the temptation to know whether the value of the building had risen since they had bought it, and spent one or two valuable hours in showing the real estate agent around. He writes: "very interested in fact we can get an offer for more than we have put in building. Nice coincidence that offer comes while treasurer is in the office. All agree it will be good for Board's morale to learn that the building will sell for a good deal more than it cost. Let's see what happens." In spite of all the pride and pleasure in the new building, it had still retained its quality as a commodity, as something expendable, and to which no full sense of possession or use is attached. The same attitude is obvious in the relationship of people to the cars they buy; the car never becomes fully a thing to which one is attached, but retains its quality as a commodity to be exchanged in a successful bargain; thus, cars are sold after a year or two, long before their use value is exhausted or even considerably diminished.

This abstractification takes place even with regard to phenomena which are not commodities sold on the market, like a flood disaster; the newspapers will headline a flood, speaking of a "million-dollar catastrophe," emphasizing the abstract quantitative element rather than the concrete aspects of human suffering.

But the abstractifying and quantifying attitude goes far beyond the realm of things. People are also experienced as the embodiment of a quantitative exchange value. To speak of a man as being "worth one million dollars," is to speak of him not any more as a concrete human person, but as an abstraction, whose essence can be expressed in a figure. It is an expression of the same attitude when a newspaper headlines an obituary with the words "Shoe Manufacturer Dies." Actually a *man* has died, a man with certain human qualities, with hopes and frustrations, with a wife and children. It is true that he manufactured shoes, or rather, that he owned and managed a factory in which workers served machines manufacturing shoes; but if it is said that a "Shoe Manufacturer Dies," the richness and concreteness of a human life is expressed in the abstract formula of economic function.

The same abstractifying approach can be seen in expressions like "Mr. Ford produced so many automobiles," or this or that general "conquered a fortress"; or if a man has a house built for himself, he says, "I built a house." Concretely speaking, Mr.

Ford did not manufacture the automobiles; he directed automobile production which was executed by thousands of workers. The general never conquered the fortress; he was sitting in his headquarters, issuing orders, and his soldiers did the conquering. The man did not build a house; he paid the money to an architect who made the plans and to workers who did the building. All this is not said to minimize the significance of the managing and directing operations, but in order to indicate that in this way of experiencing things, sight of what goes on concretely is lost, and an abstract view is taken in which one function, that of making plans, giving orders, or financing an activity, is identified with the whole concrete process of production, or of fighting, or of building, as the case may be.

The same process of abstractification takes place in all other spheres. The New York *Times* recently printed a news item under the heading: "B.Sc. + PhD = $40,000." The information under this somewhat baffling heading was that statistical data showed that a student of engineering who has acquired his Doctor's degree will earn, in a lifetime, $40,000 more than a man who has only the degree of Bachelor of Sciences. As far as this is a fact it is an interesting socio-economic datum, worth while reporting. It is mentioned here because the way of expressing the fact as an equation between a scientific degree and a certain amount of dollars is indicative of the abstractifying and quantifying thinking in which knowledge is experienced as the embodiment of a certain exchange value on the personality market. It is to the same point when a political report in a news magazine states that the Eisenhower administration feels it has so much "capital of confidence" that it can risk some unpopular measures, because it can "afford" to lose some of that confidence capital. Here again, a human quality like confidence is expressed in its abstract form, as if it were a money investment to be dealt with in terms of a market speculation. How drastically commercial categories have entered even religious thinking is shown in the following passage by Bishop Sheen, in an article on the birth of Christ. "Our reason tells us," so writes the author, "that if anyone of the claimants (for the role of God's son) came from God, the least that God could do to support His Representative's claim would be to preannounce His coming. Automobile manufacturers tell us when to expect a new model." [1] Or, even more drastically, Billy Graham, the evangelist, says: "I am selling the greatest product in the world; why shouldn't it be promoted as well as soap?" [2]

 The process of abstractification, however, has still deeper roots and manifestations than the ones described so far, roots which go back to the very beginning of the modern era; to the *dissolution* of any *concrete frame of reference* in the process of life.

In a primitive society, the "world" is identical with the tribe. The tribe is in the center of the Universe, as it were; everything outside is shadowy and has no independent existence. In the medieval world, the Universe was much wider; it comprised this globe, the sky and the stars above it; but it was seen with the earth as the center and man as the purpose of Creation. Everything had its fixed place, just as everybody had his fixed position in feudal society. With the fifteenth and sixteenth centuries, new vistas opened up. The earth lost its central place, and became one of the satellites of the sun; new continents were found, new sea lanes discovered; the static social system was more and more loosened up; everything and everybody was moving. Yet, until the end of the twentieth century, nature and society had not lost their concreteness and definiteness. Man's natural and social world was still manageable, still had definite contours. But with the progress

---

[1] From *Colliers'* magazine, 1955.
[2] *Time* magazine, October 25, 1954.

in scientific thought, technical discoveries and the dissolution of all traditional bonds, this definiteness and concreteness is in the process of being lost. Whether we think of our new cosmological picture, or of theoretical physics, or of atonal music, or abstract art—the concreteness and definiteness of our frame of reference is disappearing. We are not any more in the center of the Universe, we are not any more the purpose of Creation, we are not any more the masters of a manageable and recognizable world—we are a speck of dust, we are a nothing, somewhere in space—without any kind of concrete relatedness to anything. We speak of millions of people being killed, of one third or more of our population being wiped out if a third World War should occur; we speak of billions of dollars piling up as a national debt, of thousands of light years as interplanetary distances, of interspace travel, of artificial satellites. Tens of thousands work in one enterprise, hundreds of thousands live in hundreds of cities.

The dimensions with which we deal are figures and abstractions; they are far beyond the boundaries which would permit of any kind of concrete experience. There is no frame of reference left which is manageable, observable, which is adapted to *human dimensions*. While our eyes and ears receive impressions only in humanly manageable proportions, our concept of the world has lost just that quality; it does not any longer correspond to our human dimensions.

This is especially significant in connection with the development of modern means of destruction. In modern war, one individual can cause the destruction of hundreds of thousands of men, women and children. He could do so by pushing a button; he may not feel the emotional impact of what he is doing, since he does not see, does not know the people whom he kills; it is almost as if his act of pushing the button and their death had no real connection. The same man would probably be incapable of even slapping, not to speak of killing, a helpless person. In the latter case, the concrete situation arouses in him a conscience reaction common to all normal men; in the former, there is no such reaction, because the act and his object are alienated from the doer, his act is not *his* any more, but has, so to speak, a life and a responsibility of its own.

Science, business, politics, have lost all foundations and proportions which make sense humanly. We live in figures and abstractions; since nothing is concrete, nothing is real. Everything is possible, factually and morally. Science fiction is not different from science fact, nightmares and dreams from the events of next year. Man has been thrown out from any definite place whence he can overlook and manage his life and the life of society. He is driven faster and faster by the forces which originally were created by him. In this wild whirl he thinks, figures, busy with abstractions, more and more remote from concrete life.

b. Alienation

The foregoing discussion of the process of abstractification leads to the central issue of the effects of Capitalism on personality: the phenomenon of alienation.

By alienation is meant a mode of experience in which the person experiences himself as an alien. He has become, one might say, estranged from himself. He does not experience himself as the center of his world, as the creator of his own acts—but his acts and their consequences have become his masters, whom he obeys, or whom he may even worship. The alienated person is out of touch with himself as he is out of touch with any other person. He, like the others, are experienced as things are experienced; with the senses and with common sense, but at the same time without being related to oneself and to the world outside productively.

The older meaning in which "alienation" was used was to denote an insane person; *aliéné* in French, *alienado* in Spanish are older words for the psychotic, the thoroughly and absolutely alienated person. ("Alienist," in English, is still used for the doctor who cares for the insane.)

In the last century the word "alienation" was used by Hegel and Marx, referring not to a state of insanity, but to a less drastic form of self-estrangement, which permits the person to act reasonably in practical matters, yet which constitutes one of the most severe socially patterned defects. In Marx's system alienation is called that condition of man where his "own act becomes to him an alien power, standing over and against him, instead of being ruled by him." [1]

But while the use of the word "alienation" in this general sense is a recent one, the concept is a much older one; it is the same to which the prophets of the Old Testament referred as *idolatry*. It will help us to a better understanding of "alienation" if we begin by considering the meaning of "idolatry."

The prophets of monotheism did not denounce heathen religions as idolatrous primarily because they worshiped several gods instead of one. The essential difference between monotheism and polytheism is not one of the *number* of gods, but lies in the fact of self-alienation. Man spends his energy, his artistic capacities on building an idol, and then he worships this idol, which is nothing but the result of his own human effort. His life forces have flown into a "thing," and this thing, having become an idol,

---

[1] K. Marx, *Capital*. cf. also Marx-Engels, *Die Deutsche Ideologie* (1845/6), in K. Marx, *Der Historische Materialismus, Die Frühschriften*, S. Landshut and D. P. Mayer, Leipzig, 1932, II, p. 25.

is not experienced as a result of his own productive effort, but as something apart from himself, over and against him, which he worships and to which he submits. As the prophet Hosea says (XIV, 8) : "Assur shall not save us; we will not ride upon horses; *neither will we say any more to the work of our hands, you are our gods;* for in thee the fatherless finds love." Idolatrous man bows down to the work of his own hands. *The idol represents his own life-forces in an alienated form.*

The principle of monotheism, in contrast, is that man is infinite, that there is no partial quality in him which can be hypostatized into the whole. God, in the monotheistic concept, is unrecognizable and indefinable; God is not a "thing." If man is created in the likeness of God, he is created as the bearer of infinite qualities. In idolatry man bows down and submits to the projection of one partial quality in himself. He does not experience himself as the center from which living acts of love and reason radiate. He becomes a thing, his neighbor becomes a thing, just as his gods are things. "The idols of the heathen are silver and gold, the work of men's hands. They have mouths but they speak not; eyes have they, but they see not; they have ears but they hear not; neither is there any breath in their mouths. They that make them are like them; so is everyone that trusts in them." (Psalm 135).

Monotheistic religions themselves have, to a large extent, regressed into idolatry. Man projects his power of love and of reason unto God; he does not feel them any more as his own powers, and then he prays to God to give him back some of what he, man, has projected unto God. In early Protestantism and Calvinism, the required religious attitude is that man *should* feel himself empty and impoverished, and put his trust in the grace of God, that is, into the hope that God may return to him part of his own qualities, which he has put into God.

Man in Capitalistic Society

Every act of submissive worship is an act of alienation and idolatry in this sense. What is frequently called "love" is often nothing but this idolatrous phenomenon of alienation; only that not God or an idol, but another person is worshiped in this way. The "loving" person in this type of submissive relationship, projects all his or her love, strength, thought, into the other person, and experiences the loved person as a superior being, finding satisfaction in complete submission and worship. This does not only mean that he fails to experience the loved person as a human being in his or her reality, but that he does not experience *himself* in his full reality, as the bearer of productive human powers. Just as in the case of religious idolatry, he has projected all his richness into the other person, and experiences this richness not any more as something which is his, but as something alien from himself, deposited in somebody else, with which he can get in touch only by submission to, or submergence in the other person. The same phenomenon exists in the worshiping submission to a political leader, or to the state. The leader and the state actually are what they are by the consent of the governed. But they become idols when the individual projects all his powers into them and worships them, hoping to regain some of his powers by submission and worship.

In Rousseau's theory of the state, as in contemporary totalitarianism, the individual is supposed to abdicate his own rights and to project them unto the state as the only arbiter. In Fascism and Stalinism the absolutely alienated individual worships at the altar of an idol, and it makes little difference by what names this idol is known: state, class, collective, or what else.

We can speak of idolatry or alienation not only in relationship to other people, but also in relationship to oneself, when the person is subject to irrational passions. The person who is mainly motivated by his lust for power, does not experience himself any more in the richness and limitlessness of a human being, but he becomes a slave to one partial striving in him, which is projected into external aims, by which he is "possessed." The person who is given to the exclusive pursuit of his passion for money is possessed by his striving for it; money is the idol which he worships as the projection of one isolated power in himself, his greed for it. In this sense, the neurotic person is an alienated person. His actions are not his own; while he is under the illusion of doing what *he* wants, he is driven by forces which are separated from his self, which work behind his back; he is a stranger to himself, just as his fellow man is a stranger to him. He experiences the other and himself not as what they really are, but distorted by the unconscious forces which operate in them. The insane person is the *absolutely alienated* person; he has completely lost himself as the center of his own experience; he has lost the sense of self.

What is common to all these phenomena—the worship of idols, the idolatrous worship of God, the idolatrous love for a person, the worship of a political leader or the state, and the idolatrous worship of the externalizations of irrational passions—is the process of alienation. It is the fact that *man does not experience himself as the active bearer of his own powers and richness, but as an impoverished "thing," dependent on powers outside of himself, unto whom he has projected his living substance.*

As the reference to idolatry indicates, alienation is by no means a modern phenomenon. It would go far beyond the scope of this book to attempt a sketch on the history of alienation. Suffice it to say that it seems alienation differs from culture to culture, both in the specific spheres which are alienated, and in the thoroughness and completeness of the process.

Alienation as we find it in modern society is almost total; it pervades the relationship of man to his work, to the things he consumes, to the state, to his fellow man, and to himself. Man has created a world of man-made things as it never existed before. He has constructed a complicated social machine to administer the technical machine he built. Yet this whole creation of his stands over and above him. He does not feel himself as a creator and center, but as the servant of a Golem, which his hands have built. The more powerful and gigantic the forces are which he unleashes, the more powerless he feels himself as a human being. He confronts himself with his own forces embodied in things he has created, alienated from himself. He is owned by his own creation, and has lost ownership of himself. He has built a golden calf, and says "these are your gods who have brought you out of Egypt."

What happens to the *worker?* To put it in the words of a thoughtful and thorough observer of the industrial scene: "In industry the person becomes an economic atom that dances to the tune of atomistic management. Your place is just here, you will sit in this fashion, your arms will move x inches in a course of y radius and the time of movement will be .ooo minutes.

"Work is becoming more repetitive and thoughtless as the planners, the micromotionists, and the scientific managers further strip the worker of his right to think and move freely. Life is being denied; need to control, creativeness, curiosity, and independent thought are being baulked, and the result, the inevitable result, is flight or fight on the part of the worker, apathy or destructiveness, psychic regression." [1]

The role of the *manager* is also one of alienation. It is true, he manages the whole and not a part, but he too is alienated from his product as something concrete and useful. His aim is to employ profitably the capital invested by others, although in comparison with the older type of owner-manager, modern management is much less interested in the amount of profit to be paid

[1] J. J. Gillespie, *Free Expression in Industry*, The Pilot Press Ltd., London, 1948.

out as dividend to the stockholder than it is in the efficient operation and expansion of the enterprise. Characteristically, within
management those in charge of labor relations and of sales—that
is, of human manipulation—gain, relatively speaking, an increasing importance in comparison with those in charge of the technical
aspects of production.

The manager, like the worker, like everybody, deals with impersonal giants: with the giant competitive enterprise; with the
giant national and world market; with the giant consumer, who
has to be coaxed and manipulated; with the giant unions, and
the giant government. All these giants have their own lives, as it
were. They determine the activity of the manager and they direct
the activity of the worker and clerk.

The problem of the manager opens up one of the most significant phenomena in an alienated culture, that of *bureaucratization.*
Both big business and government administrations are conducted
by a bureaucracy. Bureaucrats are specialists in the administration of things *and of men.* Due to the bigness of the apparatus
to be administered, and the resulting abstractification, the bureaucrats' relationship to the people is one of complete alienation. They,
the people to be administered, are objects whom the bureaucrats
consider neither with love nor with hate, but completely imper-
sonally; the manager-bureaucrat must not feel, as far as his professional activity is concerned; he must manipulate people as
though they were figures, or things. Since the vastness of the
organization and the extreme division of labor prevents any single
individual from seeing the whole, since there is no organic, spontaneous co-operation between the various individuals or groups
within the industry, the managing bureaucrats are necessary;
without them the enterprise would collapse in a short time, since
nobody would know the secret which makes it function. Bureaucrats are as indispensable as the tons of paper consumed under

their leadership. Just because everybody senses, with a feeling of powerlessness, the vital role of the bureaucrats, they are given an almost godlike respect. If it were not for the bureaucrats, people feel, everything would go to pieces, and we would starve. Whereas, in the medieval world, the leaders were considered representatives of a god-intended order, in modern Capitalism the role of the bureaucrat is hardly less sacred—since he is necessary for the survival of the whole.

Marx gave a profound definition of the bureaucrat saying: "The bureaucrat relates himself to the world as a *mere object* of his activity." It is interesting to note that the spirit of bureaucracy has entered not only business and government administration, but also trade unions and the great democratic socialist parties in England, Germany and France. In Russia, too, the bureaucratic managers and their alienated spirit have conquered the country. Russia could perhaps exist without terror—if certain conditions were given—but it could not exist without the system of total bureaucratization—that is, alienation.[1]

What is the attitude of the *owner* of the enterprise, the capitalist? The small businessman seems to be in the same position as his predecessor a hundred years ago. He owns and directs his small enterprise, he is in touch with the whole commercial or industrial activity, and in personal contact with his employees and workers. But living in an alienated world in all other economic and social aspects, and furthermore being more under the constant pressure of bigger competitors, he is by no means as free as his grandfather was in the same business.

But what matters more and more in contemporary economy is big business, the large corporation. As Drucker puts it very succinctly: "In fine, it is the large corporation—the specific form in

---

[1] cf. the interesting article by W. Huhn, "Der Bolschevismus als Manager Ideologie" in Funken, Frankfurt V, 8/1954.

which Big Business is organized in a free-enterprise economy—which has emerged as the representative and determining socio-economic institution which sets the pattern and determines the behavior even of the owner of the corner cigar store who never owned a share of stock, and of his errand boy who never set foot in a mill. And thus the character of our society is determined and patterned by the structural organization of Big Business, the technology of the mass-production plant, and the degree to which our social beliefs and promises are realized in and by the large corporations." [1]

What then is the attitude of the "owner" of the big corporation to "his" property? It is one of almost complete alienation. His ownership consists in a piece of paper, representing a certain fluctuating amount of money; he has no responsibility for the enterprise and no concrete relationship to it in any way. This attitude of alienation has been most clearly expressed in Berle's and Means' description of the attitude of the stockholder to the enterprise which follows here: "(1) The position of ownership has changed from that of an active to that of a passive agent. In place of actual physical properties over which the owner could exercise direction and for which he was responsible, the owner now holds a piece of paper representing a set of rights and expectations with respect to an enterprise. But over the enterprise and over the physical property—the instruments of production—in which he has an interest, the owner has little control. At the same time he bears no responsibility with respect to the enterprise or its physical property. It has often been said that the owner of a horse is responsible. If the horse lives he must feed it. If the horse dies he must bury it. No such responsibility attaches to a share

[1] cf. Peter F. Drucker, *Concept of the Corporation*, The John Day Company, New York, 1946, pp. 8, 9.

Stock market means a long step toward alienation.

of stock. The owner is practically powerless through his own efforts to affect the underlying property.

"(2) The spiritual values that formerly went with ownership have been separated from it. Physical property capable of being shaped by its owner could bring to him direct satisfaction apart from the income it yielded in more concrete form. It represented an extension of his own personality. With the corporate revolution, this quality has been lost to the property owner much as it has been lost to the worker through the industrial revolution.

"(3) The value of an individual's wealth is coming to depend on forces entirely outside himself and his own efforts. Instead, its value is determined on the one hand by the actions of the individuals in command of the enterprise—individuals over whom the typical owner has no control, and on the other hand, by the actions of others in a sensitive and often capricious market. The value is thus subject to the vagaries and manipulations characteristic of the market place. It is further subject to the great swings in society's appraisal of its own immediate future as reflected in the general level of values in the organized market.

"(4) The value of the individual's wealth not only fluctuates constantly—the same may be said of most wealth—but it is subject to a constant appraisal. The individual can see the change in the appraised value of his estate from moment to moment, a fact which may markedly affect both the expenditure of his income and his enjoyment of that income.

"(5) Individual wealth has become extremely liquid through the organized markets. The individual owner can convert it into other forms of wealth at a moment's notice and, provided the market machinery is in working order, he may do so without serious loss due to forced sales.

"(6) Wealth is less and less in a form which can be employed directly by its owner. When wealth is in the form of land, for instance, it is capable of being used by the owner even though the value of land in the market is negligible. The physical quality of such wealth makes possible a subjective value to the owner quite apart from any market value it may have. The newer form of wealth is quite incapable of this direct use. Only through sale in the market can the owner obtain its direct use. He is thus tied to the market as never before.

"(7) Finally, in the corporate system, the 'owner' of industrial wealth is left with a mere symbol of ownership while the power, the responsibility and the substance which have been an integral part of ownership in the past are being transferred to a separate group in whose hands lies control." [1]

Another important aspect of the alienated position of the stockholder is his control over his enterprise. Legally, the stockholders control the enterprise, that is, they elect the management much as the people in a democracy elect their representatives. Factually, however, they exercise very little control, due to the fact that each individual's share is so exceedingly small, that he is not interested in coming to the meetings and participating actively. Berle and Means differentiate among five major types of control: "These include (1) control through almost complete ownership, (2) majority control, (3) control through a legal device without majority ownership, (4) minority control, and (5) management control." [2] Among the five types of control the first two—private ownership or majority ownership—exercise control in only 6 per cent (according to wealth) of the two hundred largest companies (around 1930), while in the remaining 94 per cent control is exercised either by the management, or by a legal device in col-

---

[1] cf. A. A. Berle and G. C. Means, *The Modern Corporation and Private Property*, The Macmillan Company, New York, 1940, pp. 66–68.
[2] *Ibid.*, p. 70.

130

laring a small proportion of the ownership or by a minority of the stockholders.[1] How this miracle is accomplished without force, deception or any violation of the law is most interestingly described in Berle's and Means' classic work.

The process of *consumption* is as alienated as the process of production. In the first place, we acquire things with money; we are accustomed to this and take it for granted. But actually, this is a most peculiar way of acquiring things. Money represents labor and effort in an abstract form; not necessarily *my* labor and *my* effort, since I can have acquired it by inheritance, by fraud, by luck, or any number of ways. But even if I have acquired it by *my* effort (forgetting for the moment that *my* effort might not have brought me the money were it not for the fact that I employed men), I have acquired it in a specific way, by a specific kind of effort, corresponding to my skills and capacities, while, in spending, the money is transformed into an abstract form of labor and can be exchanged against anything else. Provided I am in the possession of money, no effort or interest of mine is necessary to acquire something. If I have the money, I can acquire an exquisite painting, even though I may not have any appreciation for art; I can buy the best phonograph, even though I have no musical taste; I can buy a library, although I use it only for the purpose of ostentation. I can buy an education, even though I have no use for it except as an additional social asset. I can even destroy the painting or the books I bought, and aside from a loss of money, I suffer no damage. Mere possession of money gives me the right to acquire and to do with my acquisition whatever I like. The *human* way of acquiring would be to make an effort qualitatively commensurate with what I acquire. The acquisition of bread and clothing would depend on no other premise than that of being alive; the acquisition of books and paintings, on my effort

[1] *Ibid.*, pp. 94 and 114–117.

to understand them and my ability to use them. How this principle could be applied practically is not the point to be discussed here. What matters is that the way we acquire things is separated from the way in which we use them.

The alienating function of money in the process of acquisition and consumption has been beautifully described by Marx in the following words: "Money . . . transforms the real human and natural powers into merely abstract ideas, and hence imperfections, and on the other hand it transforms the real imperfections and imaginings, the powers which only exist in the imagination of the individual into real powers. . . . It transforms loyalty into vice, vices into virtue, the slave into the master, the master into the slave, ignorance into reason, and reason into ignorance. . . . He who can buy valour is valiant although he be cowardly. . . . Assume *man* as *man*, and his relation to the world as a human one, and you can exchange love only for love, confidence for confidence, etc. If you wish to enjoy art, you must be an artistically trained person; if you wish to have influence on other people, you must be a person who has a really stimulating and furthering influence on other people. Every one of your relationships to man and to nature must be a definite expression of your *real, individual* life corresponding to the object of your will. If you love without calling forth love, that is, if your love as such does not produce love, if by means of an *expression of life* as a loving person you do not make of yourself a *loved person,* then your love is impotent, a misfortune." [1]

But beyond the method of acquisition, how do we use things, once we have acquired them? With regard to many things, there is not even the pretense of use. We acquire them to *have* them. We are satisfied with useless possession. The expensive dining set or

---

[1] "Nationalökonomie und Philosophie," 1844, published in Karl Marx' *Die Frühschriften*, Alfred Kröner Verlag, Stuttgart, 1953, pp. 300, 301. (My translation, E.F.)

crystal vase which we never use for fear they might break, the mansion with many unused rooms, the unnecessary cars and servants, like the ugly bric-à-brac of the lower-middle-class family, are so many examples of pleasure in possession instead of in use. However, this satisfaction in possessing per se was more prominent in the nineteenth century; today most of the satisfaction is derived from possession of things-to-be-used rather than of things-to-be-kept. This does not alter the fact, however, that even in the pleasure of things-to-be-used the satisfaction of prestige is a paramount factor. The car, the refrigerator, the television set are for real, but also for conspicuous use. They confer status on the owner.

How do we use the things we acquire? Let us begin with food and drink. We eat a bread which is tasteless and not nourishing because it appeals to our phantasy of wealth and distinction—being so white and "fresh." Actually, we "eat" a phantasy and have lost contact with the real thing we eat. Our palate, our body, are excluded from an act of consumption which primarily concerns them. We drink labels. With a bottle of Coca-Cola we drink the picture of the pretty boy and girl who drink it in the advertisement, we drink the slogan of "the pause that refreshes," we drink the great American habit; least of all do we drink with our palate. All this is even worse when it comes to the consumption of things whose whole reality is mainly the fiction the advertising campaign has created, like the "healthy" soap or dental paste.

I could go on giving examples ad infinitum. But it is unnecessary to belabor the point, since everybody can think of as many illustrations as I could give. I only want to stress the principle involved: the act of consumption should be a concrete human act, in which our senses, bodily needs, our aesthetic taste—that is to say, in which *we* as concrete, sensing, feeling, judging human beings—are involved; the act of consumption should be a meaningful, human, productive experience. In our culture, there is little of that. Consuming is essentially the satisfaction of artificially stimulated phantasies, a phantasy performance alienated from our concrete, real selves.

There is another aspect of alienation from the things we consume which needs to be mentioned. We are surrounded by things of whose nature and origin we know nothing. The telephone, radio, phonograph, and all other complicated machines are almost as mysterious to us as they would be to a man from a primitive culture; we know how to use them, that is, we know which button to turn, but we do not know on what principle they function, except in the vaguest terms of something we once learned at school. And things which do not rest upon difficult scientific principles are almost equally alien to us. We do not know how bread is made, how cloth is woven, how a table is manufactured, how glass is made. We consume, as we produce, without any concrete relatedness to the objects with which we deal; we live in a world of things, and our only connection with them is that we know how to manipulate or to consume them.

Our way of consumption necessarily results in the fact that we are never satisfied, since it is not our real concrete person which consumes a real and concrete thing. We thus develop an ever-increasing need for more things, for more consumption. It is true that as long as the living standard of the population is below a dignified level of subsistence, there is a natural need for more consumption. It is also true that there is a legitimate need for more consumption as man develops culturally and has more refined needs for better food, objects of artistic pleasure, books, etc. But our craving for consumption has lost all connection with the real needs of man. Originally, the idea of consuming more and better things was meant to give man a happier, more satisfied life. Consumption was a means to an end, that of happiness. It now has become an aim in itself. The constant increase of needs forces us to an ever-increasing effort, it makes us dependent on these needs and on the people and institutions by whose help we attain them. "Each person speculates to create a new need in the other person, in order to force him into a new dependency, to a new form of pleasure, hence to his economic ruin. . . . With a multitude of commodities grows the realm of alien things which enslave man." [1]

Man today is fascinated by the possibility of buying more, better, and especially, new things. He is consumption-hungry. The act of buying and consuming has become a compulsive, irrational aim, because it is an end in itself, with little relation to the use of, or pleasure in the things bought and consumed. To buy the latest gadget, the latest model of anything that is on the market, is the dream of everybody, in comparison to which the real pleasure in use is quite secondary. Modern man, if he dared to be articulate about his concept of heaven, would describe a vision which would look like the biggest department store in the world, showing new things and gadgets, and himself having plenty of money with which to buy them. He would wander around open-mouthed in this heaven of gadgets and commodities, provided only that there were ever more and newer things to buy, and perhaps that his neighbors were just a little less privileged than he.

Significantly enough, one of the older traits of middle-class society, the attachment to possessions and property, has undergone a profound change. In the older attitude, a certain sense of loving possession existed between a man and his property. It grew on him. He was proud of it. He took good care of it, and it was painful when eventually he had to part from it because it could not be used any more. There is very little left of this sense of property today. One loves the newness of the thing bought, and is ready to betray it when something newer has appeared.

[1] K. Marx, *ibid.*, p. 254.

Expressing the same change in characterological terms, I can refer to what has been stated above with regard to the *hoarding* orientation as dominant in the picture of the nineteenth century. In the middle of the twentieth century the hoarding orientation has given way to the *receptive* orientation, in which the aim is to receive, to "drink in," to have something new all the time, to live with a continuously open mouth, as it were. This receptive orientation is blended with the marketing orientation, while in the nineteenth century the hoarding was blended with the exploitative orientation.

The alienated attitude toward consumption not only exists in our acquisition and consumption of commodities, but it determines far beyond this the employment of leisure time. What are we to expect? If a man works without genuine relatedness to what he is doing, if he buys and consumes commodities in an abstractified and alienated way, how can he make use of his leisure time in an active and meaningful way? He always remains the passive and alienated consumer. He "consumes" ball games, moving pictures, newspapers and magazines, books, lectures, natural scenery, social gatherings, in the same alienated and abstractified way in which he consumes the commodities he has bought. He does not participate actively, he wants to "take in" all there is to be had, and to have as much as possible of pleasure, culture and what not. Actually, he is not free to enjoy "his" leisure; his leisure-time consumption is determined by industry, as are the commodities he buys; his taste is manipulated, he wants to see and to hear what he is conditioned to want to see and to hear; entertainment is an industry like any other, the customer is made to buy fun as he is made to buy dresses and shoes. The value of the fun is determined by its success on the market, not by anything which could be measured in human terms.

In any productive and spontaneous activity, something happens

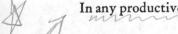

within myself while I am reading, looking at scenery, talking to friends, etcetera. I am not the same after the experience as I was before. In the alienated form of pleasure nothing happens within me; I have consumed this or that; nothing is changed within myself, and all that is left are memories of what I have done. One of the most striking examples for this kind of pleasure consumption is the taking of snapshots, which has become one of the most significant leisure activities. The Kodak slogan, "You press the button, we do the rest," which since 1889 has helped so much to popularize photography all over the world, is symbolic. It is one of the earliest appeals to push-button power-feeling; you do nothing, you do not have to know anything, everything is done for you; all you have to do is to press the button. Indeed, the taking of snapshots has become one of the most significant expressions of alienated visual perception, of sheer consumption. The "tourist" with his camera is an outstanding symbol of an alienated relationship to the world. Being constantly occupied with taking pictures, actually *he* does not see anything at all, except through the intermediary of the camera. The camera sees for him, and the outcome of his "pleasure" trip is a collection of snapshots, which are the substitute for an experience which he could have had, but did not have.

Man is not only alienated from the work he does, and the things and pleasures he consumes, but also from the *social forces* which determine our society and the life of everybody living in it.

Our actual helplessness before the forces which govern us appears more drastically in those social catastrophes which, even though they are denounced as regrettable accidents each time, so far have never failed to happen: economic depressions and wars. These social phenomena appear as if they were natural catastrophes, rather than what they really are, occurrences made by man, but without intention and awareness.

This anonymity of the social forces is inherent in the structure of the capitalist mode of production.

In contrast to most other societies in which social laws are explicit and fixed on the basis of political power or tradition— Capitalism does not have such explicit laws. It is based on the principle that if only everybody strives for himself on the market, the common good will come of it, order and not anarchy will be the result. There are, of course, economic laws which govern the market, but these laws operate behind the back of the acting individual, who is concerned only with his private interests. You try to guess these laws of the market as a Calvinist in Geneva tried to guess whether God had predestined him for salvation or not. But the laws of the market, like God's will, are beyond the reach of your will and influence.

To a large extent the development of Capitalism has proven that this principle works; and it is indeed a miracle that the antagonistic co-operation of self-contained economic entities should result in a blossoming and ever-expanding society. It is true that the capitalistic mode of production is conducive to political freedom, while any centrally planned social order is in danger of leading to political regimentation and eventually to dictatorship. While this is not the place to discuss the question of whether there are other alternatives than the choice between "free enterprise" and political regimentation, it needs to be said in this context that the very fact that we are governed by laws which we do not control, and do not even want to control, is one of the most outstanding manifestations of alienation. *We* are the producers of our economic and social arrangements, and at the same time we decline responsibility, intentionally and enthusiastically, and await hopefully or anxiously—as the case may be—what "the future" will bring. Our own actions are embodied in the laws which govern us, but these laws are above us, and we are their slaves.

Relationship ↓

The giant state and economic system are not any more controlled by man. They run wild, and their leaders are like a person on a runaway horse, who is proud of managing to keep in the saddle, even though he is powerless to direct the horse.

What is modern man's *relationship to his fellow man*? It is one between two abstractions, two living machines, who use each other. The employer uses the ones whom he employs; the salesman uses his customers. Everybody is to everybody else a commodity, always to be treated with certain friendliness, because even if he is not of use now, he may be later. There is not much love or hate to be found in human relations of our day. There is, rather, a superficial friendliness, and a more than superficial fairness, but behind that surface is distance and indifference. There is also a good deal of subtle distrust. When one man says to another, "You speak to John Smith; he is all right," it is an expression of reassurance against a general distrust. Even love and the relationship between sexes have assumed this character. The great sexual emancipation, as it occurred after the First World War, was a desperate attempt to substitute mutual sexual pleasure for a deeper feeling of love. When this turned out to be a disappointment the erotic polarity between the sexes was reduced to a minimum and replaced by a friendly partnership, a small combine which has amalgamated its forces to hold out better in the daily battle of life, and to relieve the feeling of isolation and aloneness which everybody has.

The alienation between man and man results in the loss of those general and social bonds which characterize medieval as well as most other precapitalist societies.[1] Modern society consists of "atoms" (if we use the Greek equivalent of "individual"), little particles estranged from each other but held together by selfish

---

[1] cf. the concept of "Gemeinschaft" (community) as against "Gesellschaft" (society) in Toennies' usage.

interests and by the necessity to make use of each other. Yet man is a social being with a deep need to share, to help, to feel as a member of a group. What has happened to these social strivings in man? They manifest themselves in the special sphere of the *public* realm, which is strictly separated from the private realm. Our private dealings with our fellow men are governed by the principle of egotism, "each for himself, God for us all," in flagrant contradiction to Christian teaching. The individual is motivated by egotistical interest, and not by solidarity with and love for his fellow man. The latter feelings may assert themselves secondarily as private acts of philanthropy or kindness, but they are not part of the basic structure of our social relations. Separated from our private life as individuals is the realm of our social life as "citizens." In this realm the state is the embodiment of our social existence; as citizens we are supposed to, and in fact usually do, exhibit a sense of social obligation and duty. We pay taxes, we vote, we respect the laws, and in the case of war we are willing to sacrifice our lives. What clearer example could there be of the separation between private and public existence than the fact that the same man who would not think of spending one hundred dollars to relieve the need of a stranger does not hesitate to risk his life to save this same stranger when in war they both happen to be soldiers in uniform? The uniform is the embodiment of our social nature—civilian garb, of our egotistic nature.

An interesting illustration of this thesis is to be found in S. A. Stouffer's newest work.[1] In answer to a question directed to a cross section of the American public "what kinds of things do you worry about most," the vast majority answers by mentioning personal, economic, health or other problems; only 8 per cent are worried about world problems including war—and one

---

[1] *Communism, Conformity and Civil Liberties*, Doubleday & Co., Inc. Garden City, New York, 1955.

difference between belief and what we worry about (i.e., take personally!)

per cent about the danger of Communism or the threat to civil liberties. But, on the other hand, almost half of the population of the sample thinks that Communism is a serious danger, and that war is likely to occur within two years. These social concerns, however, are not felt to be a personal reality, hence are no cause for worry, although for a good deal of intolerance. It is also interesting to note that in spite of the fact that almost the whole population believes in God, there seems to be hardly anyone who is worried about his soul, salvation, his spiritual development. God is as alienated as the world as a whole. What causes concern and worry is the private, separate sector of life, not the social, universal one which connects us with our fellow men.

The division between the community and the political state has led to the projection of all social feelings into the state, which thus becomes an idol, a power standing over and above man. Man submits to the state as to the embodiment of his own social feelings, which he worships as powers alienated from himself; in his private life as an individual he suffers from the isolation and aloneness which are the necessary result of this separation. The worship of the state can only disappear if man takes back the social powers into himself, and builds a community in which his social feelings are not something *added* to his private existence, but in which his private and social existence are one and the same.

What is the relationship of *man toward himself?* I have described elsewhere this relationship as "marketing orientation." [1] In this orientation, man experiences himself as a thing to be em-

---

[1] cf. my description of the marketing orientation in *Man for Himself*, p. 67 ff. The concept of alienation is not the same as one of the character orientations in terms of the receptive, exploitative, hoarding, marketing and productive orientations. Alienation can be found in any of these non-productive orientations, but it has a particular affinity to the marketing orientation. To the same extent it is also related to Riesman's "other-directed" personality which, however, though "developed from the marketing orientation," is a different concept in essential points. Cf. D. Riesman, *The Lonely Crowd*, Yale University Press, New Haven, 1950, p. 23.

ployed successfully on the market. He does not experience himself as an active agent, as the bearer of human powers. He is alienated from these powers. His aim is to sell himself successfully on the market. His sense of self does not stem from his activity as a loving and thinking individual, but from his socio-economic role. If things could speak, a typewriter would answer the question "Who are you?" by saying "I am a typewriter," and an automobile, by saying "I am an automobile," or more specifically by saying, "I am a Ford," or "a Buick," or "a Cadillac." If you ask a man "Who are you?", he answers "I am a manufacturer," "I am a clerk," "I am a doctor"—or "I am a married man," "I am the father of two kids," and his answer has pretty much the same meaning as that of the speaking *thing* would have. That is the way he experiences himself, not as a man, with love, fear, convictions, doubts, but as that abstraction, alienated from his real nature, which fulfills a certain function in the social system. His sense of value depends on his success: on whether he can sell himself favorably, whether he can make more of himself than he started out with, whether he is a success. His body, his mind and his soul are his capital, and his task in life is to invest it favorably, to make a profit of himself. Human qualities like friendliness, courtesy, kindness, are transformed into commodities, into assets of the "personality package," conducive to a higher price on the personality market. If the individual fails in a profitable investment of himself, he feels that *he* is a failure; if he succeeds, *he* is a success. Clearly, his sense of his own value always depends on factors extraneous to himself, on the fickle judgment of the market, which decides about his value as it decides about the value of commodities. He, like all commodities that cannot be sold profitably on the market, is worthless as far as his exchange value is concerned, even though his use value may be considerable.

The alienated personality who is for sale must lose a good deal

Sense of Self.

of the sense of dignity which is so characteristic of man even in most primitive cultures. He must lose almost all sense of self, of himself as a unique and induplicable entity. The sense of self stems from the experience of myself as the subject of *my* experiences, *my* thought, *my* feeling, *my* decision, *my* judgment, *my* action. It presupposes that my experience is my own, and not an alienated one. *Things* have no self and men who have become things can have no self.

This selflessness of modern man has appeared to one of the most gifted and original contemporary psychiatrists, the late H. S. Sullivan, as being a natural phenomenon. He spoke of those psychologists who, like myself, assume that the lack of the sense of self is a pathological phenomenon, as of people who suffer from a "delusion." The self for him is nothing but the many roles we play in relations to others, roles which have the function of eliciting approval and avoiding the anxiety which is produced by disapproval. What a remarkably fast deterioration of the concept of self since the nineteenth century, when Ibsen made the loss of self the main theme of his criticism of modern man in his Peer Gynt! Peer Gynt is described as a man who, chasing after material gain, discovers eventually that he has lost his self, that he is like an onion with layer after layer, and without a kernel. Ibsen describes the dread of nothingness by which Peer Gynt is seized when he makes this discovery, a panic which makes him desire to land in hell, rather than to be thrown back into the "casting ladle" of nothingness. Indeed, with the experience of self disappears the experience of identity—and when this happens, man could become insane if he did not save himself by acquiring a *secondary sense of self;* he does that by experiencing himself as being approved of, worth while, successful, useful—briefly, as a salable commodity which is *he* because he is looked upon by others as an entity, not unique but fitting into one of the current patterns.

Sullivan ?

Fromm calls Modern sense of self a "secondary one" based on approval.

routinization [handwritten marginalia]

One cannot fully appreciate the nature of alienation without considering one specific aspect of modern life: its *routinization*, and the *repression of the awareness of the basic problems of human existence*. We touch here upon a universal problem of life. Man has to earn his daily bread, and this is always a more or less absorbing task. He has to take care of the many time- and energy-consuming tasks of daily life, and he is enmeshed in a certain routine necessary for the fulfillment of these tasks. He builds a social order, conventions, habits and ideas, which help him to perform what is necessary, and to live with his fellow man with a minimum of friction. It is characteristic of all culture that it builds a man-made, artificial world, superimposed on the natural world in which man lives. But man can fulfill himself only if he remains in touch with the fundamental facts of his existence, if he can experience the exaltation of love and solidarity, as well as the tragic fact of his aloneness and of the fragmentary character of his existence. If he is completely enmeshed in the routine and in the artefacts of life, if he cannot see anything but the man-made, common-sense appearance of the world, he loses his touch with and the grasp of himself and the world. We find in every culture the conflict between routine and the attempt to get back to the fundamental realities of existence. To help in this attempt has been one of the functions of art and of religion, even though religion itself has eventually become a new form of routine.

art + religion [handwritten marginalia]

Art [handwritten marginalia]

Even the most primitive history of man shows us an attempt to get in touch with the essence of reality by artistic creation. Primitive man is not satisfied with the practical function of his tools and weapons, but strives to adorn and beautify them, transcending their utilitarian function. Aside from art, the most significant way of breaking through the surface of routine and of getting in touch with the ultimate realities of life is to be found in what may be called by the general term of "ritual." I am referring

144

ritual [handwritten marginalia]

here to ritual in the broad sense of the word, as we find it in the performance of a Greek drama, for instance, and not only to rituals in the narrower religious sense. What was the function of the Greek drama? Fundamental problems of human existence were presented in an artistic and dramatic form, and participating in the dramatic performance, the spectator—though not as a spectator in our modern sense of the consumer—was carried away from the sphere of daily routine and brought in touch with himself as a human being, with the roots of his existence. He touched the ground with his feet, and in this process gained strength by which he was brought back to himself. Whether we think of the Greek drama, the medieval passion play, or an Indian dance, whether we think of Hindu, Jewish or Christian religious rituals, we are dealing with various forms of dramatization of the fundamental problems of human existence, with an *acting out* of the very same problems which are *thought out* in philosophy and theology.

What is left of such dramatization of life in modern culture? Almost nothing. Man hardly ever gets out of the realm of man-made conventions and things, and hardly ever breaks through the surface of his routine, aside from grotesque attempts to satisfy the need for a ritual as we see it practiced in lodges and fraternities. The only phenomenon approaching the meaning of a ritual, is the participation of the spectator in competitive sports; here at least, one fundamental problem of human existence is dealt with: the fight between men and the vicarious experience of victory and defeat. But what a primitive and restricted aspect of human existence, reducing the richness of human life to one partial aspect!

If there is a fire, or a car collision in a big city, scores of people will gather and watch. Millions of people are fascinated daily by reportings of crimes and by detective stories. They religiously go to movies in which crime and passion are the two central themes.

All this interest and fascination is not simply an expression of bad taste and sensationalism, but of a deep longing for a dramatization of ultimate phenomena of human existence, life and death, crime and punishment, the battle between man and nature. But while Greek drama dealt with these problems on a high artistic and metaphysical level, our modern "drama" and "ritual" are crude and do not produce any cathartic effect. All this fascination with competitive sports, crime and passion, shows the need for breaking through the routine surface, but the way of its satisfaction shows the extreme poverty of our solution.

The marketing orientation is closely related to the fact that the *need to exchange* has become a paramount drive in modern man. It is, of course, true that even in a primitive economy based on a rudimentary form of division of labor, men exchange goods with each other within the tribe or among neighboring tribes. The man who produces cloth exchanges it for grain which his neighbor may have produced, or for sickles or knives made by the blacksmith. With increasing division of labor, there is increasing exchange of goods, but normally the exchange of goods is nothing but a means to an economic end. In capitalistic society *exchanging has become an end in itself*.

None other than Adam Smith saw the fundamental role of the need to exchange, and explained it as a basic drive in man. "This division of labour," he says, "from which so many advantages are derived, is not originally the effect of any human wisdom, which foresees and intends that general opulence to which it gives occasion. It is the necessary, though very slow and gradual, consequence of a certain *propensity in human nature* which has in view no such extensive utility; the propensity to truck, barter, and exchange one thing for another. Whether this propensity be one of those original principles in human nature, of which no further account can be given; or whether, as seems more probable, it be the necessary consequence of the faculties of reason and speech, it belongs not to our present subject to enquire. *It is common to all men, and to be found in no other race of animals,* which seem to know neither this nor any other species of contracts. . . . Nobody ever saw a dog make a fair and deliberate exchange of one bone for another with another dog." [1]

The principle of exchange on an ever-increasing scale on the national and world market is indeed one of the fundamental economic principles on which the capitalistic system rests, but Adam Smith foresaw here that this principle was also to become one of the deepest psychic needs of the modern, alienated personality. Exchanging has lost its rational function as a mere means for economic purposes, and has become an end in itself, extended to the noneconomic realms. Quite unwittingly, Adam Smith himself indicates the irrational nature of this need to exchange in his example of the exchange between the two dogs. There could be no possible realistic purpose in this exchange; either the two bones are alike, and then there is no reason to exchange them, or the one is better than the other, and then the dog who has the better one would not voluntarily exchange it. The example makes sense only if we assume that to exchange is a need in itself, even if it does not serve any practical purpose—and this is indeed what Adam Smith does assume.

As I have already mentioned in another context, the love of exchange has replaced the love of possession. One buys a car, or a house, intending to sell it at the first opportunity. But more important is the fact that the drive for exchange operates in the realm of interpersonal relations. Love is often nothing but a favorable exchange between two people who get the most of what they can expect, considering their value on the personality market.

---

[1] Adam Smith, *An Enquiry into the Nature and Causes of the Wealth of Nations,* The Modern Library, New York, 1937, p. 13. (Italics mine, E.F.)

Each person is a "package" in which several aspects of his exchange value are blended into one: his "personality," by which is meant those qualities which make him a good salesman of himself; his looks, education, income, and chance for success—each person strives to exchange this package for the best value obtainable. Even the function of going to a party, and of social intercourse in general, is to a large extent that of exchange. One is eager to meet the slightly higher-priced packages, in order to make contact and possibly a profitable exchange. One wishes to exchange one's social position, and that is, one's own self, for a higher one, and in this process one exchanges one's old set of friends, set of habits and feelings for the new ones, just as one exchanges one's Ford for a Buick. While Adam Smith believed this need for exchange to be an inherent part of human nature, it is actually a symptom of the abstractification and alienation inherent in the social character of modern man.

The whole process of living is experienced analogously to the profitable investment of capital, my life and my person being the capital which is invested. If a man buys a cake of soap or a pound of meat, he has the legitimate expectation that the money he pays corresponds to the value of the soap or the meat he buys. He is concerned that the equation "so much soap = so much money" makes sense in terms of the existing price structure. But this expectation has become extended to all other forms of activity. If a man goes to a concert or to the theater, he asks himself more or less explicitly whether the show is "worth the money" he paid. While this question makes some marginal sense, fundamentally the question does not make any sense, because two incommensurable things are brought together in the equation; the pleasure of listening to a concert cannot possibly be expressed in terms of money; the concert is not a commodity, nor is the experience of listening to it. The same holds true when a man makes a pleasure trip, goes to a lecture, gives a party, or any of the many activities which involve the expenditure of money. The activity in itself is a productive act of living, and incommensurable with the amount of money spent for it. The need to measure living acts in terms of something quantifiable appears also in the tendency to ask whether something was "worth the time." A young man's evening with a girl, a visit with friends, and the many other actions in which expenditure of money may or may not be involved, raise the question of whether the activity was worth the money or the time.[1] In each case one needs to justify the activity in terms of an equation which shows that it was a profitable investment of energy. Even hygiene and health have to serve for the same purpose; a man taking a walk every morning tends to look on it as a good investment for his health, rather than a pleasurable activity which does not need any justification. This attitude found its closest and most drastic expression in Bentham's concept of pleasure and pain. Starting on the assumption that the aim of life was to have pleasure, Bentham suggested a kind of bookkeeping which would show for each action whether the pleasure was greater than the pain, and if the pleasure was greater, the action was worth while doing. Thus the whole of life to him was something analogous to a business in which at any given point the favorable balance would show that it was profitable.

While Bentham's views are not very much in the minds of people any more, the attitude which they express has become ever more firmly established.[2] A new question has arisen in modern man's mind, the question, namely, whether "life is worth living," and

[1] cf. Marx' critical description of man in capitalist society: "Time is everything; man is nothing; he is no more than the carcass of time." (*The Poverty of Philosophy*, p. 57.)

[2] In Freud's concept of the pleasure principle and in his pessimistic views concerning the prevalence of suffering over pleasure in civilized society, one can detect the influence of Benthamian calculation.

correspondingly, the feeling that one's life "is a failure," or is "a success." This idea is based on the concept of life as an enterprise which should show a profit. The failure is like the bankruptcy of a business in which the losses are greater than the gains. This concept is nonsensical. We may be happy or unhappy, achieve some aims, and not achieve others; yet there is no sensible balance which could show whether life is worth while living. Maybe from the standpoint of a balance life is never worth while living. It ends necessarily with death; many of our hopes are disappointed; it involves suffering and effort; from a standpoint of the balance, it would seem to make more sense not to have been born at all, or to die in infancy. On the other hand, who will tell whether one happy moment of love, or the joy of breathing or walking on a bright morning and smelling the fresh air, is not worth all the suffering and effort which life implies? Life is a unique gift and challenge, not to be measured in terms of anything else, and no sensible answer can be given to the question whether it is "worth while" living, because the question does not make any sense.

This interpretation of life as an enterprise seems to be the basis for a typical modern phenomenon, about which a great deal of speculation exists: the *increase of suicide* in modern Western society. Between 1836 and 1890 suicide increased 140 per cent in Prussia, 355 per cent in France. England had 62 cases of suicide per million inhabitants in 1836 to 1845, and 110 between 1906 and 1910. Sweden 66, as against 150 respectively.[1] How can we explain this increase in suicide, accompanying the increasing prosperity in the nineteenth century?

No doubt that the motives for suicide are highly complex, and that there is not a single motivation which we can assume to be

---

[1] Quoted from *Les Causes du Suicide* by Maurice Halbwachs, Félix Alcan, Paris, 1930, pp. 92 and 481.

the cause. We find "revenge suicide" as a pattern in China; we find suicide caused by melancholia all over the world; but neither of these motivations play much of a role in the increase of suicide rates in the nineteenth century. Durkheim, in his classic work on suicide, assumed that the cause is to be found in a phenomenon which he called "anomie." He referred by that term to the destruction of all the traditional social bonds, to the fact that all truly collective organization has become secondary to the state, and that all genuine social life has been annihilated.[1] He believed that the people living in the modern political state are "a disorganized dust of individuals."[2] Durkheim's explanation lies in the direction of assumptions made in this book, and I shall return to discuss them later on. I believe also that the boredom and monotony of life which is engendered by the alienated way of living is an additional factor. The suicide figures for the Scandinavian countries, Switzerland and the United States, together with the figures on alcoholism seem to support this hypothesis.[3] But there is another reason which has been ignored by Durkheim and other students of suicide. It has to do with the whole "balance" concept of life as an enterprise which can fail. Many cases of suicide are caused by the feeling that "life has been a failure," that "it is not worth while living any more"; one commits suicide just as a businessman declares his bankruptcy when losses exceed gains, and when there is no more hope of recuperating the losses.

[1] cf. Emil Durkheim, *Le Suicide*, Felix Alcan, Paris, 1897, p. 446.
[2] *loc. cit.*, p. 448.
[3] All figures show also that Protestant countries have a much higher suicide rate than Catholic countries. This may be due to a number of factors inherent in the differences between the Catholic and Protestant religions, such as the greater influence which the Catholic religion has on the life of its adherents, the more adequate means to deal with a sense of guilt employed by the Catholic Church, etc. But it must also be taken into account that the Protestant countries are the ones in which the capitalistic mode of production is developed further, and has molded the character of the population more completely than in the Catholic countries, so that the difference between Protestant and Catholic countries is also largely the difference between various stages in the development of modern Capitalism.

c. Various Other Aspects

Thus far I have tried to give a general picture of the alienation of modern man from himself and his fellow man in the process of producing, consuming and leisure activities. I want now to deal with some specific aspects of the contemporary social character which are closely related to the phenomenon of alienation, the treatment of which, however, is facilitated by dealing with them separately rather than as subheadings of alienation.

i. *Anonymous Authority—Conformity*

The first such aspect to be dealt with is modern man's attitude toward *authority*.

We have discussed the difference between rational and irrational, furthering and inhibiting authority, and stated that Western society in the eighteenth and nineteenth centuries was characterized by the mixture of both kinds of authority. What is common to both rational and irrational authority is that it is *overt authority*. You know who orders and forbids: the father, the teacher, the boss, the king, the officer, the priest, God, the law, the moral conscience. The demands or prohibitions may be reasonable or not, strict or lenient, I may obey or rebel; I always know that there is an authority, who it is, what it wants, and what results from my compliance or my rebellion.

Authority in the middle of the twentieth century has changed its character; it is not overt authority, but *anonymous, invisible, alienated authority*. Nobody makes a demand, neither a person, nor an idea, nor a moral law. Yet we all conform as much or more than people in an intensely authoritarian society would. Indeed, nobody is an authority except *"It."* What is *It*? Profit, economic necessities, the market, common sense, public opinion, what *"one"* does, thinks, feels. The laws of anonymous authority are as invisible as the laws of the market—and just as unassailable. Who can attack the invisible? Who can rebel against Nobody?

The disappearance of overt authority is clearly visible in all spheres of life. Parents do not give commands any more; they suggest that the child "will want to do this." Since they have no principles or convictions themselves, they try to guide the children do what the law of conformity expects, and often, being older and hence less in touch with "the latest," they learn from the children what attitude is required. The same holds true in business and in industry; you do not give orders, you "suggest"; you do not command, you coax and manipulate. Even the American army has accepted much of the new form of authority. The army is propagandized as if it were an attractive business enterprise; the soldier should feel like a member of a "team," even though the hard fact remains that he must be trained to kill and be killed.

As long as there was overt authority, there was conflict, and there was rebellion—against irrational authority. In the conflict with the commands of one's conscience, in the fight against irrational authority, the personality developed—specifically the sense of self developed. I experience myself as "I" because I doubt, I protest, I rebel. Even if I submit and sense defeat, I experience myself as "I"—I, the defeated one. But if I am not aware of submitting or rebelling, if I am ruled by an anonymous authority, I lose the sense of self, I become a "one," a part of the "It."

The mechanism through which the anonymous authority operates is *conformity*. I ought to do what everybody does, hence, I must conform, not be different, not "stick out"; I must be ready and willing to change according to the changes in the pattern; I must not ask whether I am right or wrong, but whether I am adjusted, whether I am not "peculiar," not different. The only thing which is permanent in me is just this readiness for change. Nobody has power over me, except the herd of which I am a part, yet to which I am subjected.

It is hardly necessary to demonstrate to the reader the degree which this submission to anonymous authority by conformity has reached. However, I want to give a few illustrations taken from the very interesting and illuminating report on a settlement in Park Forest, Illinois, which seems to justify a formulation which the author puts at the head of one of his chapters, "The Future, c/o Park Forest." [1] This development near Chicago was made to house 30,000 people, partly in clusters of rental garden apartments (rent for two-bedroom duplex, $92), partly in ranch-type houses for sale ($11,995). The inhabitants are mostly junior executives, with a sprinkling of chemists and engineers, with an average income of $6,000 to $7,000, between 25 and 35 years of age, married, and with one or two children.

What are the social relations, and the "adjustment" in this package community? While people move there mainly out of "a simple economic necessity and not because of any yen for a womb image," the author notes "that after exposure to such an environment some people find a warmth and support in it that makes other environments seem unduly cold—it is somewhat unsettling, for example, to hear the way residents of the new suburbs occasionally refer to 'the outside.' " This feeling of warmth is more or less the same as the feeling of being accepted: "I could afford a better place than the development we are going to" says one of the people, "and I must say it isn't the kind of place where you have the boss or a customer to dinner. But you get real acceptance in a community like that." This craving for acceptance is indeed a very characteristic feeling in the alienated person. Why should

[1] The following quotations are taken from the article by William H. Whyte, Jr., "The Transients," *Fortune*, May, June, July and August 1953. Copyright 1953 Time Inc.

anyone be so grateful for acceptance unless he doubts that he is acceptable, and why should a young, educated, successful couple have such doubts, if not due to the fact that they cannot accept themselves—because they *are not* themselves. The only haven for having a sense of identity is conformity. Being acceptable really means not being different from anybody else. Feeling inferior stems from feeling different, and no question is asked whether the difference is for the better or the worse.

Adjustment begins early. One parent expresses the concept of anonymous authority quite succinctly: "The adjustment to the group does not seem to involve so many problems for them [the children]. I have noticed that they seem to get the feeling that nobody is the boss—there is a feeling of complete co-operation. Partly this comes from early exposure to court play." The ideological concept in which this phenomenon is expressed here is that of absence of authority, a positive value in terms of eighteenth- and nineteenth-century freedom. The reality behind this concept of freedom is the presence of anonymous authority and the absence of individuality. What could be clearer for this concept of conformity than the statement made by one mother: "Johnny has not been doing so well at school. The teacher told me he was doing fine in some respects but *that his social adjustment was not as good as it might be.* He would *pick one or two friends to play with—and sometimes he was happy to remain by himself.*" (Italics mine.) Indeed, the alienated person finds it almost impossible to remain by himself, because he is seized by the panic of experiencing nothingness. That it should be formulated so frankly is nevertheless surprising, and shows that we have even ceased to be ashamed of our herdlike inclinations.

The parents sometimes complain that the school might be a bit too "permissive," and that the children lack discipline, but "whatever the faults of Park Forest parents may be, harshness and authoritarianism are not among them." Indeed not, but why would you need authoritarianism in its overt forms if the anonymous authority of conformism makes your children submit completely to the It, even if they do not submit to their individual parents? The complaint of the parents, however, about lack of discipline is not meant too seriously, for "What we have in Park Forest, it is becoming evident, is the apotheosis of pragmatism. It would be an exaggeration, perhaps, to say that the transients have come to deify society—and the job of adjusting to it—but certainly they have remarkably little yen to quarrel with society. They are, as one puts it, the practical generation."

Another aspect of alienated conformity is the leveling-out process of taste and judgment which the author describes under the heading "The Melting Pot." " 'When I first came here I was pretty rarefied,' a self-styled 'egghead' explained to a recent visitor. 'I remember how shocked I was one day when I told the girls in the court how much I had enjoyed listening to 'The Magic Flute' the night before. They didn't know what I was talking about. I began to learn that diaper talk is a lot more important to them. I still listen to 'The Magic Flute' but now I realize that for most people other things in life seem as important.' " Another woman reports that she was discovered reading Plato when one of the girls made a surprise visit. The visitor " 'almost fell over from surprise. Now all of them are sure I'm strange.' " Actually, the author tells us, the poor woman overestimates the damage. The others do not think her overly odd, "for her deviance is accompanied by enough tact, enough observance of the little customs that oil court life, so that equilibrium is maintained." What matters is to transform value judgment into matters of opinion, whether it is listening to "The Magic Flute" as against diaper talk, or whether it is being a Republican as against being a Democrat. All that matters is that nothing is too serious, that one exchanges views, and that one is ready to accept any opinion or conviction (if there is such a thing) as being as good as the other. On the market of opinions everybody is supposed to have a commodity of the same value, and it is indecent and not fair to doubt it.

The word which is used for alienated conformity and sociability is of course one which expresses the phenomenon in terms of a very positive value. Indiscriminating sociability and lack of individuality is called being *outgoing*. The language here becomes psychiatrically tinged with the philosophy of Dewey thrown in for good measure. " 'You can really help make a lot of people happy here,' says one social activist. 'I've brought out two couples myself; I saw potentialities in them they didn't realize they had. Whenever we see someone who is shy and withdrawn, we make a special effort with them.' "

Another aspect of social "adjustment" is the complete lack of privacy, and the indiscriminate talking about one's "problems." Here again, one sees the influence of modern psychiatry and psychoanalysis. Even the thin walls are greeted as a help from feeling alone. " 'I never feel lonely, even when Jim's away,' goes a typical comment. 'You know friends are nearby, because at night you hear the neighbors through the walls.' " Marriages which might break up otherwise are saved, depressed moods are kept from becoming worse, by talking, talking, talking. " 'It's wonderful,' says one young wife. 'You find yourself discussing all your problems with your neighbors—things that back in South Dakota we would have kept to ourselves.' As time goes on, this capacity for self-revelation grows; and on the most intimate details of family life, court people become amazingly frank with each other. No one, they point out, ever need face a problem alone." We may add that it would be more correct to say that never do they face a problem.

Even the architecture becomes functional in the battle against loneliness. "Just as doors inside houses—which are sometimes said to have marked the birth of the middle class—are disappearing, so are the barriers against neighbors. The picture in the picture window, for example, is what is going on *inside*—or, what is going on inside other people's picture windows."

The conformity pattern develops a new morality, a new kind of super-ego. But the new morality is not the conscience of the humanistic tradition nor is the new super-ego made in the image of an authoritarian father. Virtue is to be adjusted and to be like the rest. Vice, to be different. Often this is expressed in psychiatric terms, where "virtuous" means being healthy, and "evil," being neurotic. "From the eye of the court there is no escape." Love affairs are rare for that reason, rather than for moral reasons or the fact that the marriages are so satisfactory. There are feeble attempts at privacy. While the rule is that you walk into the house without knocking, or making any other sign, some people gain a little privacy by moving the chair to the front, rather than the court side of the apartment, to show that they do not want to be disturbed. "But there is an important corollary of such efforts at privacy—*people feel a little guilty about making them.* Except very occasionally, to shut oneself off from others like this is regarded as either a childish prank or, more likely, an indication of some inner neurosis. The individual, not the group has erred. So, at any rate, many errants seem to feel, and they are often penitent about what elsewhere would be regarded as one's own business, and rather normal business at that. 'I've promised myself to make it up to them,' one court resident recently told a confidant. 'I was feeling bad and just plain didn't make the effort to ask the others in later. I don't blame them, really, for reacting the way they did. I'll make it up to them somehow.' "

Indeed, "privacy has become clandestine." Again the terms which are used are taken from the progressive political and philosophic tradition; what could sound finer than the sentence "Not in solitary and selfish contemplation but in doing things with other people does one fulfill oneself." What it really means, however, is giving up oneself, becoming part and parcel of the herd, and liking it. This state is often called by another pleasant word, "togetherness." The favorite way of expressing the same state of mind is that of putting it in psychiatric terms: " 'We have learned not to be so introverted,' one junior executive, and a very thoughtful and successful one, describes the lesson. 'Before we came here we used to live pretty much to ourselves. On Sundays, for instance, we used to stay in bed until around maybe two o'clock, reading the paper and listening to the symphony on the radio. Now we stop around and visit with people, or they visit with us. I really think Park Forest has broadened us.' "

Lack of conformity is not only punished by disapproving words like "neurotic," but sometimes by cruel sanctions. " 'Estelle is a case,' says one resident of a highly active block. 'She was dying to get in with the gang when she moved in. She is a very warm-hearted gal and is always trying to help people, but she's well—sort of elaborate about it. One day she decided to win over everybody by giving an afternoon party for the gals. Poor thing, she did it all wrong. The girls turned up in their bathing suits and slacks, as usual, and here she had little doilies and silver and everything spread around. Ever since then it's been almost like a planned campaign to keep her out of things. It's really pitiful. She sits there in her beach chair out front just dying for someone to come and kaffeeklatsch with her, and right across the street four or five of the girls will be yakking away. Every time they suddenly all laugh at some jokes she thinks they are laughing at her. She came over here yesterday and cried all afternoon. She told me she and her husband are thinking about moving somewhere else so they can make a fresh start.' " Other cultures have punished deviants from the prescribed political or religious creed by prison or the stake. Here the punishment is only ostracism which drives a poor woman into despair and an intense feeling of guilt. What is the crime? One act of error, one single sin toward the god of conformity.

It is only another aspect of the alienated kind of interpersonal relationship that friendships are not formed on the basis of individual liking or attraction, but that they are determined by the location of one's own house or apartment in relation to the others. This is the way it works. "It begins with the children. The new suburbs are matriarchies, yet the children are in effect so dictatorial that a term like *filiarchy* would not be entirely facetious. It is the children who set the basic design; their friendships are translated into the mother's friendships, and these, in turn, to the family's. Fathers just tag along.

"It is the flow of wheeled juvenile traffic, . . . that determines which is to be the functional door; i.e., in the homes, the front door; in the courts, the back door. It determines, further, the route one takes from the functional door; for when wives go visiting with neighbors they gravitate toward the houses within sight and hearing of their children and the telephone. This crystallizes into the court 'checkerboard movement' (i.e., the regular kaffeeklatsch route) and this forms the basis of adult friendships." Actually, this determination of friendship goes so far that the reader of the article is invited by the author to pick out the clusters of friendship in one sector of the settlement, just from the picture of the location of the houses, their entrance and exit doors in this sector.

What is important in this picture is not only the fact of alienated friendships, and automaton conformity, but the reaction of people to this fact. Consciously it seems people fully accept the new form of adjustment. "Once people hated to concede that their behavior was determined by anything except their own free will. Not so with the new suburbanites; they are fully aware of the all-pervading power of the environment over them. As a matter of fact, there are few subjects they like so much to talk about; and with the increasing lay curiosity about psychology, psychiatry, and sociology, they discuss their social life in surprisingly clinical terms. But they have no sense of plight; this, they seem to say, is the way things are, and the trick is not to fight it but to understand it."

This young generation has also its philosophy to explain their way of life. "Not merely as an instinctive wish, but as an articulate set of values to be passed on to one's children, the next generation of leaders are coming to deify social utility. *Does it work*, not why, has become the key question. With society having become so complex, the individual can have meaning only as he contributes to the harmony of the group, transients explain— and for them, constantly on the move, ever exposed to new groups, the adapting to groups has become particularly necessary. They are all, as they themselves so often put it, in the same boat." On the other hand, the author tells us: "The value of solitary thought, the fact that conflict is sometimes necessary, and other such disturbing thoughts rarely intrude." The most important, or really the only important thing children as well as adults have to learn, is to get along with other people which, if taught in school is called "citizenship," the equivalent for "outgoingness" and "togetherness" as the adults call it.

Are people really happy, are they as satisfied, unconsciously, as they believe themselves to be? Considering the nature of man, and the conditions for happiness, this can hardly be so. But they even have some doubts consciously. While they feel that conformity and merging with the group is their duty, many of them sense that they are "frustrating other urges." They feel that "responding to the group mores is akin to a moral duty—and so they continue, hesitant and unsure, *imprisoned in brotherhood*. (My italics) 'Every once in a while I wonder,' says one transient in an almost furtive moment of contemplation. 'I don't want to do anything to offend the people here: they're kind and decent, and I'm proud we've been able to get along with each other—with all our differences—so well. But then, once in a while, I *think of myself and my husband and what we are not doing, and I get depressed. Is is just enough not to be bad?*' " (Italics mine.) Indeed, this life of compromise, this "outgoing" life, is the life of imprisonment, selflessness and depression. They *are* all "in the same boat," but, as the author says very pointedly, "*where is the boat going? No one seems to have the faintest idea;* nor, for that matter, do they see much point in even raising the question."

The picture of conformity as we have illustrated it with the "outgoing" inhabitants of Park Forest is certainly not the same all over America. The reasons are obvious. These people are young, they are middle class and they move upwards, they are mostly people who in their work career manipulate symbols and men, and whose advancement depends on whether they permit themselves to be manipulated. There are undoubtedly many older people of the same occupational group, and many equally young people of different occupational groups who are less "advanced," as for instance those engineers, chemists and physicists, more interested in their work than in the hope of jumping into an executive career as soon as possible; furthermore, there are millions of farmers and farm-hands, whose style of life has only been changed partly by the conditions of the twentieth century; eventually the industrial workers, whose income is not too different from the white-collar workers, but whose work situation is. Although this is not the place to discuss the meaning of work for the industrial worker today, this much can be said here: there is undoubtedly a difference between people who manipulate other people and people who create things, even though their role in the process of production is a partial and in many ways an alienated one. The worker in a big steel mill co-operates with others, and has to do so if he is to protect his life; he faces dangers, and shares them with others; his colleagues as well as the foreman can judge and appreciate his skill rather than his smile and "pleasant personality"; he has a considerable amount of freedom outside of work; he has paid vacations, he may be busy in his garden, with a hobby, with local and union politics.[1] However, even taking into account all these factors which differentiate the industrial worker from the white-collar worker and the higher strata of the middle classes, there seems little chance that eventually the industrial worker will escape being molded by the dominant conformity pattern. In the first place, even the most positive aspects of his work situation, like the ones just mentioned, do not alter the fact that his work is alienated and only to a limited extent a meaningful expression of his energy and reason; secondly, the trend for increasing automatization of industrial work diminishes this latter factor rapidly. Eventually, he is under the influence of our whole cultural apparatus, the advertisements, movies, television, newspapers, just as everybody else, and can hardly escape being driven into conformity, although perhaps more slowly than other sectors of the population.[2] What holds true for the industrial worker holds true also for the farmer.

[1] Cf. Warner Bloomberg Jr.'s article "The Monstrous Machine and the Worried Workers," in *The Reporter*, September 28, 1953, and his lectures at the University of Chicago, "Modern Times in the Factory," 1934, a transcript of which he was kind enough to let me have.
[2] A detailed analysis of modern industrial work follows later.

ii. *The Principle of Nonfrustration*

As I have pointed out before, anonymous authority and automaton conformity are largely the result of our mode of production, which requires quick adaptation to the machine, disciplined mass behavior, common taste and obedience without the use of force. Another facet of our economic system, the need for mass consumption, has been instrumental in creating a feature in the social character of modern man which constitutes one of the most striking contrasts to the social character of the nineteenth century. I am referring to *the principle that every desire must be satisfied immediately, no wish must be frustrated.* The most obvious illustration of this principle is to be found in our system of buying on the installment plan. In the nineteenth century you bought what you needed, when you had saved the money for it; today you buy what you need, or do not need, on credit, and the function of advertising is largely to coax you into buying and to whet your appetite for things, so that you can be coaxed. You live in a circle. You buy on the installment plan, and about the time you have finished paying, you sell and you buy again —the latest model.

The principle that desires must be satisfied without much delay has also determined sexual behavior, especially since the end of the First World War. A crude form of misunderstood Freudianism used to furnish the appropriate rationalizations; the idea being that neuroses result from "repressed" sexual strivings, that frustrations were "traumatic," and the less you repressed the healthier you were. Even parents anxious to give their children everything they wanted lest they be frustrated, acquired a "complex." Unfortunately, many of these children as well as their parents landed on the analyst's couch, provided they could afford it.

The greed for things and the inability to postpone the satisfaction of wishes as characteristic of modern man has been stressed by thoughtful observers, such as Max Scheler and Bergson. It has been given its most poignant expression by Aldous Huxley in the *Brave New World*. Among the slogans by which the adolescents in the Brave New World are conditioned, one of the most important ones is *"Never put off till tomorrow the fun you can have today."* It is hammered into them, "two hundred repetitions, twice a week from fourteen to sixteen and a half." This instant realization of wishes is felt as happiness. "Everybody's happy nowadays" is another of the Brave New World slogans; people "get what they want and they never want what they can't get." This need for the immediate consumption of commodities and the immediate consummation of sexual desires is coupled in the Brave New World, as in our own. It is considered immoral to keep one "love" partner beyond a relatively short time. "Love" is short-lived sexual desire, which must be satisfied immediately. "The greatest care is taken to prevent you from loving anyone too much. There's no such thing as a divided allegiance; you're so conditioned that you can't help doing what you ought to do. And what you ought to do is on the whole so pleasant, so many of the natural impulses are allowed free play, that there really aren't any temptations to resist." [1]

This lack of inhibition of desires leads to the same result as the lack of overt authority—the paralysis and eventually the destruction of the self. If I do not postpone the satisfaction of my wish (and am conditioned only to wish for what I can get), I have no conflicts, no doubts; no decision has to be made; I am never alone with myself, because I am always busy—either working, or having fun. I have no need to be aware of myself as myself because I am constantly absorbed having pleasure. *I am—a system*

[1] cf. Aldous Huxley, *Brave New World*, The Vanguard Library, p. 196.

of desires and satisfactions; I have to work in order to fulfill my desires—and these very desires are constantly stimulated and directed by the economic machine. Most of these appetites are synthetic; even sexual appetite is by far not as "natural" as it is made out to be. It is to some extent stimulated artificially. And it needs to be if we want to have people as the contemporary system needs them—people who feel "happy," who have no doubts, who have no conflicts, who are guided without the use of force.

Having fun consists mainly in the satisfaction of consuming and "taking in"; commodities, sights, food, drinks, cigarettes, people, lectures, books, movies—all are consumed, swallowed. The world is one great object for our appetite, a big apple, a big bottle, a big breast; we are the sucklers, the eternally expectant ones, the hopeful ones—and the eternally disappointed ones. How can we help being disappointed if our birth stops at the breast of the mother, if we are never weaned, if we remain over-grown babes, if we never go beyond the receptive orientation?

So people do worry, feel inferior, inadequate, guilty. They sense that they live without living, that life runs through their hands like sand. How do they deal with their troubles, which stem from the passivity of constant taking in? By another form of passivity, a constant spilling out, as it were: by *talking*. Here, as in the case of authority and consumption, an idea which once was productive has been turned into its opposite.

iii. *Free Association and Free Talk*

Freud had discovered the principle of *free association*. By giving up the control of your thoughts in the presence of a skilled listener, you can discover your unconscious feelings and thoughts without being asleep, or crazy, or drunk, or hypnotized. The psycholanalyst reads between your lines, he is capable of understanding you better than you understand yourself because you have freed your thinking from the limitations of conventional thought control. But free association soon deteriorated, like freedom and happiness. First it deteriorated in the orthodox psychoanalytic procedure itself. Not always, but often. Instead of giving rise to a meaningful expression of imprisoned thoughts, it became meaningless chatter. Other therapeutic schools reduced the role of the analyst to that of a sympathetic listener, who repeats in a slightly different version the words of the patient, without trying to interpret or to explain. All this is done with the idea that the patient's freedom must not be interfered with. The Freudian idea of free association has become the instrument of many psychologists who call themselves counselors, although the only thing they do not do is to counsel. These counselors play an increasingly large role as private practitioners and as advisers in industry.[1] What is the effect of the procedure? Obviously not a cure which Freud had in mind when he devised free association as a basis for understanding the unconscious. Rather a release of tension which results from talking things out in the presence of a sympathetic listener. Your thoughts, as long as you keep them within yourself, may disturb you—but something fruitful may come out of this disturbance; you mull them over, you think, you feel, you may arrive at a new thought born out of this travail. But when you talk right away, when you do not let your thoughts and feelings build up pressure, as it were, they do not become fruitful. It is exactly the same as with unobstructed consumption. You are a system in which things go in and out continuously—and within it is nothing, no tension, no digestion, no self. Freud's discovery of free association had

[1] cf. W. J. Dickson, *The New Industrial Relations*, Cornell University Press, 1948, and G. Friedmann's discussion in *Où va le Travail Humain?*, Gallimard, Paris, 1950, p. 142 ff. Also H. W. Harrell, *Industrial Psychology*, Rinehart & Company, Inc., New York, 1949, p. 372 ff.

the aim of finding out what went on in you underneath the surface, of *discovering who you* really were; the modern talking to the sympathetic listener has the opposite, although unavowed aim; its function is to make a man *forget* who he is (provided he has still some memory), to lose all tension, and with it all sense of self. Just as one oils machines, one oils people and especially those in the mass organizations of work. One oils them with pleasant slogans, material advantages, and with the sympathetic understanding of the psychologists.

The talking and listening to eventually has become the indoor sport of those who cannot afford a professional listener, or prefer the layman for one reason or another. It has become fashionable, sophisticated, to "talk things out." There is no inhibition, no sense of shame, no holding back. One speaks about the tragic occurrences of one's own life with the same ease as one would talk about another person of no particular interest, or as one would speak about the various troubles one has had with one's car.

Indeed, psychology and psychiatry are in the process of changing their function fundamentally. From the Delphic Oracle's "Know thyself!" to Freud's psychoanalytic therapy, the function of psychology was to discover the self, to understand the individual, to find the "truth that makes you free." Today the function of psychiatry, psychology and psychoanalysis threatens to become the tool in the manipulation of men. The specialists in this field tell you what the "normal" person is, and, correspondingly, what is wrong with you; they devise the methods to help you adjust, be happy, be normal. In the Brave New World this conditioning is done from the first month of fertilization (by chemical means), until after puberty. With us, it begins a little later. Constant repetition by newspaper, radio, television, does most of the conditioning. But the crowning achievement of manipulation is modern psychology. What Taylor did for industrial work, the psychologists do for the whole personality —all in the name of understanding and freedom. There are many exceptions to this among psychiatrists, psychologists and psychoanalysts, but it becomes increasingly clear that these professions are in the process of becoming a serious danger to the development of man, that their practitioners are evolving into the priests of the new religion of fun, consumption and self-lessness, into the specialists of manipulation, into the spokesmen for the alienated personality.

iv. *Reason, Conscience, Religion*

What becomes of *reason, conscience* and *religion* in an alienated world? Superficially seen, they prosper. There is hardly any illiteracy to speak of in the Western countries; more and more people go to college in the United States; everybody reads the newspapers and talks reasonably about world affairs. As to conscience, most people act quite decently in their narrow personal sphere, in fact surprisingly so, considering their general confusion. As far as religion is concerned, it is well known that church affiliation is higher than ever, and the vast majority of Americans believe in God—or so they say in public-opinion polls. However, one does not need to dig too deeply to arrive at less pleasant findings.

If we talk about reason, we must first decide what human capacity we are referring to. As I have suggested before, we must differentiate between intelligence and reason. By intelligence I mean the ability to manipulate concepts for the purpose of achieving some practical end. The chimpanzee—who puts the two sticks together in order to get at the banana because no one of the two is long enough to do the job—uses intelligence. So do we all when we go about our business, "figuring out" how to do things. *Intelligence,* in this sense, is taking things for granted as they are, making combinations which have the purpose of facilitating their manipulation; intelligence is thought in the service of biological survival. *Reason,* on the other hand, aims at understanding; it tries to find out what is behind the surface, to recognize the kernel, the essence of the reality which surrounds us. Reason is not without a function, but its function is not to further physical as much as mental and spiritual existence. However, often in individual and social life, reason is required in order to predict (considering that prediction often depends on recognition of forces which operate underneath the surface), and prediction sometimes is necessary even for physical survival.

Reason requires relatedness and a sense of self. If I am only the passive receptor of impressions, thoughts, opinions, I can compare them, manipulate them—but I cannot penetrate them. Descartes deduced the existence of myself as an individual from the fact that I think. I doubt, so he argued, hence I think; I think, hence I am. The reverse is true, too. Only if I am I, if I have not lost my individuality in the It, can I think, that is, can I make use of my reason.

Closely related to this is the lacking sense of reality which is characteristic of the alienated personality. To speak of the "lacking sense of reality" in modern man is contrary to the widely held idea that we are distinguished from most periods of history by our greater realism. But to speak of our realism is almost like a paranoid distortion. What realists, who are playing with weapons which may lead to the destruction of all modern civilization, if not of our earth itself! If an individual were found doing just that, he would be locked up immediately, and if he prided himself on his realism, the psychiatrists would consider this an additional and rather serious symptom of a diseased mind. But quite aside from this—the fact is that modern man exhibits an amazing lack of realism for all that matters. For the meaning of life and death, for happiness and suffering, for feeling and serious thought. He has covered up the whole reality of human existence and replaced it with his artificial, prettified picture of a pseudo-reality, not too different from the savages who lost their land and freedom for glittering glass beads. Indeed, he is so far away from human reality, that he can say with the inhabitants of the Brave New World: "When the individual feels, the community reels.".

Another factor in contemporary society already mentioned is destructive to reason. Since nobody ever does the whole job, but only a fraction of it, since the dimension of things and of the organization of people is too vast to be understood as a whole, nothing can be seen in its totality. Hence the laws underlying the phenomena cannot be observed. Intelligence is sufficient to manipulate properly one sector of a larger unit, whether it is a machine or a state. But reason can develop only if it is geared to the whole, if it deals with observable and manageable entities. Just as our ears and eyes function only within certain quantitative limits of wave length, our reason too is bound by what is observable as a whole and in its total functioning. To put it differently, beyond a certain order of bigness, concreteness is necessarily lost and abstractification takes place; with it, the sense for reality fades out. The first one to see this problem was Aristotle, who thought that a city which transcended in number what we would call today a small town was not livable.

In observing the quality of thinking in alienated man, it is striking to see how his intelligence has developed and how his reason has deteriorated. He takes his reality for granted; he wants to eat it, consume it, touch it, manipulate it. He does not even ask what is behind it, why things are as they are, and where they are going. You cannot eat the meaning, you cannot consume the sense, and as far as the future is concerned—*après nous le déluge!* Even from the nineteenth century to our day, there seems to have occurred an observable increase in stupidity, if by this we mean the opposite to reason, rather than to intelligence. In spite of the fact that everybody reads the daily paper religiously, there is an absence of understanding of the meaning of political events which is truly frightening, because our intelligence helps us to produce weapons which our reason is not capable of controlling. Indeed, we have the know-how, but we do not have the know-why, nor the know-what-for. We have many persons with good and high intelligence quotients, but our intelligence tests measure the ability to memorize, to manipulate thoughts quickly—but not to reason. All this is true notwithstanding the fact that there are men of outstanding reason in our midst, whose thinking is as profound and vigorous as ever existed in the history of the human race. But they think apart from the general herd thought, and they are looked upon with suspicion—even if they are needed for their extraordinary achievements in the natural sciences.

The new automatic brains are indeed a good illustration of what is meant here by intelligence. They manipulate data which are fed into them; they compare, select, and eventually come out with results more quickly or more error-proof than human intelligence could. However, the condition of all this is that the basic data are fed into them beforehand. What the electric brain cannot do is think creatively, to arrive at an insight into the essence of the observed facts, to go beyond the data with which it has been fed. The machine can duplicate or even improve on intelligence, but it cannot simulate reason.

Ethics, at least in the meaning of the Greco-Judaeo-Christian tradition, is inseparable from reason. Ethical behavior is based on the faculty of making value judgments on the basis of reason; it means deciding between good and evil, and to act upon the decision. Use of reason presupposes the presence of self; so does ethical judgment and action. Furthermore, ethics, whether it is that of monotheistic religion or that of secular humanism, is based on the principle that no institution and no thing is higher than any human individual; that the aim of life is to unfold man's love and reason and that every other human activity has to be subordinated to this aim. How then can ethics be a significant part of a life in which the individual becomes an automaton, in which he serves the big It? Furthermore, how can conscience develop when the principle of life is conformity? Conscience, by its very nature is nonconforming; it must be able to say no, when everybody else says yes; in order to say this "no" it must be certain in the rightness of the judgment on which the no is based. To the degree to which a person conforms he cannot hear the voice of his conscience, much less act upon it. Conscience exists only when man experiences himself as man, not as a thing, as a commodity. Concerning *things* which are exchanged on the market there exists another quasi ethical code, that of *fairness*. The question is, whether they are exchanged at a fair price, no tricks and no force interfering with the fairness of the bargain; this fairness, not good and evil, is the ethical principle of the market and it is the ethical principle governing the life of the marketing personality.

This principle of fairness, no doubt, makes for a certain type of ethical behavior. You do not lie, cheat or use force; you even give the other person a chance—if you act according to the code of fairness. But to love your neighbor, to feel one with him, to devote your life to the aim of developing your spiritual powers, is not part of the fairness ethics. We live in a paradoxical situation: we practice fairness ethics, and profess Christian ethics. Must we not stumble over this obvious contradiction? Obviously, we do not stumble. What is the reason? Partly, it is to be found in the fact that the heritage of four thousand years of the development of conscience is by no means completely lost. On the contrary, in many ways the liberation of man from the powers of the feudal state and the Church, made it possible for this heritage to be brought to fruition and in the period between the eighteenth century and now it blossomed as perhaps never before. We still are part of this process—but given our own twentieth-century condition of life, it seems that there is no new bud which will blossom when this flower has wilted.

Another reason why we do not stumble over the contradiction between humanistic ethics and fairness ethics lies in the fact that we reinterpret religious and humanistic ethics in the light of fairness ethics. A good illustration of this interpretation is the Golden Rule. In its original Jewish and Christian meaning, it was a popular phrasing of the Biblical maxim to "love thy neighbor as thyself." In the system of fairness ethics, it means simply "Be fair when you exchange. Give what you expect to get. Don't cheat!" No wonder the Golden Rule is the most popular religious phrase of today. It combines two opposite systems of ethics and helps us to forget the contradiction.

While we still live from the Christian-humanistic heritage it is not surprising that the younger generation exhibits less and less of the traditional ethics and that we come across a moral barbarism among our youth which is in complete contrast to the economic and educational level society has reached. Today, while revising this manuscript, I read two items. One in the *New York Times,* regarding the fact of the murder of a man, cruelly trampled to death by four teen-agers of average middle-class families. The other in *Time* magazine, a description of the new Guatemalan chief of police, who as former chief of police under the Ubico dictatorship had "perfected a head-shrinking steel skull cap to pry loose secrets and crush improper political thoughts." [1] His picture is published with the caption "For improper thought, a crusher." Could anything be more insanely insensitive to extremes of sadism than this flippant line? Is it surprising when in a culture in which the most popular news magazine can write this, teen-agers have no scruples about beating a man to death? Is the fact that we show brutality and cruelty in comic books and movies, because money is made with these commodities, not enough of an explanation for the growing barbarism and vandalism in our youth? Our movie censors watch that no sexual scenes are shown, since this could suggest illicit sexual desires. How innocent would this result be in comparison with the dehumanizing effect of what the censors permit and the churches seem to object to less than to the traditional sins. Yes, we still have an ethical heritage, but it will soon be spent and will be replaced by the ethics of the Brave New World, or "1984," unless it ceases to be a heritage and is re-created in our whole mode of life. At the moment, it seems that ethical behavior is still to be found in the concrete situation of many individuals, while society is marching toward barbarism. [2]

Much of what has been said about ethics is to be said about *religion.* Of course, speaking of the role of religion among alienated men, everything depends on what we call religion. If we are referring to religion in its widest sense, as a system of orientation and an object of devotion, then, indeed, every human being is religious, since nobody can live without such a system and remain sane. Then, our culture is as religious as any. Our gods are the machine, and the idea of efficiency; the meaning of our life is to move, to forge ahead, to arrive as near to the top as possible. But if by religion we mean monotheism, then, indeed,

[1] *Time,* August 23, 1954.
[2] cf. the similar point of view made by A. Gehlen in his very thoughtful and profound *Sozialpsychologische Probleme in der Industriellen Gesellschaft.* I. C. B. Mohr, 1949.

our religion is not more than one of the commodities in our show windows. Monotheism is incompatible with alienation and with our ethics of fairness. It makes man's unfolding, his salvation, the supreme aim of life, an aim which never can be subordinated to any other. Inasmuch as God is unrecognizable, indefinable, and inasmuch as man is made in the likeness of God, *man* is indefinable—which means he is not and can never be considered a *thing*. The fight between monotheism and idolatry is exactly the fight between the productive and the alienated way of life. Our culture is perhaps the first completely secularized culture in human history. We have shoved away awareness of and concern with the fundamental problems of human existence. We are not concerned with the meaning of life, with the solution to it; we start out with the conviction that there is no purpose except to invest life successfully and to get it over with without major mishaps. The majority of us believe in God, take it for granted that God exists. The rest, who do not believe, take it for granted that God does not exist. Either way, God is taken for granted. Neither belief nor disbelief cause any sleepless nights, nor any serious concern. In fact, whether a man in our culture believes in God or not makes hardly any difference either from a psychological or from a truly religious standpoint. In both instances he does not care—either about God or about the answer to the problem of his own existence. Just as brotherly love has been replaced by impersonal fairness, God has been transformed into a remote General Director of Universe, Inc.; you know that He is there, He runs the show, (although it probably would run without Him too), you never see Him, but you acknowledge His leadership while you are "doing your part."

The religious 'renaissance' which we witness in these days is perhaps the worst blow monotheism has yet received. Is there any greater sacrilege than to speak of "the Man upstairs," to teach to pray in order to make God your partner in business, to "sell" religion with the methods and appeals used to sell soap?

In view of the fact that the alienation of modern man is incompatible with monotheism, one might expect that ministers, priests and rabbis would form the spearhead of criticism of modern Capitalism. While it is true that from high Catholic quarters and from a number of less highly placed ministers and rabbis such criticism has been voiced, all churches belong essentially to the conservative forces in modern society and use religion to keep man going and satisfied with a profoundly ir-religious system. The majority of them do not seem to recognize that this type of religion will eventually degenerate into overt idolatry, unless they begin to define and then to fight against modern idolatry, rather than to make pronouncements about God and thus to use His name in vain—in more than one sense.

v. *Work*

What becomes the meaning of *work* in an alienated society?

We have already made some brief comments about this question in the general discussion of alienation. But since this problem is of utmost importance, not only for the understanding of present-day society, but also for any attempt to create a saner society, I want to deal with the nature of work separately and more extensively in the following pages.

Unless man exploits others, he has to work in order to live. However primitive and simple his method of work may be, by the very fact of production, he has risen above the animal kingdom; rightly has he been defined as "the animal that produces." But work is not only an inescapable necessity for man. Work is also his liberator from nature, his creator as a social and independent being. *In the process of work, that is, the molding and*

*changing of nature outside of himself, man molds and changes
himself.* He emerges from nature by mastering her; he develops
his powers of co-operation, of reason, his sense of beauty. He
separates himself from nature, from the original unity with
her, but at the same time unites himself with her again as her
master and builder. The more his work develops, the more his
individuality develops. In molding nature and re-creating her,
he learns to make use of his powers, increasing his skill and
creativeness. Whether we think of the beautiful paintings in the
caves of Southern France, the ornaments on weapons among
primitive people, the statues and temples of Greece, the cathe-
drals of the Middle Ages, the chairs and tables made by skilled
craftsmen, or the cultivation of flowers, trees or corn by peasants
—all are expressions of the creative transformation of nature by
man's reason and skill.

In Western history, craftsmanship, especially as it developed
in the thirteenth and fourteenth centuries, constitutes one of
the peaks in the evolution of creative work. Work was not only
a useful activity, but one which carried with it a profound
satisfaction. The main features of craftsmanship have been very
lucidly expressed by C. W. Mills. "There is no ulterior motive
in work other than the product being made and the processes of
its creation. The details of daily work are meaningful because
they are not detached in the worker's mind from the product of
the work. The worker is free to control his own working action.
The craftsman is thus able to learn from his work; and to use
and develop his capacities and skills in its prosecution. There is
no split of work and play, or work and culture. The craftsman's
way of livelihood determines and infuses his entire mode of
living." [1]

With the collapse of the medieval structure, and the begin-

[1] C. W. Mills, *White Collar,* Oxford University Press, New York, 1951, p. 220.

ning of the modern mode of production, the meaning and function of work changed fundamentally, especially in the Protestant countries. Man, being afraid of his newly won freedom, was obsessed by the need to subdue his doubts and fears by developing a feverish activity. The outcome of this activity, success or failure, decided his salvation, indicating whether he was among the saved or the lost souls. *Work, instead of being an activity satisfying in itself and pleasureable, became a duty and an obsession.* The more it was possible to gain riches by work, the more it became a pure means to the aim of wealth and success. Work became, in Max Weber's terms, the chief factor in a system of "inner-worldly asceticism," an answer to man's sense of aloneness and isolation.

However, work in this sense existed only for the upper and middle classes, those who could amass some capital and employ the work of others. For the vast majority of those who had only their physical energy to sell, work became nothing but forced labor. The worker in the eighteenth or nineteenth century who had to work sixteen hours if he did not want to starve was not doing it because he served the Lord in this way, nor because his success would show that he was among the "chosen" ones, but because he was forced to sell his energy to those who had the means of exploiting it. The first centuries of the modern era find the meaning of work divided into that of *duty* among the middle class, and that of *forced labor* among those without property.

The religious attitude toward work as a duty, which was still so prevalent in the nineteenth century, has been changing considerably in the last decades. Modern man does not know what to do with himself, how to spend his lifetime meaningfully, and he is driven to work in order to avoid an unbearable boredom. But work has ceased to be a moral and religious obligation in the sense of the middle-class attitude of the eighteenth and nineteenth centuries. Something new has emerged. Ever-increasing production, the drive to make bigger and better things, have become aims in themselves, new ideals. Work has become alienated from the working person.

What happens to the industrial worker? He spends his best energy for seven or eight hours a day in producing "something." He needs his work in order to make a living, but his role is essentially a passive one. He fulfills a small isolated function in a complicated and highly organized process of production, and is never confronted with "his" product as a whole, at least not as a producer, but only as a consumer, provided he has the money to buy "his" product in a store. He is concerned neither with the whole product in its physical aspects nor with its wider economic and social aspects. He is put in a certain place, has to carry out a certain task, but does not participate in the organization or management of the work. He is not interested, nor does he know why one produces this, instead of another commodity—what relation it has to the needs of society as a whole. The shoes, the cars, the electric bulbs, are produced by "the enterprise," using the machines. He is a part of the machine, rather than its master as an active agent. The machine, instead of being in his service to do work for him which once had to be performed by sheer physical energy, has become his master. Instead of the machine being the substitute for human energy, man has become a substitute for the machine. *His work can be defined as the performance of acts which cannot yet be performed by machines.*

Work is a means of getting money, not in itself a meaningful human activity. P. Drucker, observing workers in the automobile industry, expresses this idea very succinctly: "For the great majority of automobile workers, the only meaning of the job is in the pay check, not in anything connected with the work or the product. Work appears as something unnatural, a disagreeable, meaningless and stultifying condition of getting the pay check, devoid of dignity as well as of importance. No wonder that this puts a premium on slovenly work, on slow-downs, and on other tricks to get the same pay check with less work. No wonder that this results in an unhappy and discontented worker—because a pay check is not enough to base one's self-respect on." [1]

This relationship of the worker to his work is an outcome of the whole social organization of which he is a part. Being "employed," [2] he is not an active agent, has no responsibility except the proper performance of the isolated piece of work he is doing, and has little interest except the one of bringing home enough money to support himself and his family. Nothing more is expected of him, or wanted from him. He is part of the equipment hired by capital, and his role and function are determined by this quality of being a piece of equipment. In recent decades, increasing attention has been paid to the psychology of the worker, and to his attitude toward his work, to the "human problem of industry"; but this very formulation is indicative of the underlying attitude; there is a human being spending most of his life-time at work, and what should be discussed is the *"industrial problem of human beings," rather than "the human problem of industry."*

Most investigations in the field of industrial psychology are concerned with the question of how the productivity of the individual worker can be increased, and how he can be made to work with less friction; psychology has lent its services to "hu-

[1] cf. Peter F. Drucker, *Concept of the Corporation,* The John Day Company, New York, 1946, p. 179.

[2] The English "employed" like the German *angestellt* are terms which refer to things rather than to human beings.

man engineering," an attempt to treat the worker and employee like a machine which runs better when it is well oiled. While Taylor was primarily concerned with a better organization of the technical use of the worker's physical powers, most industrial psychologists are mainly concerned with the manipulation of the worker's psyche. The underlying idea can be formulated like this: if he works better when he is happy, then let us make him happy, secure, satisfied, or anything else, provided it raises his output and diminishes friction. In the name of "human relations," the worker is treated with all devices which suit a completely alienated person; even happiness and human values are recommended in the interest of better relations with the public. Thus, for instance, according to *Time* magazine, one of the best-known American psychiatrists said to a group of fifteen hundred Supermarket executives: "It's going to be an increased satisfaction to our customers if we are happy. . . . It is going to pay off in cold dollars and cents to management, if we could put some of these general principles of values, human relationships, really into practice." One speaks of "human relations" and one means the most in-human relations, those between alienated automatons; one speaks of happiness and means the perfect routinization which has driven out the last doubt and all spontaneity.[1]

The alienated and profoundly unsatisfactory character of work results in two reactions: one, the ideal of complete *laziness;* the other a deep-seated, though often unconscious *hostility* toward work and everything and everybody connected with it.

It is not difficult to recognize the widespread longing for the state of complete laziness and passivity. Our advertising appeals to it even more than to sex. There are, of course, many useful and labor saving gadgets. But this usefulness often serves only as a

[1] The problem of work will be dealt with further in Chapter VIII.

rationalization for the appeal to complete passivity and receptivity. A package of breakfast cereal is being advertised as *"new— easier to eat."* An electric toaster is advertised with these words: ". . . the most distinctly different toaster in the world! Everything is done *for* you with this new toaster. You need not even bother to lower the bread. Power-action, though a unique electric motor, *gently takes the bread right out of your fingers!"* How many courses in languages, or other subjects are announced with the slogan "effortless learning, no more of the old drudgery." Everybody knows the picture of the elderly couple in the advertisement of a life-insurance company, who have retired at the age of sixty, and spend their life in the complete bliss of having nothing to do except just travel.

Radio and television exhibit another element of this yearning for laziness: the idea of "push-button power"; by pushing a button, or turning a knob on my machine, I have the power to produce music, speeches, ball games, and on the television set, to command events of the world to appear before my eyes. The pleasure of driving cars certainly rests partly upon this same satisfaction of the wish for push-button power. By the effortless pushing of a button, a powerful machine is set in motion; little skill and effort is needed to make the driver feel that he is the ruler of space.

But there is far more serious and deep-seated reaction to the meaninglessness and boredom of work. It is a hostility toward work which is much less conscious than our craving for laziness and inactivity. Many a businessman feels himself the prisoner of his business and the commodities he sells; he has a feeling of fraudulency about his product and a secret contempt for it. He hates his customers, who force him to put up a show in order to sell. He hates his competitors because they are a threat; his employees as well as his superiors, because he is in a constant competitive fight with them. Most important of all, he hates himself, because he sees his life passing by, without making any sense beyond the momentary intoxication of success. Of course, this hate and contempt for others and for oneself, and for the very things one produces, is mainly unconscious, and only occasionally comes up to awareness in a fleeting thought, which is sufficiently disturbing to be set aside as quickly as possible.

vi. *Democracy*

Just as work has become alienated, the expression of the will of the voter in modern democracy is an alienated expression. The principle of *democracy* is the idea that not a ruler or a small group, but the people as a whole, determine their own fate and make their decisions pertaining to matters of common concern. By electing his own representatives, who in a parliament decide on the laws of the land, each citizen is supposed to exercise the function of responsible participation in the affairs of the community. By the principle of the division of powers, an ingenious system was created that served to retain the integrity and independence of the judiciary system, and to balance the respective functions of the legislature and executive. Ideally, every citizen is equally responsible for and influential in making decisions.

In reality, the emerging democratic system was beset by one important contradiction. Operating in states with tremendous inequalities of opportunity and income, the privileged classes naturally did not want to lose the privileges which the status quo gave them, and which they could easily have lost if the will of the majority, who were without property, had found its full expression. To avoid such a danger, many among the property-less population were excluded from the franchise, and only very slowly was the principle accepted that every citizen, without restrictions and qualifications, had the right to vote.

In the nineteenth century it seemed as if universal franchise would solve all problems of democracy. O'Connor, one of the Chartist leaders, said in 1838: "Universal suffrage would at once change the whole character of society from a state of watchfulness, doubt and suspicion to that of brotherly love, reciprocal interest and universal confidence," and in 1842 he said: ". . . six months after the Charter is passed, every man, woman and child in the country will be well fed, well housed and well clothed." [1] Since then, all great democracies have established general suffrage for men, and with the exception of Switzerland, for women, but even in the richest country in the world, one third of the population was still "ill fed, ill housed, and ill clothed," to quote Franklin D. Roosevelt.

The introduction of universal suffrage not only disappointed the hopes of the Chartists, it disappointed all those who believed that universal suffrage would help to transform the citizenry into responsible, active, independent personalities. It became clear that the *problem of democracy today is not any more the restriction of franchise but the manner in which the franchise is exercised.*

How can people express "their" will if they do not have any will or conviction of their own, if they are alienated automatons, whose tastes, opinions and preferences are manipulated by the big conditioning machines? Under these circumstances universal suffrage becomes a fetish. If a government can prove that everybody has a right to vote, and that the votes are counted honestly, it is democratic. If everybody votes, but the votes are not counted honestly, or if the voter is afraid of voting against the governing party, the country is undemocratic. It is true indeed that there is a considerable and important difference between free and ma-

[1] Quoted from J. R. M. Butler, *History of England*, Oxford University Press, London, 1928, p. 86.

nipulated elections, but noting this difference must not lead us to forget the fact that even free elections do not necessarily express "the will of the people." If a highly advertised brand of toothpaste is used by the majority of people because of some fantastic claims it makes in its propaganda, nobody with any sense would say that the people have "made a decision" in favor of the toothpaste. All that could be claimed is that the propaganda was sufficiently effective to coax millions of people into believing its claims.

In an alienated society the mode in which people express their will is not very different from that of their choice in buying commodities. They are listening to the drums of propaganda and facts mean little in comparison with the suggestive noise which hammers at them. In recent years we see more and more how the wisdom of public relations' counsels determines political propaganda. Accustomed to make the public buy anything for the build-up of which there is enough money, they think of political ideas and political leaders in the same terms. They use television to build up political personalities as they use it to build up a soap; what matters is the effect, in sales or votes, not the rationality or usefulness of what is presented. This phenomenon found a remarkably frank expression in recent statements about the future of the Republican Party. They are to the effect that since one cannot hope the majority of voters will vote for the Republican Party, one must find a personality who wants to represent the Party—then *he* will get the votes. In principle this is not different from the endorsement of a cigarette by a famous sportsman or movie actor.

Actually, the functioning of the political machinery in a democratic country is not essentially different from the procedure on the commodity market. The political parties are not too different from big commercial enterprises, and the professional politicians try to sell their wares to the public. Their method is more and more like that of high-pressure advertising. A particularly clear formulation of this process has been given by a keen observer of the political and economic scene, J. A. Schumpeter. He starts out with the formulation of the classical eighteenth-century concept of democracy. "The democratic method is that institutional arrangement for arriving at political decisions which realizes the common good by making the people itself decide issues through the election of individuals who are to assemble in order to carry out its will." [1] Schumpeter then analyzes modern man's attitudes toward the problem of public welfare, and arrives at a result not too different from the ones outlined above. "However, when we move still farther away from the private concerns of the family and the business office into those regions of national and international affairs that lack a direct and unmistakable link with those private concerns, individual volition, command of facts and method of inference soon cease to fulfill the requirements of the classical doctrine. What strikes me most of all and seems to me to be the core of the trouble is the fact that the sense of reality is so completely lost. Normally, the great political questions take their place in the psychic economy of the typical citizen with those leisure-hour interests that have not attained the rank of hobbies, and with the subjects of irresponsible conversation. These things seem so far off; they are not at all like a business proposition; dangers may not materialize at all and if they should they may not prove so very serious; one feels oneself to be moving in a fictitious world.

"This reduced sense of reality accounts not only for a reduced sense of responsibility but also for the absence of effective volition. One has one's phrases, of course, and one's wishes and daydreams

---

[1] Joseph A. Schumpeter, *Capitalism, Socialism, and Democracy*, Harper and Brothers New York and London, 1947, p. 250.

and grumbles; especially, one has one's likes and dislikes. But ordinarily they do not amount to what we call a will—the psychic counterpart of purposeful responsible action. In fact, for the private citizen musing over national affairs there is no scope for such a will and no task at which it could develop. He is a member of an unworkable committee, the committee of the whole nation, and this is why he expends less disciplined effort on mastering a political problem than he expends on a game of bridge.

"The reduced sense of responsibility and the absence of effective volition in turn explain the ordinary citizen's ignorance and lack of judgment in matters of domestic and foreign policy which are if anything more shocking in the case of educated people and of people who are successfully active in non-political walks of life than it is with uneducated people in humble situations. Information is plentiful and readily available. But this does not seem to make any difference. Nor should we wonder at it. We need only compare a lawyer's attitude to his brief and the same lawyer's attitude to the statements of political fact presented in his newspaper in order to see what is the matter. In the one case the lawyer has qualified for appreciating the relevance of his facts by years of purposeful labor done under the definite stimulus of interest in his professional competence; and under a stimulus that is no less powerful he then bends his acquirements, his intellect, his will to the contents of the brief. In the other case, he has not taken the trouble to qualify; he does not care to absorb the information or to apply to it the canons of criticism he knows so well how to handle; and he is impatient of long or complicated argument. All of this goes to show that without the initiative that comes from immediate responsibility, ignorance will persist in the face of masses of information however complete and correct. It persists even in the face of the meritorious efforts that are being made to go beyond presenting information and to teach the use of it by means of lectures, classes, discussion groups. Results are not zero. But they are small. People cannot be carried up the ladder.

"Thus the typical citizen drops down to a lower level of mental performance as soon as he enters the political field. He argues and analyzes in a way which he would readily recognize as infantile within the sphere of his real interests. He becomes a primitive again." [1]

Schumpeter too points to the similarity between the manufacturing of the popular will in political issues and that in commercial advertising. "The ways," he says, "in which issues and the popular will on any issue are being manufactured is exactly analogous to the ways of commercial advertising. We find the same attempts to contact the subconscious. We find the same technique of creating favorable and unfavorable associations which are the more effective the less rational they are. We find the same evasions and reticences and the same trick of producing opinion by reiterated assertion that is successful precisely to the extent to which it avoids rational argument and the danger of awakening the critical faculties of the people. And so on. Only, all these arts have infinitely more scope in the sphere of public affairs than they have in the sphere of private and professional life. The picture of the prettiest girl that ever lived will in the long run prove powerless to maintain the sales of a bad cigarette. There is no equally effective safeguard in the case of political decisions. Many decisions of fateful importance are of a nature that makes it impossible for the public to experiment with them at its leisure and at moderate cost. Even if that is possible, however, judgment is as a rule not so easy to arrive at as it is in the case of the cigarette, because effects are less easy to interpret." [2]

[1] *Ibid.*, pp. 261, 262.
[2] *Ibid.*, p. 263.

On the basis of his analysis, Schumpeter arrives at a definition of democracy which, while less lofty than the first one, is undoubtedly more realistic. "The democratic method is that institutional arrangement for arriving at political decisions *in which individuals acquire the power to decide by means of a competitive struggle for the people's vote.*" [1] (My italics.)

The comparison between the process of opinion formation in politics with that in the commodity market can be supplemented with another one dealing not so much with the formation of opinion, but rather with its expression. I am referring to the role of the stockholder in America's big corporations, and of the influence of his will on the management.

As has been pointed out above, ownership in the big corporations rests today in the hands of hundreds of thousands of individuals, each of whom owns an exceedingly small fraction of the total stocks. Legally speaking, the stockholders own the enterprise and hence have the right to determine its policy and to appoint the management. Practically speaking, they feel little responsibility for their ownership, and acquiesce in what the management does, satisfied to have a regular income. The vast majority of the stockholders do not bother to go to the meetings and are willing to send the required proxies to the management. As has been pointed out above, only in 6 per cent of the big corporations (in 1930) is control exercised by total or majority ownership.

The situation of control in a modern democracy is not too different from the control in a big corporation. It is true, over 50 per cent of the voters cast their votes personally. They make the decision between two party machines competing for their votes. Once one of the machines is voted into office, the relationship to the voter becomes remote. The real decisions often do not lie any more with individual members of the parliament, representing the

[1] *Ibid.*, p. 269.

interests and wishes of their constituency, but with the party.[1] But even there decisions are made by influential key personalities, often little known to the public. The fact is that while the individual citizen believes that he directs the decisions of his country, he does it only a little more than the average stockholder participates in the controlling of "his" company. Between the act of voting and the most momentous high-level political decisions is a connection which is mysterious. One cannot say that there is none at all, nor can one say that the final decision is an outcome of the voter's will. This is exactly the situation of an alienated expression of the citizen's will. He does something, voting, and is under the illusion that he is the creator of decisions which he accepts as if they were his own, while in reality they are largely determined by forces beyond his control and knowledge. No wonder this situation gives the average citizen a deep sense of powerlessness in political matters (though not necessarily consciously so) and hence that his political intelligence is reduced more and more. For while it is true that one must think *before* one acts, it is also true that if one has no chance to act, the thinking becomes impoverished; in other words, if one cannot act effectively—one cannot think productively either.

3. Alienation and Mental Health

What is the effect of alienation on mental health? The answer depends of course on what is meant by health; if it means that man can fulfill his social function, carry on with production, and reproduce himself, alienated man can quite obviously be healthy. After all, we have created the most powerful production machine which has existed so far on earth—even though we have also created the most powerful destruction machine, accessible to the

---

[1] cf. R. H. S. Crossman's article "The Party Oligarchies," in *The New Statesman* and *Nation*, London, August 21, 1954.

grasp of the madman. If we look into the current psychiatric definition of mental health, then one should think too that we are healthy. Quite naturally the concepts of health and illness are the products of those men who formulate them—hence of the culture in which these men live. Alienated psychiatrists will define mental health in terms of the alienated personality, and therefore consider healthy what might be considered sick from the standpoint of normative humanism. In this respect what H. G. Wells has described so beautifully for the psychiatrists and surgeons in the "Country of the Blind," also holds true for many psychiatrists in our culture. The young man who has found an abode in an isolated tribe of congenitally blind people, is examined by their doctors.

"Then afterwards one of the elders, who thought deeply, had an idea. He was the great doctor among these people, their medicine-man, and he had a very philosophical and inventive mind, and the idea of curing Nunez of his peculiarities appealed to him. One day when Yacob was present he returned to the topic of Nunez.

" 'I have examined Bogota,' he said, 'and the case is clearer to me. I think very probably he might be cured.'

" 'That is what I have always hoped,' said old Yacob.

" 'His brain is affected,' said the blind doctor.

"The elders murmured assent.

" 'Now, *what* affects it?'

" 'Ah!' said old Yacob.

" '*This*,' said the doctor, answering his own question. 'Those queer things that are called the eyes, and which exist to make an agreeable soft depression in the face, are diseased, in the case of Bogota, in such a way as to affect his brain. They are greatly distended, he has eyelashes, and his eyelids move, and consequently his brain is in a state of constant irritation and distraction.'

" 'Yes?' said old Yacob. 'Yes?'

" 'And I think I may say with reasonable certainty that, in order to cure him completely, all that we need do is a simple and easy surgical operation—namely, to remove these irritant bodies.'

" 'And then he will be sane?'

" 'Then he will be perfectly sane, and a quite admirable citizen.'

" 'Thank Heaven for science!' said old Yacob, and went forth at once to tell Nunez of his happy hopes." [1]

Our current psychiatric definitions of mental health stress those qualities which are part of the alienated social character of our time: adjustment, co-operativeness, aggressiveness, tolerance, ambition, etc. I quoted above Strecker's definition of "maturity," as an illustration for the naïve translation of an ad for a junior executive into psychiatric parlance. But as was already briefly mentioned in another context, even one of the most profound and brilliant psychoanalysts of our period, H. S. Sullivan, was influenced in his theoretical concepts by the all pervasive alienation. Just because of his eminence and the important contribution he made to psychiatry, it will be enlightening to dwell somewhat on this point. Sullivan took the fact that the alienated person lacks a feeling of selfhood and experiences himself in terms of a response to the expectation of others, as part of human nature, just as Freud had taken the competitiveness characteristic of the beginning of the century as a natural phenomenon. Sullivan thus called the view that there exists a unique individual self the "delusion of unique individuality." [2] Equally clear is the influence of alienated thinking on his formulation of the basic needs of man. They are, according to him, "the need for personal

---

[1] H. G. Wells, *In the Days of the Comet and Seventeen Short Stories*, New York, Charles Scribner's Sons, 1925.

[2] H. S. Sullivan, *The Interpersonal Theory of Psychiatry*, W. W. Norton & Company, Inc., New York, 1953, p. 140.

security—that is for freedom from anxiety; the need for intimacy—that is, for collaboration with at least one other person; and the need for lustful satisfaction, which is concerned with genital activity in pursuit of the orgasm." [1] The three criteria for mental health which Sullivan postulates here are quite generally accepted. At first glance, nobody will have any quarrel with the idea that love, security and sexual satisfaction are perfectly normal goals of mental health. A critical examination of these concepts, however, shows that they mean something different in an alienated world than what they might have meant in other cultures.

Perhaps the most popular modern concept in the arsenal of psychiatric formulae is that of *security*. In recent years there is an increasing emphasis on the concept of security as the paramount aim of life, and as the essence of mental health. One reason for this attitude lies, perhaps, in the fact that the threat of war hanging over the world for many years has increased the longing for security. Another, more important reason, lies in the fact that people feel increasingly more insecure as the result of an increasing automatization and overconformity.

The problem becomes more complicated by the confusion between *psychic* and *economic* security. It is one of the fundamental changes of the last fifty years that in all Western countries the principle has been adopted that every citizen must have a minimum material security in case of unemployment, sickness and old age. Yet, while this principle has been adopted, there is still, among many businessmen, intense hostility against it, and especially its widening application; they speak contemptuously of the "welfare state" as killing private initiative and the spirit of adventure, and in fighting social security measures, they pretend to fight for the freedom and initiative of the worker. That these

[1] *Ibid.* p. 264.

194

arguments are sheer rationalizations is evidenced by the fact that the same people have no qualms about praising economic security as one of the chief aims of life. One needs only to read the advertisements of insurance companies, with their promises to free their customers from insecurity which could be caused by accidents, death, sickness, old age, etc., to be aware of the important role which the ideal of economic security plays for the moneyed class, and what else is the idea of saving, but practicing the aim of economic security? This contradiction between the denunciation of the striving for security among the working class, and the praise of the same aim for those in the higher income brackets is another example of man's unlimited capacity for thinking contradictory thoughts, without even making a feeble attempt to become aware of the contradiction.

Yet the propaganda against the "welfare state" and the principle of economic security is more effective than it would otherwise be, because of the widespread confusion between *economic* and *emotional* security.

Increasingly people feel that they should have no doubts, no problems, that they should have to take no risks, and that they should always feel "secure." Psychiatry and psychoanalysis have lent considerable support to this aim. Many writers in this field postulate security as the main aim of psychic development and consider a sense of security more or less equivalent with mental health. (Sullivan is the most profound and the most searching among these.) Thus parents, especially those who follow this literature, get worried that their little son or daughter may, at an early age, acquire a sense of "insecurity." They try to help them avoid conflicts, to make everything easy, to do away with as many obstacles as they can, in order to make the child feel "secure." Just as they try to inoculate the child against all illnesses, and to prevent it from getting in touch with any germ, they think they can banish insecurity by preventing any contact with it. The result is often as unfortunate as exaggerated hygiene sometimes is: once an infection occurs, the person becomes more vulnerable and helpless before it.

How can a sensitive and alive person ever feel secure? Because of the very conditions of our existence, we cannot feel secure about anything. Our thoughts and insights are at best partial truths, mixed with a great deal of error, not to speak of the unnecessary misinformation about life and society to which we are exposed almost from the day of birth. Our life and health are subject to accidents beyond our control. If we make a decision, we can never be certain of the outcome; any decision implies a risk of failure, and if it does not imply it, it has not been a decision in the true sense of the word. We can never be certain of the outcome of our best efforts. The result always depends on many factors which transcend our capacity of control. Just as a sensitive and alive person cannot avoid being sad, he cannot avoid feeling insecure. The psychic task which a person can and must set for himself, *is not to feel secure, but to be able to tolerate insecurity, without panic and undue fear.*

Life, in its mental and spiritual aspects, is by necessity insecure and uncertain. There is certainty only about the fact that we are born and that we shall die; there is complete security only in an equally complete submission to powers which are supposed to be strong and enduring, and which relieve man from the necessity of making decisions, taking risks, and having responsibilities. *Free man is by necessity insecure; thinking man by necessity uncertain.*

How, then, can man tolerate this insecurity inherent in human existence? One way is to be rooted in the group in such a way that the feeling of identity is guaranteed by the membership to the group, be it family, clan, nation, class. As long as the process of individualism has not reached a stage where the individual emerges from these primary bonds, he is still "we," and as long as the group functions he is certain of his own identity by his membership in it. The development of modern society has led to the dissolution of these primary bonds. Modern man is essentially alone, he is put on his own feet, expected to stand all by himself. He can achieve a sense of identity only by developing the unique and particular entity which is "he" to a point where he can truly sense "I am I." This accomplishment is possible only if he develops his active powers to such an extent that he can be related to the world without having to submerge in it; if he can achieve a productive orientation. The alienated person, however, tries to solve the problem in a different way, namely by conforming. He feels secure in being as similar as possible to his fellow man. His paramount aim is to be approved of by others; his central fear, that he may not be approved of. To be different, to find himself in a minority, are the dangers which threaten his sense of security; hence a craving for limitless conformity. It is obvious that this craving for conformity produces in turn a continuously operating, though hidden, sense of insecurity. Any deviation from the pattern, any criticism, arouses fear and insecurity; one is always dependent on the approval of others, just as a drug addict is dependent on his drug, and similarly, one's own sense of self and "self"-reliance becomes ever increasingly weaker. The sense of guilt, which some generations ago pervaded the life of man with reference to sin, has been replaced by a sense of uneasiness and inadequacy with regard to being different.

Another goal of mental health, *love*, like that of security, has assumed a new meaning in the alienated situation. For Freud, according to the spirit of his time, love was basically a sexual phenomenon. "Man having found by experience that sexual (genital) love afforded him his greatest gratification, so that it became in fact a prototype of all happiness to him, must have been thereby impelled to seek his happiness further along the path of sexual relations, to make genital eroticism the central point of his life. . . . In doing so he becomes to a very dangerous degree dependent on a part of the outer world, namely, on his chosen love object, and this exposes him to most painful suffering if he is rejected by it, or loses it by death or defection." [1] In order to protect himself from the danger of suffering by love, man, but only a "small minority," can transform the erotic functions of love by transferring "the main value from the fact of being loved to their own act of loving," and "by attaching their love not to individual objects, but to all men equally." Thus "they avoid the uncertainties and disappointments of genital love by turning away from its sexual aim and modifying the instinct into an impulse with an *inhibited aim*. . . . Love with an inhibited aim was indeed originally full sensual love, and in men's unconscious minds is so still." [2] The feeling of oneness and fusion with the world (the "oceanic feeling") which is the essence of religious experience and specifically of mystical experience, and the experience of oneness and union with the beloved person is interpreted by Freud as a regression to a state of an early "limitless narcissism." [3]

In accordance with his basic concepts, mental health for Freud is the full achievement of the capacity for love, which is attained if the libido development has reached the genital stage.

In H. S. Sullivan's psychoanalytic system we find, in contrast to Freud, a strict division between sexuality and love. What is the meaning of love and intimacy in Sullivan's concept? "In-

[1] S. Freud, *Civilization and Its Discontents, loc. cit.*, p. 69.
[2] *Ibid.*, p. 69 ff.
[3] *Ibid.*, p. 21.

timacy is that type of situation involving two people which permits validation of all components of personal worth. Validation of personal worth requires a type of relationship which I call collaboration, by which I mean clearly formulated adjustments of one's behavior to the expressed needs of the other person in the pursuit of increasingly identical—that is, more and more nearly mutual satisfactions, and in the maintenance of increasingly similar security operations." [1] Sullivan, putting it more simply, defined the essence of love as a situation of collaboration, in which two people feel: 'we play according to the rules of the game to preserve our prestige and feeling of superiority and merit.' [2]

Just as Freud's concept of love is a description of the experience of the patriarchal male in terms of nineteenth-century materialism, Sullivan's description refers to the experience of the alienated, marketing personality of the twentieth century. It is a description of an *"egotism à deux,"* of two people pooling their common interests, and standing together against a hostile and alienated world. Actually his definition of intimacy is in principle valid for the feeling of any co-operating team, in which everybody "adjusts his behavior to the expressed needs of the other person in the pursuit of common aims." (It is remarkable that Sullivan speaks here of *expressed* needs, when the least one could say about love is that it implies a reaction to *unexpressed* needs between two people.)

In more popular terms one can discover the marketing connotation of love in discussions on marital love and on the need for children for love and affection. In numerous articles, in counseling, in lectures, marital love is described as a state of

[1] *Ibid.*, p. 246.

[2] *Ibid.*, p. 246. Another definition of love by Sullivan, that love begins when a person feels another person's needs to be as important as his own, is less colored by the marketing aspect than the above mentioned formulation.

mutual fairness and mutual manipulation, called "understanding each other." The wife is supposed to consider the needs and sensibilities of the husband, and vice versa. If he comes home tired and disgruntled, she should not ask him questions—or should ask him questions—according to what the authors think is best for "oiling" him. And he should say appreciative words about her cooking or her new dress—and all this in the name of love. Every day now one can hear that a child must "get affection" in order to feel secure, or that another child "did not get enough love from his parents," and that is why he became a criminal or schizophrenic. Love and affection have assumed the same meaning as that of the formula for the baby, or the college education one should get, or the latest film one should "take in." You feed love, as you feed security, knowledge and everything else—and you have a happy person!

Happiness is another, and one of the more popular concepts by which mental health is defined today. As the formula runs in the *Brave New World*: "everybody is happy nowadays."

What is meant by happiness? Most people today would probably answer the question by saying that to be happy is to have "fun," or "to have a good time." The answer to the question, "What is fun?" depends somewhat on the economic situation of the individual, and more, on his education and personality structure. Economic differences, however, are not as important as they may seem. The "good time" of society's upper strata is the fun model for those not yet able to pay for it while earnestly hoping for that happy eventuality—and the "good time" of society's lower strata is increasingly a cheaper imitation of the upper strata's, differing in cost, but not so much in quality.

What does this fun consist in? Going to the movies, parties, ball games, listening to the radio and watching television, taking a ride in the car on Sundays, making love, sleeping late on Sunday mornings, and traveling, for those who can afford it. If we use a more respectable term, instead of the word "fun," and "having a good time," we might say that the concept of happiness is, at best, identified with that of pleasure. Taking into consideration our discussion of the problem of consumption, we can define the concept somewhat more accurately as the pleasure of unrestricted consumption, push-button power and laziness.

From this standpoint, happiness could be defined as the opposite of sadness or sorrow, and indeed, the average person defines happiness as a state of mind which is free from sadness or sorrow. This definition, however, shows that there is something profoundly wrong in this concept of happiness. A person who is alive and sensitive cannot fail to be sad, and to feel sorrow many times in his life. This is so, not only because of the amount of unnecessary suffering produced by the imperfection of our social arrangements, but because of the nature of human existence, which makes it impossible not to react to life with a good deal of pain and sorrow. Since we are living beings, we must be sadly aware of the necessary gap between our aspirations and what can be achieved in our short and troubled life. Since death confronts us with the inevitable fact that either we shall die before our loved ones or they before us—since we see suffering, the unavoidable as well as the unnecessary and wasteful, around us every day, how can we avoid the experience of pain and sorrow? The effort to avoid it is only possible if we reduce our sensitivity, responsiveness and love, if we harden our hearts and withdraw our attention and our feeling from others, as well as from ourselves.

If we want to define happiness by its opposite, we must define it not in contrast to *sadness*, but in contrast to *depression*.

What is depression? It is the inability to feel, it is the sense of being dead, while our body is alive. It is the inability to experience joy, as well as the inability to experience sadness. A depressed person would be greatly relieved if he could feel sad. A state of depression is so unbearable because one is incapable of feeling anything, either joy or sadness. If we try to define happiness in contrast to depression, we approach Spinoza's definition of joy and happiness as that state of intensified vitality that fuses into one whole our effort both to understand our fellow men and be one with them. Happiness results from the experience of productive living, and the use of the powers of love and reason which unite us with the world. Happiness consists in our touching the rock bottom of reality, in the discovery of our self and our oneness with others as well as our difference from them. Happiness is a state of intense inner activity and the experience of the increasing vital energy which occurs in productive relatedness to the world and to ourselves.

It follows that happiness cannot be found in the state of inner passivity, and in the consumer attitude which pervades the life of alienated man. Happiness is to experience fullness, not emptiness which needs to be filled. The average man today may have a good deal of fun and pleasure, but in spite of this, he is fundamentally depressed. Perhaps it clarifies the issue if instead of using the word "depressed" we use the word "bored." Actually there is very little difference between the two, except a difference in degree, because boredom is nothing but the experience of a paralysis of our productive powers and the sense of un-aliveness. Among the evils of life, there are few which are as painful as boredom, and consequently every attempt is made to avoid it.

It can be avoided in two ways; either fundamentally, by being productive, and in this manner experiencing happiness, or by trying to avoid its manifestations. The latter attempt seems to characterize the chasing after fun and pleasure in the average person today. He senses his depression and boredom, which becomes manifest when he is alone with himself or with those closest to him. All our amusements serve the purpose of making it easy for him to run away from himself and from the threatening boredom by taking refuge in the many ways of escape which our culture offers him; yet covering up a symptom does not do away with the conditions which produce it. Aside from the fear of physical illness, or of being humiliated by the loss of status and prestige, the fear of boredom plays a paramount role among the fears of modern man. In a world of fun and amusement, he is afraid of boredom, and glad when another day has passed without mishap, another hour has been killed without his having become aware of the lurking boredom.

From the standpoint of normative humanism we must arrive at a different concept of mental health; the very person who is considered healthy in the categories of an alienated world, from the humanistic standpoint appears as the sickest one—although not in terms of individual sickness, but of the socially patterned defect. Mental health, in the humanistic sense, is characterized by the ability to love and to create, by the emergence from the incestuous ties to family and nature, by a sense of identity based on one's experience of self as the subject and agent of one's powers, by the grasp of reality inside and outside of ourselves, that is, by the development of objectivity and reason. The aim of life is to live it intensely, to be fully born, to be fully awake. To emerge from the ideas of infantile grandiosity into the conviction of one's real though limited strength; to be able to accept the paradox that every one of us is the most important thing there is in the universe—and at the same time not more important than a fly or a blade of grass. To be able to love life, and yet to accept death without terror; to tolerate uncertainty about the most important questions with which life confronts us—and yet to have faith in our thought and feeling, inasmuch as they are truly ours. To be able to be alone, and at the same time one with a loved person, with every brother on this earth, with all that is alive; to follow the voice of our conscience, the voice that calls us to ourselves, yet not to indulge in self hate when the voice of conscience was not loud enough to be heard and followed. The mentally healthy person is the person who lives by love, reason and faith, who respects life, his own and that of his fellow man.

The alienated person, as we have tried to describe him in this chapter, cannot be healthy. Since he experiences himself as a thing, an investment, to be manipulated by himself and by others, he is lacking in a sense of self. This lack of self creates deep anxiety. The anxiety engendered by confronting him with the abyss of nothingness is more terrifying than even the tortures of hell. In the vision of hell, *I* am punished and tortured—in the vision of nothingness I am driven to the border of madness—because I cannot say "I" any more. If the modern age has been rightly called the age of anxiety, it is primarily because of this anxiety engendered by the lack of self. Inasmuch as "I am as you desire me"—*I* am *not*; I am anxious, dependent on approval of others, constantly trying to please. The alienated person feels inferior whenever he suspects himself of not being in line. Since his sense of worth is based on approval as the reward for conformity, he feels naturally threatened in his sense of self and in his self-esteem by any feeling, thought or action which could be suspected of being a deviation. Yet, inasmuch as he *is* human and not an automaton, he cannot help deviating, hence he must feel afraid of disapproval all the time. As a result he has to try all the harder to conform, to be approved of, to be successful. Not the voice of his conscience gives him strength and security but the feeling of not having lost the close touch with the herd.

Another result of alienation is the prevalence of a feeling of guilt. It is, indeed, amazing that in as fundamentally irreligious a culture as ours, the sense of guilt should be so widespread and deep-rooted as it is. The main difference from, let us say, a Calvinistic community, is the fact that the feeling of guilt is neither very conscious, nor does it refer to a religiously patterned concept of sin. But if we scratch the surface, we find that people feel guilty about hundreds of things; for not having worked hard enough, for having been too protective—or not protective enough —toward their children, for not having done enough for Mother, or for having been too kindhearted to a debtor; people feel guilty for having done good things, as well as for having done bad things; it is almost as if they had to find something to feel guilty about.

What could be the cause of so much guilt feeling? It seems that there are two main sources which, though entirely different in themselves, lead to the same result. The one source is the same as that from which the feelings of inferiority spring. Not to be like the rest, not to be totally adjusted, makes one feel guilty toward the commands of the great It. The other source of guilt feeling is man's one conscience; he senses his gifts or talents, his ability to love, to think, to laugh, to cry, to wonder and to create, he senses that his life is the one chance he is given, and that if he loses this chance he has lost everything. He lives in a world with more comfort and ease than his ancestors ever knew—yet he senses that, chasing after more comfort, his life runs through his fingers like sand. He cannot help feeling guilty for the waste, for the lost chance. This feeling of guilt is much less conscious than the first one, but one reinforces the other, the one often serving as a rationalization for the other. Thus, alienated man feels guilty for being himself, and for not being himself, for being alive and for being an automaton, for being a person and for being a thing.

Alienated man is unhappy. Consumption of fun serves to repress the awareness of his unhappiness. He tries to save time, and yet he is eager to kill the time he has saved. He is glad to have finished another day without failure or humiliation, rather than to greet the new day with the enthusiasm which only the "I am I" experience can give. He is lacking the constant flow of energy which stems from productive relatedness to the world.

Having no faith, being deaf to the voice of conscience, and having a manipulating intelligence but little reason, he is bewildered, disquieted and willing to appoint to the position of a leader anyone who offers him a total solution.

Can the picture of alienation be connected with any of the established pictures of mental illness? In answering this question we must remember that man has two ways of relating himself to the world. One in which he sees the world as he needs to see it in order to manipulate or use it. Essentially this is sense experience and common-sense experience. Our eye sees that which we have to see, our ear hears what we have to hear in order to live; our common sense perceives things in a manner which enables us to act; both senses and common sense work in the service of survival. In the matter of sense and common sense and for the logic built upon them, things are the same for all people because the laws of their use are the same.

The other faculty of man is to see things from within, as it were; subjectively, formed by *my* inner éxperience, feeling, mood.[1] Ten painters paint the same tree in one sense, yet they paint ten different trees in another. Each tree is an expression of their individuality while also being the same tree. In the dream we see the world entirely from within; it loses its objective meaning and is transformed into a symbol of our own purely individual experience. The person who dreams while

---

[1] See a more detailed discussion of this point in E. Fromm, *The Forgotten Language*, Rinehart & Company, Inc., New York, 1952.

awake, that is, the person who is in touch only with his inner world and who is incapable of perceiving the outer world in its objective-action context, is insane. The person who can only experience the outer world photographically, but is out of touch with his inner world, with himself, is the alienated person. Schizophrenia and alienation are complementary. In both forms of sickness one pole of human experience is lacking. If both poles are present, we can speak of the productive person, whose very productiveness results from the polarity between an inner and an outer form of perception.

Our description of the alienated character of contemporary man is somewhat one-sided; there are a number of positive factors which I have failed to mention. There is in the first place still a humanistic tradition alive, which has not been destroyed by the in-human process of alienation. But beyond that, there are signs that people are increasingly dissatisfied and disappointed with their way of life and trying to regain some of their lost selfhood and productivity. Millions of people listen to good music in concert halls or over the radio, an ever-increasing number of people paint, do gardening, build their own boats or houses, indulge in any number of "do it yourself" activities. Adult education is spreading, and even in business the awareness is growing that an executive should have reason and not only intelligence.[1]

But promising and real as all these trends are, they are not enough to justify an attitude which is to be found among a number of very sophisticated writers who claim that criticisms of our society, such as the one which has been offered here, are dated and old-fashioned; that we have already passed the peak of alienation and are now on our way to a better world. Appeal-

---

[1] An impressive example of this new trend is the course in literature and philosophy for junior executives of the Bell Telephone Co., under the directorship of Professors Morse Peckham and Rex Crawford at the University of Pennsylvania.

ing as this type of optimism is, it is nevertheless only a more sophisticated form of the defense of the status quo, a translation of the praise of the American Way of Life into the concepts of a cultural anthropology which, enriched by Marx and Freud, has "gone beyond" them and is reassuring man that there is no reason for serious worry.

· 6 ·

VARIOUS OTHER DIAGNOSES

NINETEENTH CENTURY

The diagnosis of the illness of present-day Western culture, as we tried to give it in the previous chapter, is by no means new; its only claim toward furthering the understanding of the problem is the attempt to apply the concept of alienation more empirically to various observable phenomena, and to establish the connection between the illnesses of alienation and the humanistic concept of human nature and mental health. In fact, it is most remarkable that a critical view of twentieth-century society was already held by a number of thinkers living in the nineteenth century, long before the symptomatology which seems so apparent today had become fully manifest. It is also remarkable that their critical diagnosis and prognosis should have so much in common among themselves and with the critics of the twentieth century.

The prognosis of the decay and barbarism into which the twentieth century will sink was made by people of the most varied philosophical and political views. The Swiss conservative, Burckhardt; the Russian religious radical, Tolstoy; the French anarchist, Proudhon, as well as his conservative compatriot, Baudelaire; the American anarchist, Thoreau, and later his more politically minded compatriot, Jack London; the German revolutionary, Karl Marx—they all agreed in the most severe criticism of the modern culture and most of the them visualized the possibility of the advent of an age of barbarism. Marx's predictions were mitigated by his assumption that Socialism was a possible and even probable alternative to it. Burckhardt, from his conservative perspective, colored by the Swiss capacity for a stubborn refusal to be impressed by words and glamour, stated in a letter written in 1876, that perhaps Europe might still enjoy a few peaceful decades before it transformed itself by a number of terrible wars and revolutions into a new kind of Imperium Romanum, into a military and economic despotism: "The 20th century is chosen for everything else but for a true democracy." In 1872, Burckhardt writes to a friend: "I have a premonition which still sounds like folly, and yet it will not leave me alone: the military state must become a big industrialist. Those concentrations of people in the big workshops must not forever be left to their greed and want; the logical consequence would be a predetermined and supervised amount of misery with advancement and in uniform, begun and completed daily with the accompaniment of drums. . . . There is the prospect of long and voluntary submission to single leaders and usurpers. The people no longer believe in principles, but will probably periodically believe in saviours. Because of this reason, authority will again raise its head in the delightful 20th century and a frightful head it will be." [1]

In his prediction of systems like Fascism and Stalinism for the twentieth century, Burckhardt differs little from the predictions of the revolutionary Proudhon. The threat for the future

---

[1] J. Burckhardt's *Briefe*, ed. F. Kaplan, Leipzig, 1935, letters of April 26th, 1872; April 13, 1882; July 24, 1899. (My translation, E.F.)

is, Proudhon writes, ". . . a compact democracy having the appearance of being founded on the dictatorship of the masses, but in which the masses have no more power than is necessary to ensure a general serfdom in accordance with the following precepts and principles borrowed from the old absolutism: indivisibility of public power, all-consuming centralization, systematic destruction of all individual, corporative and regional thought (regarded as disruptive), inquisitorial police. . . ." "We should no longer deceive ourselves," he wrote. "Europe is sick of thought and order; it is entering into an era of brute force and contempt of principles." And later on: "Then the great war of the six great powers will begin. . . . Carnage will come and the enfeeblement that will follow these bloodbaths will be terrible. We shall not live to see the work of the new age, we shall fight in the darkness; we must prepare ourselves to endure this life without too much sadness, by doing our duty. Let us help one another, call to one another in the gloom, and practice justice wherever opportunity offers." And finally: "To-day civilization is in the grip of a crisis for which one can only find a single analogy in history—that is the crisis which brought the coming of Christianity. All the traditions are worn out, all the creeds abolished; but the new programme is not yet *ready,* by which I mean that it has not yet entered the consciousness of the masses. Hence what I call *the dissolution.* This is the cruellest moment in the life of societies. . . . I am under no illusions and do not expect to wake up one morning to see the resurrection of freedom in our country, as if by a stroke of magic. . . . No, no; decay, and decay for a period whose end I cannot fix and which will last for not less than one or two generations—is our lot. . . . I shall witness the evil only, I shall die in the midst of the darkness." [1]

[1] Quoted from E. Dolleans' *Proudhon,* Gallimard, Paris, 1948, p. 96 ff. (My translation, E.F.)

While Burckhardt and Proudhon visualized Fascism and Stalinism as the outcome of nineteenth-century culture (a prophecy
repeated more specifically in 1907 by Jack London in his *Iron
Heel*), others centered their diagnosis on the spiritual poverty
and alienation of contemporary society, which, according to them
must lead to an increasing dehumanization and decay of culture.

How similar are two statements made by two authors as
different from each other as Baudelaire and Tolstoy. Baudelaire
writes in 1851 in some fragments entitled "Fusées": "The world
is drawing to a close. Only for one reason can it last longer:
just because it happens to exist. But how weak a reason is this
compared with all that forebodes the contrary, particularly with
the question: What is left to the world of man in the future?
Supposing it should continue materially, would that be an existence worthy of its name and of the historical dictionary? I do
not say the world would fall back into a spectral condition and
the odd disorder of South American republics; nor do I say
that we should return to primitive savagery and, with a rifle
in our arms, hunt for food through the grass-covered ruins of
our civilization. No, such adventures would still call for a certain
vital energy, an echo from primordial times. We shall furnish a
new example of the inexorability of the spiritual and moral laws
and shall be their new victims: *we shall perish by the very thing
by which we fancy that we live.* Technocracy will Americanize
us, progress will starve our spirituality so far that nothing of the
bloodthirsty, frivolous or unnatural dreams of the utopist will
be comparable to those positive facts. I invite any thinking person
to show me what is left of life. Religion! It is useless to talk
about it, or to look for its remnants; it is a scandal that one
takes the trouble even of denying God. Private property! It was
—strictly speaking—abolished with the suppression of the right
of primogeniture; yet the time will come when mankind like a

revengeful cannibal will snatch the last piece from those who rightfully deemed themselves the heirs of revolutions. And even this will not be the worst. . . . Universal ruin will manifest itself not solely or particularly in political institutions or general progress or whatever else might be a proper name for it; it will be seen, above all, in the baseness of hearts. Shall I add that that little left-over of sociability will hardly resist the sweeping brutality, and that the rulers, in order to hold their own and to produce a sham order, will ruthlessly resort to measures which will make us, who already are callous, shudder?" [1]

Tolstoy wrote some years later: "The medieval theology, or the Roman corruption of morals, poisoned only their own people, a small part of mankind; today, electricity, railways and telegraphs spoil the whole world. Everyone makes these things his own. He simply cannot help making them his own. Everyone suffers in the same way, is forced to the same extent to change his way of life. All are under the necessity of betraying what is most important for their lives, the understanding of life itself, religion. Machines—to produce what? The telegraph—to despatch what? Books, papers—to spread what kind of news? Railways—to go to whom and to what place? Millions of people herded together and subject to a supreme power—to accomplish what? Hospitals, physicians, dispensaries in order to prolong life—for what? How easily do individuals as well as whole nations take their own so-called civilization as the true civilization: finishing one's studies, keeping one's nails clean, using the tailor's and the barber's services, travelling abroad, and the most civilized man is complete. And with regard to nations: as many railways as possible, academies, industrial works, battleships, forts, newspapers, books, parties, parliaments. Thus the most civilized nation is complete.

[1] Quoted from K. Löwith, *Meaning in History*, The University of Chicago Press, Chicago, 1949, pp. 97, 98.

Enough individuals therefore, as well as nations, can be interested in civilization but not in true enlightenment. The former is easy and meets with approval; the latter requires rigorous efforts and therefore, from the great majority, always meets with nothing but contempt and hatred, for it exposes the lie of civilization." [1]

Less drastic, yet just as clear as the foregoing writer's, is Thoreau's criticism of modern culture. In his "Life without Principle" (1861) [2] he says: "Let us consider the way in which we spend our lives. This world is a place of business. What an infinite bustle! I am awaked almost every night by the panting of the locomotive. It interrupts my dreams. There is no sabbath. It would be glorious to see mankind at leisure for once. It is nothing but work, work, work. I cannot easily buy a blankbook to write thoughts in; they are commonly ruled for dollars and cents. An Irishman, seeing me making a minute in the fields, took it for granted that I was calculating my wages. If a man was tossed out of a window when an infant, and so made a cripple for life, or scared out of his wits by the Indians, it is regretted chiefly because he was thus incapacitated for—business! I think that there is nothing, not even crime, more opposed to poetry, to philosophy, ay, to life itself, than this incessant business. . . .

"If a man walk in the woods for love of them half of each day, he is in danger of being regarded as a loafer; but if he spends his whole day as a speculator, shearing off those woods and making earth bald before her time, he is esteemed an industrious and enterprising citizen. As if a town had no interest in its forests but to cut them down! . . .

"The ways by which you may get money almost without exception lead downward. To have done anything by which you

---

[1] Quoted from Löwith, *loc. cit.*, p. 99. From *Tolstois Flucht und Tod*, ed. by R. Fülöp-Miller and F. Eckstein, Berlin, 1925, p. 103.

[2] Published in *The Portable Thoreau*, ed. by Carl Bode, The Viking Press, New York, 1947, pp. 631–655.

earned money *merely* is to have been truly idle or worse. If the laborer gets no more than the wages which his employer pays him, he is cheated, he cheats himself. If you would get money as a writer or lecturer, you must be popular, which is to go down perpendicularly. . . .

"The aim of the laborer should be, not to get his living, to get 'a good job,' but to perform well a certain work; and, even in a pecuniary sense, it would be economy for a town to pay its laborers so well that they would not feel that they were working for low ends, as for a livelihood merely, but for scientific, or even moral ends. Do not hire a man who does your work for money, but him who does it for love of it. . . . The ways in which most men get their living, that is, live, are mere makeshifts, and a shirking of the real business of life—chiefly because they do not know, but partly because they do not mean, any better. . . ."

In summing up his views he says: "America is said to be the arena on which the battle of freedom is to be fought; but surely it cannot be freedom in a merely political sense that is meant. Even if we grant that the American has freed himself from a political tyrant, he is still the slave of an economical and moral tyrant. Now that the republic—*the res-publica*—has been settled, it is time to look after the *res-privata*—the private state—to see, as the Roman senate charged its consuls, *'ne quid res-privata detrimenti caperet,'* that the *private* state receive no detriment.

"Do we call this the land of the free? What is it to be free from King George and continue the slaves of King Prejudice? What is it to be born free and not to live free? What is the value of any political freedom, but as a means to moral freedom? Is it a freedom to be slaves, or a freedom to be free, of which we boast? We are a nation of politicians, concerned about the outmost defenses only of freedom. It is our children's children who may perchance be really free. We tax ourselves unjustly. There is a part of us which is not represented. It is taxation without representation. We quarter troops, we quarter fools and cattle of all sorts upon ourselves. We quarter our gross bodies on our poor souls, till the former eat up all the latter's substance. . . .

"Those things which now most engage the attention of men, as politics and the daily routine, are, it is true, vital functions of human society, but should be unconsciously performed, like the corresponding functions of the physical body. They are *infra-*human, a kind of vegetation. I sometimes awake to a half-consciousness of them going on about me, as a man may become conscious of some of the processes of digestion in a morbid state, and so have the dyspepsia, as it is called. It is as if a thinker submitted himself to be rasped by the great gizzard of creation. Politics is, as it were, the gizzard of society, full of grit and gravel, and the two political parties are its two opposite halves—sometimes split into quarters, it may be, which grind on each other. Not only individuals, but states, have thus a confirmed dyspepsia, which expresses itself, you can imagine by what sort of eloquence. Thus our life is not altogether a forgetting, but also, alas! to a great extent, a remembering, of that which we should never have been conscious of, certainly not in our waking hours. Why should we not meet, not always as dyspeptics, to tell our bad dreams, but sometimes as *eu*peptics, to congratulate each other on the ever-glorious morning? I do not make an exorbitant demand, surely."

One of the most penetrating diagnoses of the capitalist culture in the nineteenth century was made by a sociologist, E. Durkheim, who was neither a political nor a religious radical. He states that in modern industrial society the individual and the group have ceased to function satisfactorily; that they live in a condition of "anomie," that is, a lack of meaningful and structuralized social life; that the individual follows more and more "a restless movement, a planless self-development, an aim of living which has no criterion of value and in which happiness lies always in the future, and never in any present achievement." The ambition of man, having the whole world for his customer, becomes unlimited, and he is filled with disgust, with the "futility of endless pursuit." Durkheim points out that only the *political state* survived the French Revolution as a solitary factor of collective organization. As a result, a genuine social order has disappeared, the state emerging as the only collective organizing activity of a social character. The individual, free from all genuine social bonds, finds himself abandoned, isolated, and demoralized.[1] Society becomes *"a disorganized dust of individuals."* [2]

TWENTIETH CENTURY

Turning now to the twentieth century there is also a remarkable similarity in the criticisms and diagnosis of the mental ill health of contemporary society, just as in the nineteenth century, remarkable particularly in view of the fact that it comes from people with different philosophical and political views. Although I leave out from this survey most of the socialist critics of the nineteenth and twentieth centuries, because I shall deal with them separately in the next chapter, I shall begin here with the views of the British socialist, R. H. Tawney, because they are in many ways related to the views expressed in this book. In his classic work, *The Acquisitive Society* [3] (originally published under the title *The Sickness of an Acquisitive Society*), he points to the fact that the principle on which capitalistic society is based, is the domination of man by things. In our society, he

[1] Emil Durkheim, *Le Suicide*, Felix Alcan, Paris, 1897, p. 449.
[2] *Ibid.*, p. 448. (My italics, E.F.)
[3] R. H. Tawney, *The Acquisitive Society*, Harcourt, Brace & Company, Inc., New York, 1920.

says, ". . . even sensible men are persuaded that capital 'employs' labour, such as our pagan ancestors imagined that the other pieces of wood and iron, which they deified in their day, sent their crops, and won their battles. When men have gone so far as to talk as though their idols have come to life, it is time that some-one broke them. Labour consists of persons, capital of things. The only use of things is to be applied to the service of persons." [1] He points out that the worker in modern industry does not give his best energies because he lacks in interest in his work, owing to his nonparticipation in control.[2] He postulates, as the only way out of the crisis of modern society, a change in moral values. It is necessary to assign ". . . to economic activity itself its proper place as the servant, not a master, of society. The burden of our civilization is not merely, as many suppose, that the product of industry is ill-distributed, or its conduct tyrannical, or its opera-tion interrupted by embittered disagreements. It is that industry itself has come to hold a position of exclusive predominance among human interests, which no single interest, and least of all the provision of the material means of existence, is fit to occupy. Like a hypochondriac who is so absorbed in the processes of his own digestion that he goes to his grave before he has begun to live, industrialized communities neglect the very objects for which it is worth while to acquire riches in their feverish preoccupation with the means by which riches can be acquired.

"That obsession by economic issues is as local and transitory as it is repulsive and disturbing. To future generations it will appear as pitiable as the obsession of the seventeenth century by religious quarrels appears to-day; indeed, it is less rational, since the object with which it is concerned is less important. And it is a poison which inflames every wound and turns each trivial

[1] *Ibid.*, p. 99.
[2] *Ibid.*, pp. 106, 107.

scratch into a malignant ulcer. Society will not solve the particular problems of industry which afflict it, until that poison is expelled, and it has learned to see industry itself in the right perspective. If it is to do that, it must rearrange its scale of values. It must regard economic interests as one element in life, not as the whole of life. It must persuade its members to renounce the opportunity of gains which accrue without any corresponding service, because the struggle for them keeps the whole community in a fever. It must so organize industry that the instrumental character of economic activity is emphasized by its subordination to the social purpose for which it is carried on." [1]

One of the most outstanding contemporary students of the industrial civilization in the United States, Elton Mayo, shared, although somewhat more cautiously, Durkheim's viewpoint. "It is true," he said, "that the problem of social disorganization, with its consequent *anomie*, probably exists in a more acute form in Chicago than in other parts of the United States. It is probable that it is a more immediate issue in the United States than in Europe. But it is a problem of order in social development with which the whole world is concerned." [2] Discussing the modern preoccupation with economic activities, Mayo says: "Just as our political and economic studies have for 200 years tended to take account only of the economic functions involved in living, so also in our actual living we have inadvertently allowed pursuit of economic development to lead us in a condition of extensive social disintegration. . . . It is probable that the work a man does represents his most important function in the society; but unless there is some sort of integral social background to his life, he cannot even assign a value to his work. Durkheim's findings in

---

[1] *Ibid.*, pp. 183, 184.
[2] E. Mayo, *The Human Problems of an Industrial Civilization*, The Macmillan Company, New York, 1933, p. 125.

19th century France would seem to apply to 20th century America." [1] Referring to his comprehensive study of the attitude of the Hawthorne workers toward their work, he comes to the following conclusion: "The failure of workers and supervisors to understand their work and working conditions, the wide-spread sense of personal futility is general to the civilized world, and not merely characteristic of Chicago. The belief of the individual in his social function and solidarity with the group—his capacity for collaboration in work—these are disappearing, destroyed in part by rapid scientific and technical advance. With this belief, his sense of security and of well-being also vanishes, and he begins to manifest those exaggerated demands of life which Durkheim has described." [2] Mayo not only agrees with Durkheim in the essential point of his diagnosis, but he also comes to the critical conclusion that in the half century of scientific effort after Durkheim, very little progress has been made in the understanding of the problem. "Whereas" he writes, "in the material and scientific spheres we have been careful to develop knowledge and technique, in the human and socio-political, we have contented ourselves with haphazard guess and opportunist fumbling." [3] And further, ". . . we are faced with the fact, then, that in the important domain of human understanding and control we are ignorant of the facts and their nature; our opportunism in administration and social enquiry has left us incapable of anything but impotent inspection of a cumulative disaster. . . . So we are compelled to wait for the social organism to recover or perish, without adequate medical aid." [4] Speaking more specifically of the backwardness of our political theory, he states: "Political theory has tended to relate itself for the most part to its historic origins;

[1] *Ibid.*, p. 131.
[2] *Ibid.*, p. 159.
[3] *Ibid.*, p. 132.
[4] *Ibid.*, pp. 169, 170.

it has failed to originate and sustain a vigorous enquiry into the changing structure of society. In the meantime the social context, the actual condition of civilized peoples has undergone so great a variety of changes that any mere announcement of the ancient formulae rings hollow and carries no conviction to anyone." [1]

Another thoughtful student of the contemporary social scene, F. Tannenbaum, arrives at conclusions which are not unrelated to those of Tawney, in spite of the fact that Tannenbaum emphasizes the central role of the trade union, in contrast to Tawney's socialist insistence on the direct participation of the workers. Concluding his "Philosophy of Labor," Tannenbaum writes: "The major error of the last century has been the assumption that a total society can be organized upon an economic motive, upon profit. The trade-union has proved that notion to be false. It has demonstrated once again that men do not live by bread alone. Because the corporation can offer only bread or cake, it has proved incompetent to meet the demands for the good life. The union, with all its faults, may yet save the corporation and its great efficiencies by incorporating it into its own natural 'society,' its own cohesive labor force, and by endowing it with the meanings that all real societies possess, meanings that give some substance of idealism to man in his journey between the cradle and the grave. Those meanings cannot be embraced by expanding the economic motive. If the corporation is to survive, it will have to be endowed with a moral role in the world, not merely an economic one. From this point of view, the challenge to management by the trade-union is salutary and hopeful. It is a route, perhaps the only available one, for saving the values of our democratic society, and the contemporary industrial system as well. In some way the corporation and its labor

[1] *Ibid.*, p. 138.

force must become one corporate group and cease to be a house divided and seemingly at war." [1]

Lewis Mumford, with whose writings my own ideas have many points in common, says this about our contemporary civilization: "The most deadly criticism one could make of modern civilization is that apart from its man-made crises and catastrophes, it is not humanly *interesting*. . . .

"In the end, such a civilization can produce only a mass man: incapable of choice, incapable of spontaneous, self-directed activities: at best patient, docile, disciplined to monotonous work to an almost pathetic degree, but increasingly irresponsible as his choices become fewer and fewer: finally, a creature governed mainly by his conditioned reflexes—the ideal type desired, if never quite achieved, by the advertising agency and the sales organizations of modern business, or by the propaganda office and the planning bureaus of totalitarian and quasi-totalitarian governments. The handsomest encomium for such creatures is: 'They do not make trouble'. Their highest virtue is: 'They do not stick their necks out'. Ultimately, such a society produces only two groups of men: the conditioners and the conditioned; the active and the passive barbarians. The exposure of this web of falsehood, self-deception, and emptiness is perhaps what made *Death of a Salesman* so poignant to the metropolitan American audiences that witnessed it.

"Now this mechanical chaos is plainly not self-perpetuating, for it affronts and humiliates the human spirit; and the tighter and more efficient it becomes as a mechanical system, the more stubborn will be the human reaction against it. Eventually, it must drive modern man to blind rebellion, to suicide, or to renewal: and so far it has worked in the first two ways. On this

[1] Frank Tannenbaum, *A Philosophy of Labor*, Alfred A. Knopf, Inc., New York, 1952, p. 168.

analysis, the crisis we now face would be inherent in our culture even if it had not, by some miracle, also unleashed the more active disintegrations that have taken place in recent history." [1]

A. R. Heron, a convinced supporter of Capitalism and a writer with a much more conservative bent than the ones quoted so far, nevertheless comes to critical conclusions which are essentially very close to those of Durkheim and Mayo. In his *Why Men Work*, a 1948 selection of the Executive Book Club of New York, he writes: "It is fantastic to picture a great multitude of workers committing mass suicide because of boredom, a sense of futility, and frustration. But the fantastic nature of the picture disappears when we broaden our concept of suicide beyond the killing of the physical life of the body. The human being who has resigned himself to a life devoid of thinking, ambition, pride, and personal achievement, has resigned himself to the death of attributes which are distinctive elements of human life. Filling a space in the factory or office with his physical body, making motions designed by the minds of others, applying physical strength, or releasing the power of steam or electricity, are not in themselves contributions of the essential abilities of human beings.

"This inadequate demand upon human abilities can be no more forcibly indicated than by reference to modern techniques for the placement of workers. Experience has shown that there are jobs, a startling number of them, which cannot be satisfactorily filled by persons of average or superior intelligence. It is no answer to say that large numbers of persons with inferior intelligence need the jobs. Management shares responsibility with statesmen, ministers, and educators for the improvement of the intelligence of all of us. We shall always be governed in a democ-

---

[1] L. Mumford, *The Conduct of Life*, Harcourt, Brace & Company, New York, 1951, pp. 14 and 16.

racy by the votes of people as people, including those whose native intelligence is low or whose potential mental and spiritual development have been cramped.

"We must never abandon the material benefits we have gained from technology and mass production and specialization of tasks. But we shall never achieve the ideals of America if we create a class of workers denied the satisfactions of significant work. We shall not be able to maintain those ideals if we do not apply every tool of government, education, and industry to the improvement of the human abilities of those who are our rulers —the tens of millions of ordinary men and women. The part of this task assigned to management is the provision of working conditions which will release the creative instinct of every worker, and which will give play to his divine-human ability to think." [1]

After having heard the voices of various social scientists, let us conclude this chapter by listening to three men outside of the field of social science: A. Huxley, A. Schweitzer, and A. Einstein. Huxley's indictment of twentieth-century Capitalism is contained in his *Brave New World*. In this novel (1931), he describes a picture of an automatized world which is clearly insane and yet which only in details and somewhat in degree is different from the reality of 1954. The only alternative he sees is the life of the savage with a religion which is half fertility cult and half penitente ferocity. In a foreword written for the new edition of the *Brave New World* (1946) he writes: "Assuming, then, that we are capable of learning as much from Hiroshima as our forefathers learned from Magdeburg, we may look forward to a period, not indeed of peace, but of limited and only partially ruinous warfare. During that period it may

[1] A. R. Heron, *Why Men Work,* Stanford University Press, Stanford, 1948, pp. 121, 122.

be assumed that nuclear energy will be harnessed to industrial uses. The result, pretty obviously, will be a series of economic and social changes unprecedented in rapidity and completeness. All the existing patterns of human life will be disrupted and new patterns will have to be improvised to conform with the non-human fact of atomic power. Procrustes in modern dress, the nuclear scientist will prepare the bed on which mankind must lie; and if mankind doesn't fit—well, that will be just too bad for mankind. There will have to be some stretching and a bit of amputation—the same sort of stretching and amputation as have been going on ever since applied science really got into its stride, only this time they will be a good deal more drastic than in the past. These far from painless operations will be directed by highly centralized totalitarian governments. Inevitably so; for the immediate future is likely to resemble the immediate past, and in the immediate past rapid technological changes, taking place in a mass-producing economy and among a population predominantly propertyless, have always tended to produce economic and social confusion. To deal with confusion, power has been centralized and government control increased. It is probable that all the world's governments will be more or less completely totalitarian even before the harnessing of atomic energy; that they will be totalitarian during and after the harnessing seems almost certain. *Only a large-scale popular movement toward decentralization and self-help can arrest the present tendency toward statism.*[1] At present there is no sign that such a movement will take place.

"There is, of course, no reason why the new totalitarianisms should resemble the old. Government by clubs and firing squads, by artificial famine, mass imprisonment and mass deportation, is not merely inhumane (nobody cares much about that nowa-

[1] My italics. E.F.

225

days) ; it is demonstrably inefficient—and in an age of advanced technology, inefficiency is the sin against the Holy Ghost. A really efficient totalitarian state would be one in which the all-powerful executive of political bosses and their army of managers control a population of slaves who do not have to be coerced, because they love their servitude. To make them love it is the task assigned, in present-day totalitarian states, to ministries of propaganda, newspaper editors and schoolteachers. But their methods are still crude and unscientific. The old Jesuits' boast that, if they were given the schooling of the child, they could answer for the man's religious opinions, was a product of wishful thinking. And the modern pedagogue is probably rather less efficient at conditioning his pupils' reflexes than were the reverend fathers who educated Voltaire. The greatest triumphs of propaganda have been accomplished, not by doing something, but by refraining from doing. Great is the truth, but still greater, from a practical point of view, is silence about truth. By simply not mentioning certain subjects, by lowering what Mr. Churchill calls an 'iron curtain' between the masses and such facts or arguments as the local political bosses regard as undesirable, totalitarian propagandists have influenced opinion much more effectively than they could have done by the most eloquent denunciations, the most compelling of logical rebuttals. But silence is not enough. If persecution, liquidation and other symptoms of social friction are to be avoided, the positive sides of propaganda must be made as effective as the negative. The most important Manhattan Projects of the future will be vast government-sponsored enquiries into what the politicians and the participating scientists will call "the problem of happiness"—in other words, the problem of making people love their servitude. Without economic security, the love of servitude cannot possibly come into existence; for the sake of brevity, I assume that the all-powerful executive and its managers will succeed in solving the problem of permanent security. But security tends very quickly to be taken for granted. Its achievement is merely a superficial, external revolution. The love of servitude cannot be established except as the result of a deep, personal revolution in human minds and bodies. To bring about that revolution we require, among others, the following discoveries and inventions. First, a greatly improved technique of suggestion—through infant conditioning and, later, with the aid of drugs, such as scopolamine. Second, a fully developed science of human differences, enabling government managers to assign any given individual to his or her proper place in the social and economic hierarchy. (Round pegs in square holes tend to have dangerous thoughts about the social system and to infect others with their discontents.) Third (since reality, however utopian, is something from which people feel the need of taking pretty frequent holidays), a substitute for alcohol and the other narcotics, something at once less harmful and more pleasure-giving than gin or heroin. And fourth (but this would be a long-term project, which would take generations of totalitarian control to bring to a successful conclusion), a foolproof system of eugenics, designed to standardize the human product and so to facilitate the task of the managers. In *Brave New World* this standardization of the human product has been pushed to fantastic, though not perhaps impossible, extremes. Technically and ideologically we are still a long way from bottled babies and Bokanovsky groups of semi-morons. But by A.F. 600, who knows what may not be happening? Meanwhile the other characteristic features of that happier and more stable world—the equivalents of soma and hypnopaedia and the scientific caste system—are probably not more than three or four generations away. Nor does the sexual promiscuity of *Brave New World* seem so very distant. There are already certain American cities in which the number of divorces is equal to the number of marriages. In a few years, no doubt, marriage licenses will be sold like dog licenses, good for a period of twelve months, with no law against changing dogs or keeping more than one animal at a time. As political and economic freedom diminishes, sexual freedom tends compensatingly to increase. And the dictator (unless he needs cannon fodder and families with which to colonize empty or conquered territory) will do well to encourage that freedom. In conjunction with the freedom to daydream under the influence of dope and movies and the radio, it will help to reconcile his subjects to the servitude which is their fate.

"All things considered, it looks as though Utopia were far closer to us than anyone, only fifteen years ago, could have imagined. Then, I projected it six hundred years into the future. To-day, it seems quite possible that the horror may be upon us within a single century. That is, if we refrain from blowing ourselves to smithereens in the interval. Indeed, unless we choose to decentralize and to use applied science, not as the end to which human beings are to be made the means, but as the means to producing a race of free individuals, we have only two alternatives to choose from: either a number of national, militarized totalitarianisms, having as their root the terror of the atomic bomb and as their consequence the destruction of civilization (or, if the warfare is limited, the perpetuation of militarism); or else one supra-national totalitarianism, called into existence by the social chaos resulting from rapid technological progress in general and the atom revolution in particular, and developing, under the need for efficiency and stability, into the welfare-tyranny of Utopia. You pays your money and you takes your choice." [1]

[1] A. Huxley, *Brave New World*, The Vanguard Library, London, 1952, pp. 11–15.

Albert Schweitzer and Albert Einstein, who perhaps more than any living person manifest the highest development of the intellectual and moral traditions of Western culture have this to say on present-day culture.

Albert Schweitzer writes: "A new public opinion must be created privately and unobtrusively. The existing one is maintained by the press, by propaganda, by organization, and by financial and other influences which are at its disposal. This unnatural way of spreading ideas must be opposed by the natural one, which goes from man to man and relies solely on the truth of our thoughts and the hearer's receptiveness for new truth. Unarmed, and following the human spirit's primitive and natural fighting method, it must attack the other, which faces it, as Goliath faced David, in the mighty armour of the age.

"About the struggle which must needs ensue no historical analogy can tell us much. The past has, no doubt, seen the struggle of the free-thinking individual against the fettered spirit of a whole society, but the problem has never presented itself on the scale on which it does to-day, because the fettering of the collective spirit as it is fettered to-day by modern organizations, modern unreflectiveness, and modern popular passions, is a phenomenon without precedent in history.

"Will the man of to-day have strength to carry out what the spirit demands from him, and what the age would like to make impossible?

"In the over-organized societies which in a hundred ways have him in their power, he must somehow become once more an independent personality and so exert influence back upon them. They will use every means to keep him in that condition of impersonality which suits them. They fear personality because the spirit and the truth, which they would like to muzzle, find in it a means of expressing themselves. And their power is, unfortunately, as great as their fear.

"There is a tragic alliance between society as a whole and its economic conditions. With a grim relentlessness those conditions tend to bring up the man of to-day as a being without freedom, without self-collectedness, without independence, in short as a human being so full of deficiencies that he lacks the qualities of humanity. And they are the last things that we can change. Even if it should be granted us that the spirit should begin its work, we shall only slowly and incompletely gain power over these forces. There is, in fact, being demanded from the will that which our conditions of life refuse to allow.

"And how heavy the tasks that the spirit has to take in hand! It has to create the power of understanding the truth that is really true where at present nothing is current but propagandist truth. It has to depose ignoble patriotism, and enthrone the noble kind of patriotism which aims at ends that are worthy of the whole of mankind, in circles where the hopeless issues of past and present political activities keep nationalist passions aglow even among those who in their hearts would fain be free from them. It has to get the fact that civilization is an interest of all men and of humanity as a whole recognized again in places where national civilization is to-day worshipped as an idol, and the notion of a humanity with a common civilization lies broken to fragments. It has to maintain our faith in the civilized State, even though our modern States, spiritually and economically ruined by the war, have no time to think about the tasks of civilization, and dare not devote their attention to anything but how to use every possible means, even those which undermine the conception of justice, to collect money with which to prolong their own existence. It has to unite us by giving us a single ideal of civilized men, and this in a world where one nation has robbed its neighbour of all faith in humanity, idealism, righteousness, reasonableness, and truthfulness, and all alike have come under the domination of powers which are plunging us ever deeper into barbarism. It has to get attention concentrated on civilization while the growing difficulty of making a living absorbs the masses more and more in material cares, and makes all other things seem to them to be mere shadows. It has to give us faith in the possibility of progress while the reaction of the economic on the spiritual becomes more pernicious every day and contributes to an ever growing demoralization. It has to provide us with reasons for hope at a time when not only secular and religious institutions and associations, but the men, too, who are looked upon as leaders, continually fail us, when artists and men of learning show themselves as supporters of barbarism, and notabilities who pass for thinkers, and behave outwardly as such, are revealed, when crises come, as being nothing more than writers and members of academies.

"All these hindrances stand in the path of the will to civilization. A dull despair hovers about us. How well we now understand the men of the Greco-Roman decadence, who stood before events incapable of resistance, and, leaving the world to its fate, withdrew upon their inner selves! Like them, we are bewildered by our experience of life. Like them, we hear enticing voices which say to us that the one thing which can still make life tolerable is to live for the day. We must, we are told, renounce every wish to think or hope about anything beyond our own fate. We must find rest in resignation.

"The recognition that civilization is founded on some sort of theory of the universe, can be restored only through a spiritual awakening, and a will for ethical good in the mass of mankind, compels us to make clear to ourselves those difficulties in the way of a rebirth of civilization which ordinary reflection would overlook. But at the same time it raises us above all considerations of possibility or impossibility. If the ethical spirit provides a sufficient standing ground in the sphere of events for making civilization a reality, then we shall get back to civilization, if we return to a suitable theory of the universe and the convictions to which this properly gives birth." [1]

In a short article, "Why Socialism," Einstein writes: "I have now reached the point where I may indicate briefly what to me constitutes the essence of the crisis of our time. It concerns the relationship of the individual to society. The individual has become more conscious than ever of his dependence upon society. But he does not experience this dependence as a positive asset, as an organic tie, as a protective force, but rather as a threat to his natural rights, or even to his economic existence. Moreover, his position in society is such that the egotistical drives of his make-up are constantly being accentuated, while his social drives, which are by nature weaker, progressively deteriorate. All human beings, whatever their position in society, are suffering from this process of deterioration. Unknowingly prisoners of their own egotism, they feel insecure, lonely, and deprived of the naïve, simple, and unsophisticated enjoyment of life. Man can find meaning in life, short and perilous as it is, only through devoting himself to society." [2]

[1] Quoted from *The Philosophy of Civilization*, by Albert Schweitzer, The Macmillan Company, New York, and A & C Black Ltd., London, England.
[2] A. Einstein, "Why Socialism," in *Monthly Review*, Vol. I, i 1949, pp. 9–15.

VARIOUS ANSWERS

In the nineteenth century men with vision saw the process of decay and dehumanization behind the glamour and wealth and political power of Western society. Some of them were resigned to the necessity of such a turn toward barbarism, others stated an alternative. But whether they took the one or the other position, their criticism was based on a religious-humanistic concept of man and history. By criticizing their own society they transcended it. They were not relativists who said, as long as the society functions it is a sane and good society—and as long as the individual is adjusted to his society he is a sane and healthy individual. Whether we think of Burckhardt or Proudhon, of Tolstoy or Baudelaire, of Marx or Kropotkin, they had a concept of man which was essentially a religious and moral one. Man is the end, and must never be used as a means; material production is for man, not man for material production; the aim of life is the unfolding of man's creative powers; the aim of history is a transformation of society into one governed by justice and truth—these are the principles on which explicitly and implicitly, all criticism of modern Capitalism was based.

These religious-humanistic principles were also the basis for the proposals for a better society. In fact, the main expression of religious enthusiasm in the last two hundred years is to be found exactly in those movements which had broken with traditional religion. Religion as an organization and a profession of dogma was carried on in the churches; religion in the sense of religious fervor and living faith was largely carried on by the anti-religionists.

In order to give more substance to the statements just made, it is necessary to consider some salient features in the development of Christian Western culture. While for the Greeks history had no aim, purpose or end, the Judaeo-Christian concept of history was characterized by the idea that its inherent meaning was the salvation of man. The symbol for this final salvation was the Messiah; the time itself, the Messianic time. There are, however, two different concepts of what constitutes the *eschaton*, the "end of days," the aim of history. One connects the biblical myth of Adam and Eve with the concept of salvation. Briefly stated, the essence of this idea is that originally man was one with nature. There was no conflict between him and nature, or between man and woman. But man also lacked the most essential human trait: that of knowledge of good and evil. Hence he was incapable of free decision and responsibility. The first act of disobedience became also the first act of freedom, thus the beginning of human history. Man is expelled from paradise, he has lost his harmony with nature, he is put on his own feet. But he is weak, his reason is still undeveloped, his power to resist temptation is still small. He has to develop his reason, to grow into full humanity in order to achieve a new harmony with nature, with himself and with his fellow men. The aim of history is the full birth of man, his full humanization. Then "the earth shall be full of the knowledge of the Lord, as the waters cover the sea." All nations will form a single community and swords will be transformed into ploughs. In this concept, God does not perform an act of grace. Man has to go through many errors, he has to sin and to take the consequences. God does not solve his problems for him except by revealing to him the aims of life. Man has to achieve his own salvation, he has to give birth to himself, and at the end of the days, the new harmony, the new peace [1] will be established, the curse pronounced against Adam and Eve will be repealed, as it were, by man's own unfolding in the historical process.

The other Messianic concept of salvation, which became predominant in the Christian Church, is that man can never absolve himself from the corruption he underwent as a consequence of Adam's disobedience. Only God, by an act of grace, can save man, and He saved him by becoming human in the person of Christ, who died the sacrificial death of the Saviour. Man, through the sacraments of the church, becomes a participant in this salvation—and thus obtains the gift of God's grace. The end of history is the second coming of Christ—which is a supernatural and not a historical event.

This tradition continued in that part of the Western world in which the Catholic Church remained dominant. But for the rest of Europe and America in the eighteenth and nineteenth centuries, theological thinking lost more and more in vitality. The age of enlightenment was characterized by its fight against the Church, and clericalism, and the further development by a growing doubt and eventually the negation of all religious concepts. But this negation of religion was only a new form of thought expressing the old religious enthusiasm, especially as far as the meaning and purpose of history was concerned. In the name of reason and happiness, of human dignity and freedom, the Messianic idea found a new expression.

[1] In Hebrew "Schalom" means both harmony (completeness) and peace.

In France, Condorcet, in his *Esquisse d'un Tableau Historique des Progrès de l'Esprit Humain* (1793), laid the foundation for the faith in the eventual perfection of the human race, which would bring about a new era of reason and happiness, and to which there were no limitations. The coming of the Messianic realm was Condorcet's message, which was to influence St. Simon, Comte and Proudhon. Indeed, the fervor of the French Revolution was Messianic fervor in secular language.

In German enlightenment philosophy the same translation from the theological concept of salvation into secular language occurred. Lessing's *Die Erziehung des Menschengeschlechts* became most influential on German, but also on French thinking. To Lessing the future was to be the age of reason and self-realization, brought about by the education of mankind, thus realizing the promise of Christian revelation. Fichte believed in the coming of a spiritual millenium, Hegel in the realization of God's realm in history, thus translating Christian theology into this-worldly philosophy. Hegel's philosophy found its most significant historical continuation in Marx. More clearly perhaps than that of many other enlightenment philosophers, Marx' thought is Messianic-religious, in secular language. All past history is only "prehistory," it is the history of self-alienation; with Socialism the realm of *human* history, of human freedom will be ushered in. The classless society of justice, brotherliness and reason will be the beginning of a new world, toward the formation of which all previous history was moving.[1]

While it is the main purpose of this chapter to present the ideas of Socialism as the most important attempt to find an answer to the ills of Capitalism, I shall first discuss briefly the Totalitarian answers, and one which may be properly called Super-Capitalism.

[1] Cf. K. Löwith, *loc. cit.*, p. 191 ff.

AUTHORITARIAN IDOLATRY

Fascism, Nazism and Stalinism have in common that they offered the atomized individual a new refuge and security. These systems are the culmination of alienation. The individual is made to feel powerless and insignificant, but taught to project all his human powers into the figure of the leader, the state, the "fatherland," to whom he has to submit and whom he has to worship. He escapes from freedom into a new idolatry. All the achievements of individuality and reason, from the late Middle Ages to the nineteenth century are sacrificed on the altars of the new idols. The new systems were built on the most flagrant lies, both with regard to their programs and to their leaders. In their program they claimed to fulfill some sort of Socialism, when what they were doing was the negation of everything that was meant by this word in the socialist tradition. The figures of their leaders only emphasize the great deception. Mussolini, a cowardly braggart, became a symbol for manliness and courage. Hitler, a maniac of destruction, was praised as the builder of a new Germany. Stalin, a cold-blooded, ambitious schemer, was painted as the loving father of his people.

Nevertheless, in spite of the common element, one must not ignore certain important differences between the three forms of dictatorship. Italy, industrially the weakest of the great *Western* European powers, remained relatively weak and powerless in spite of her victory in the First World War. Her upper classes were unwilling to undertake any of the necessary reforms, especially in the agricultural sphere, and her population was seized by a deep dissatisfaction with the status quo. Fascism was to cure the hurt national vanity by its bragging slogans and to channel the resentment of the masses away from its original objectives; at the same time, it wanted to convert Italy into a more advanced industrial power. It failed in all its realistic aims, because Fascism never made a serious attempt to solve the pressing economic and social problems of Italy.

Germany, on the contrary, was the most developed and progressive industrial country in Europe. While Fascism could have had at least an economic function, Nazism had none. It was the insurrection of the lower middle class, and jobless officers and students, based on the demoralization brought about by military defeat and inflation, and more specifically by the mass unemployment during the depression after 1929. But it could not have been victorious without the active support of important sectors of financial and industrial capital, who felt threatened by an ever-increasing dissatisfaction of the masses with the capitalist system. The German Reichstag in the early 1930's had a majority of those parties which partly sincerely, and partly insincerely, had a program of some kind of anti-Capitalism. This threat led important sectors of German Capitalism to support Hitler.

Russia was the exact opposite of Germany. She was industrially the most backward of all the European great powers, just emerging from a semifeudal state, even though her industrial sector in itself was highly developed and centralized. The sudden collapse of the Czarist system had created a vacuum, so that Lenin, disbanding the only other force which could have filled this vacuum, the Constituent Assembly, hoped to be able to jump directly from the semifeudal phase into that of an industrialized socialist system. However, Lenin's policy was not a product of the moment, it was the logical consequence of his political thinking, conceived many years before the outbreak of the Russian revolution. He, like Marx, believed in the historic mission of the working class to emancipate society, but he had little faith in the will and ability of the working class to achieve this aim spontaneously. Only if the working class was led, so he thought, by a small well-disciplined group of professional revolutionaries, only if it was forced by this group to execute the laws of history, as Lenin saw them, could the revolution succeed and be prevented from ending up in a new version of a class society. The crucial point in Lenin's position was the fact that he had no faith in the spontaneous action of the workers and peasants—and he had no faith in them *because he had no faith in man.* It is this lack of faith in man which antiliberal and clerical ideas have in common with Lenin's concept; on the other hand faith in man is the basis for all genuinely progressive movements throughout history; it is the most essential condition of Democracy and of Socialism. Faith in *mankind* without faith in *man* is either insincere or, if sincere, it leads to the very results which we see in the tragic history of the Inquisition, Robespierre's terror and Lenin's dictatorship. Many democratic socialist and socialist revolutionaries saw the dangers in Lenin's concept; nobody saw it more clearly than Rosa Luxemburg. She warned that the choice to be made was between *democratism* and *bureaucratism,* and the development in Russia proved the correctness of her prediction. While an ardent and uncompromising critic of Capitalism, she was a person with an unshakable and profound faith in man. When she and Gustav Landauer were murdered by the soldiers of the German counter-revolution, the humanistic tradition of faith in man was meant to be killed with them. It was this lack of faith in man which made it possible for the authoritarian systems to conquer man, leading him on to have faith in an idol rather than in himself.

Between the exploitation in early Capitalism and that of Stalinism, there is not a small difference; the brutal exploitation of the worker in early Capitalism, even though it was backed by the political power of the state apparatus, did not prevent the rise of new and progressive ideas; in fact, all great socialist ideas had their birth in this very period, a period in which Owenism could flourish and in which the Chartist movement was destroyed by force only after ten years. Indeed, the most reactionary government in Europe, that of the Czar, did not use methods of repression which could be compared with those of Stalinism. Since the brutal destruction of the Kronstadt rebellion, Russia offered no chance for any progressive development, such as even the darkest periods of early Capitalism did. Under Stalin, the Soviet system lost the last remnants of its original socialist intentions; the killing of the Old Guard of Bolsheviks in the thirties was only the final dramatic expression of this fact. In many respects the Stalinist system shows similarities with the earlier phase of European Capitalism, characterized by a quick accumulation of capital and by a ruthless exploitation of the workers, with the difference, however, that political terror is used in place of the economic laws which forced the nineteenth-century worker to accept the economic conditions to which he was exposed.

SUPER-CAPITALISM

Exactly the opposite pole is represented by certain ideas proposed by a group of industrialists in the United States (and also in France), seeking for a solution of the industrial problem. The philosophy of this group, which is united into a "Council of Profit Sharing Industries" is clearly and lucidly expressed in *Incentive Management*, by James F. Lincoln, for the past thirty-eight years the executive head of the Lincoln Electric Company. The thinking of this group starts out on premises which, in some ways, are reminiscent of the above-quoted critics of Capitalism. "The industrialist," writes Lincoln, "*concentrates on machines and neg-*

lects man, who is the producer and developer of the machine and, obviously, has far greater potentialities. He will not consider the fact that undeveloped geniuses are doing manual jobs in his plant where they have neither the opportunity nor are given the incentive to develop themselves to genius *or even to normal intelligence and skill.*" [1] The author feels that the lack of interest of the worker in his work creates dissatisfaction which either leads to a decrease in the productiveness of the worker, or to industrial strife and class struggle. He considers his solution not as an embellishment for our industrial system, but as a matter vital to the survival of Capitalism. "America," he writes, "is at the crossroads in this matter. A decision must be made, and soon. There is much lack of understanding by the people generally, yet they must choose. On their decision rests the future of the United States, and of the individual." [2] He criticizes, quite in contrast to most defenders of the capitalist system, the prevalence of the profit motive in the industrial system. "In industry," he writes, "the goal of the company's operation that is stated in the by-laws is to make a 'profit,' and profit only. There is no one outside of the stockholders, who gets that profit, and few stockholders generally are workers for the company. As long as that is true, the goal of profit will engender no enthusiasm in the workers. That goal will not do; in fact, most workers feel that too much profit is already given to the stockholder." [3]

"He, the worker, resents being fooled by economic theories about paying for the tools of production, when he often sees these costs being frittered away by incompetence and selfishness in high places." [4] These criticisms are very much the same as

[1] J. F. Lincoln, *Incentive Management*, published by the Lincoln Electric Co., Cleveland, 1951, pp. 113, 114. (Italics mine, E.F.)
[2] *Ibid.*, p. 117.
[3] *Ibid.*, pp. 106, 107.
[4] *Ibid.*, p. 108.

they have been made by many socialist critics of Capitalism, and they show a sober and realistic appreciation of the economic and human facts. The philosophy behind it, however, is quite the contrary of socialist ideas. Lincoln is convinced "that development of the individual can only take place in the fiercely competitive game of life." [1] *"Selfishness is the driving force that makes the human race what it is,* for good or evil. Hence, it is the force that we must depend on, and properly guide, if the human race is to progress." [2] He then goes on to differentiate between "stupid" and "intelligent" selfishness, the former being the selfishness that permits man to steal, the latter that causes a man to struggle toward perfection, so that he becomes more prosperous. [3] Discussing the incentives for work, Lincoln states that just as with the amateur athlete the incentive is not money, we can conclude that money is not necessarily an incentive for the industrial workers, nor are short hours, safety, seniority, security and bargaining power an incentive for work. [4] The only potent incentive, according to him, is "recognition of our abilities by our contemporaries and ourselves." [5] As a practical consequence of these ideas, Lincoln suggests a method of industrial organization in which the worker is "rewarded for all the things he does that are of help, and penalized if he does not do as well as others in all these same ways. He is a member of the team, and is rewarded or penalized, depending on what he can do and does do in all opportunities to win the game." [6] In applying this system, ". . . the man is rated by all those who have accurate knowledge of some phase of his work. On this rating, he is rewarded or penalized. This program runs parallel to the write-ups following the playing of a

[1] *Ibid.,* p. 72.
[2] *Ibid.,* p. 89.
[3] *Ibid.,* p. 91.
[4] *Ibid.,* p. 99.
[5] *Ibid.,* p. 101.
[6] *Ibid.,* p. 109.

game, or the selecting of an All-American team. The best man gets the praise and the standing he warrants and craves. In the bonus plan described here, man is rewarded in direct proportion to his contribution to the success of the company. The parallel is obvious. Each man is advanced or retarded in his standing by his current record. He is rated three times per year. The sum of these ratings determines his share in the bonus and advancement. At the time of giving each man his rating, any question that he may want to ask as to why the rating is as it is and how it can be improved is answered in complete detail by the executives responsible." [1] The size of the bonus is determined in this way: 6 per cent of the profit is paid to the stockholders as a dividend. "After the dividend is provided for, we set aside 'seed money' for the future of the company. The amount of this 'seed money' is determined by the directors, based on current operations." [2] The "seed money" is used for expansion and replacement. After these deductions from the profits, all the balance is divided as a bonus among the workers and management. The bonus has represented a total amount of from 20 per cent of wages and salaries per year as a minimum, to a maximum of 28 per cent a year, over the last 16 years. The average total bonus for each employee was around $40,000 in 16 years, that is, $2,500 per year. All workers have, aside from the bonus, the same basic wage rates as those usual for comparable operations. The average employment costs for the employee at the Lincoln factory for 1950 was $7,701, as compared with $3,705 at the General Electric Co. [3] Under this system the Lincoln company, which employs

[1] *Ibid.*, p. 109, 110.
[2] *Ibid.*, p. 111.
[3] Since the bonus is divided among the workers and managers, one would want to know how much of this average figure refers to wages, and how much to the sums paid to higher employees and managers, and also whether the figure for the General Electric Co. refers only to workers, or also to employees in the higher strata of the company bureaucracy.

around 1,000 workers and employees has been very prosperous, and the sales value of products per employee has been about twice as high as that of the rest of the electrical machinery industry. The number of work stoppages in the Lincoln factory between 1934 and 1945 was zero, as against a minimum of 11 to a maximum of 96 in the rest of the electrical machinery industry. The labor turnover rates were more or less only 25 per cent of those of all other manufacturing industries.[1]

The principle involved in incentive management is in one respect drastically different from that of traditional Capitalism. The worker's wages, instead of being independent from the efforts and results of his work, are related to it. He participates in increasing profits, while the stockholder gets a regular income which is not quite as directly related to the earnings of the company.[2] The company records show clearly that this system led to increased productivity of the worker, low labor turnover, and absence of strikes. But while this system differs in one important respect from the concept and practice of traditional Capitalism, it is, at the same time, the expression of some of its most important principles, especially as far as the human aspect is concerned. It is based on the principle of selfishness and competition, of monetary reward as the expression of social recognition, and it does not change essentially the position of the worker in the process of work, as far as the meaningfulness of the work for him is concerned. As Lincoln points out again and again, the model for this system is the football team, a group of men fiercely competing with all others outside of the group, competing with each other within the group, and producing results in this spirit of competitive co-operation. Actually, the

---

[1] cf. Lincoln, *loc. cit.*, p. 254 ff.

[2] It is, however, not unrelated either, since dividends paid per share increased from $2.00 in 1933 to $8.00 in 1941, going back to an average of $6.00 since then.

system of incentive management is the most logical consequence of the capitalistic system. It tends to make every man, the worker and employee as well as the manager, into a small capitalist; it tends to encourage the spirit of competition and selfishness in everybody, to transform Capitalism in such a way that it comprises the whole of the nation.[1]

The profit-sharing system is not as different from traditional capitalistic practices as it pretends to be. It is a glorified form of the piece-work system, combined with a certain disregard for

[1] There are quite a number of enterprises organized in the Council of Profit Sharing Industries, which have a more or less radical plan of profit sharing in their business. Their principles are expressed in the following paragraphs:

"1. The Council defines profit sharing as any procedure under which an employer pays to all employees, in addition to good rates of regular pay, special current or deferred sums, based not only upon individual or group performance, but on the prosperity of the business as a whole.

"2. The Council considers as the essential factor of economic life the human person. A free company must be based on freedom of opportunity for each to achieve his maximum personal development.

"3. The Council holds that profit sharing affords a most significant means of granting workers freedom of opportunity to participate in the rewards of their cooperation with capital and management.

"4. While the Council feels that profit sharing is entirely justified as a principle in its own right, the Council considers well-planned profit sharing to be the best means of developing group cooperation and efficiency.

"5. The Council holds that widespread profit sharing should assist in stabilizing the economy. Flexibility in compensations as well as in prices and profits affords the best insurance of ready adjustment to changing conditions, either upward or downward.

"6. The Council maintains that stabilized prosperity can be maintained only under a fair relationship between prices, pay and profits. It believes that if our free economy is to survive, management must accept the responsibility of trusteeship to see that this relationship prevails.

"7. The Council holds of paramount importance the true spirit of partnership which sound profit sharing engenders. The only solution to industrial strife is the spreading of this spirit. The council is convinced, through the experience of its members, that this approach will be reciprocated by a large body of labor.

"8. The Council is dedicated to the purpose of extending profit sharing in every practical way. At the same time it does not offer profit sharing as a panacea. No policy or plan in the industrial relation field can succeed unless it is well adapted and unless it has behind it the sincere desire of management to be fair and the faith of management in the importance, dignity and response of the human individual."

the importance of the rates of profit paid to the stockholders. In spite of the talk about the "human person," everything, the rating of the work as well as the amount of the worker's bonus and of the dividends, is determined by the management in an autocratic fashion. The essential principle is 'sharing of profits,' not 'sharing of work.' However, even if the principles are not new, the profit-sharing concept is interesting because it is the most logical aim for a super-Capitalism in which the dissatisfaction of the worker is overcome by making him feel that he too is a capitalist, and an active participant in the system.

SOCIALISM

Aside from Fascist or Stalinist authoritarianism and super-Capitalism of the "incentive management" type, the third great reaction to and criticism of Capitalism is the socialist theory. It is essentially a theoretical vision, in contrast to Fascism and Stalinism, which became political and social realities. This is so in spite of the fact that socialist governments were in power for a shorter or longer time in England and in Scandinavian countries, since the majority upon which their power rested was so small that they could not transform society beyond the most tentative beginnings of the realization of their program.

Unfortunately, at the time of this writing the words "Socialism" and "Marxism" have been charged with such an emotional impact that it is difficult to discuss these problems in a calm atmosphere. The association which these words evoke today in many people are those of "materialism," "godlessness," "bloodshed," or the like—briefly, of the bad and evil. One can understand such a reaction only if one appreciates the degree to which words can assume a magical function, and if one takes into account the decrease in reasonable thought, that is to say, in objectivity, which is so characteristic of our age.

The irrational response which is evoked by the words Socialism and Marxism is furthered by an astounding ignorance on the part of most of those who become hysterical when they hear these words. In spite of the fact that all of Marx's and other socialist's writings are available to be read by everybody, most of those who feel most violently about Socialism and Marxism have never read a word by Marx, and many others have only a very superficial knowledge. If this were not so, it would seem impossible that men with some degree of insight and reason could have distorted the idea of Socialism and Marxism to the degree which is current today. Even many Liberals, and those who are relatively free from hysterical reactions, believe that "Marxism" is a system based on the idea that the interest in material gain is the most active power in man, and that it aims at furthering material greed and its satisfaction. If we only remind ourselves that the main argument in favor of Capitalism is the idea that interest in material gain is the main incentive for work, it can easily be seen that the very materialism which is ascribed to Socialism is the most characteristic feature of Capitalism, and if anyone takes the trouble to study the socialist writers with a modicum of objectivity, he will find that their orientation is exactly the opposite, that they criticize Capitalism for its materialism, for its crippling effect on the genuinely human powers in man. Indeed, Socialism in all its various schools can be understood only as one of the most significant, idealistic and moral movements of our age.

Aside from everything else, one cannot help deploring the political stupidity of this misrepresentation of Socialism on the part of the Western democracies. Stalinism won its victories in Russia and Asia by the very appeal which the idea of Socialism has on vast masses of the population of the world. The appeal lies in the very idealism of the socialist concept, in the spiritual and moral encouragement which it gives. Just as Hitler used the word "Socialism" to give added appeal to his racial and nationalistic ideas, Stalin misappropriated the concept of Socialism and of Marxism for the purpose of his propaganda. His claim is false in the essential points. He separated the purely economic aspect of Socialism, that of the socialization of the means of production, from the whole concept of Socialism, and perverted its human and social aims into their opposite. The Stalinist system today, in spite of its state ownership of the means of production, is perhaps closer to the early and purely exploitative forms of Western Capitalism than to any conceivable idea of a socialist society. An obsessional striving for industrial advance, ruthless disregard for the individual and greed for personal power are its mainsprings. By accepting the thesis that Socialism and Marxism are more or less identical with Stalinism, we do the greatest service in the field of propaganda which the Stalinists could wish to obtain. Instead of showing the falsity of their claims, we confirm them. This may not be an important problem in the United States, where socialist concepts have no strong hold on the minds of the people, but it is a very serious problem for Europe and especially for Asia, where the opposite is true. To combat the appeal of Stalinism in those parts of the world, we must uncover this deception, and not confirm it.

There are considerable differences between the various schools of socialist thought, as they have developed since the end of the eighteenth century, and these differences are significant. However, as happens so often in the history of human thought, the arguments between the representatives of the various schools obscure the fact that the common element among the various socialist thinkers is by far greater and more decisive than are the differences.

Socialism as a political movement, and at the same time as a theory dealing with the laws of society and a diagnosis of its ills, may be said to have been started in the French Revolution, by Babeuf. He speaks in favor of the abolition of private ownership of the soil, and demands the common consumption of the fruits of the earth, the abolition of the difference between rich and poor, ruler and ruled. He believes that the time has come for a Republic of the Equals (*égalitaires*), "the great hospitable house (*hospice*) open for all."

In contrast to the relatively simple and primitive theory of Babeuf, Charles Fourier, whose first publication, "Théorie de Quatre Movements," appeared in 1808, offers a most complex and elaborate theory and diagnosis of society. He makes man and his passions a basis of all understanding of society, and believes that a healthy society must serve, not so much the aim of increasing material wealth, as a realization of our basic passion, brotherly love. Among the human passions, he emphasizes particularly the "butterfly passion," man's need for change, which corresponds to the many and diverse potentialities present in every human being. Work should be a pleasure (*"travail attrayant"*) and two daily hours of work should be sufficient. Against the universal organization of great monopolies in all branches of industry, he postulates communal associations in the field of production and consumption, free and voluntary associations in which individualism will combine spontaneously with collectivism. Only in this way can the third historical phase, that of harmony, supersede the two previous ones: that of societies based on relations between slave and master, and that between wage-earners and entrepreneurs.[1]

While Fourier was a theoretician with a somewhat obsessional mind, Robert Owen was a man of practice, manager and owner of one of the best-managed textile mills in Scotland. For Owen,

[1] cf. Charles Fourier, *The Passions of the Human Soul*, with a general introduction by H. Doherty, translated by J. R. Morell, H. Bailliere, London, 1851.

too, the aim of a new society was not primarily that of increasing production, but the improvement of the most precious thing there is, man. Like Fourier's, his thinking is based on psychological considerations of man's character. While men are born with certain characteristic traits, their character is definitely determined only by the circumstances under which they live. If the social conditions of life are satisfactory, man's character will develop its inherent virtues. He believed that men were trained in all previous history only to defend themselves or to destroy others. A new social order must be created, in which men are trained in principles that would permit them to act in union, and to create real and genuine bonds between individuals. Federal groups of three hundred and up to two thousand persons will cover the earth and be organized according to the principle of collective help, within each other, and among each other. In each community, the local government will work in closest harmony with each individual.

An even more drastic condemnation of the principle of authority and hierarchy is to be found in Proudhon's writings. For him the central problem is not the substitution of one political regime for another, but the building of a political order which is expressive of society itself. He sees as the prime cause of all disorders and ills of society the single and hierarchical organization of authority, and he believes: "The limitations of the State's task is a matter of life and death for freedom, both collective and individual."

"Through monopoly," he says, "mankind has taken possession of the globe, and through association it will become its real master." His vision of a new social order is based on the idea of ". . . reciprocity, where all workers instead of working for an entrepreneur who pays them and keeps the products, work for one another and thus collaborate in the making of a common product whose profits they share amongst themselves." What is essential for him is that these associations are free and spontaneous, and not state imposed, like the state-financed social workshops demanded by Louis Blanc. Such a state-controlled system, he says, would mean a number of large associations "in which labour would be regimented and ultimately enslaved through a state policy of Capitalism. What would freedom, universal happiness, civilization, have gained? Nothing. We would merely have exchanged our chains and the social idea would have made no step forward; we would still be under the same arbitrary power, not to say under the same economic fatalism." Nobody has seen the danger which has come to pass under Stalinism more clearly than Proudhon, in the middle of the nineteenth century, as the passage already quoted clearly indicates. He was also aware of the danger of dogmatism, which should prove so disastrous in the development of the Marxist theory, and he expressed it clearly in a letter to Marx. "Let us," he writes, "if you wish, search together for the laws of society, the manner in which they are realized, the method according to which we can discover them, but, for God's sake, after having demolished all dogmas, let us not think of indoctrinating the people ourselves; let us not fall into the contradiction of your compatriot Luther, who began with excommunications and anathemas to found the Protestant theology, after having over-thrown the Catholic theology." [1] Proudhon's thinking is based on an ethical concept in which self-respect is the first maxim of ethics. From self-respect follows respect of one's neighbor as the second maxim of morality. This concern with the inner change in man as the basis of a new social order was expressed by Proudhon in a letter, saying, "The Old World is in a

[1] Quoted from E. Dolleans *Proudhon*, Gallimard, Paris, 1948, p. 96. (My translation, E.F.)

process of dissolution . . . one can change it only by the *integral revolution in the ideas and in the hearts. . . ."* [1]

The same awareness of the dangers of centralization, and the same belief in the productive powers of man, although mixed with a romantic glorification of destruction, is to be found in the writings of Michael Bakunin; in a letter of 1868 he says: "The great teacher of us all, Proudhon, said that the unhappiest combination which might occur, could be that Socialism should unite itself to Absolutism; the striving of the people for economic freedom, and material well-being, through dictatorship and the concentration of all political and social powers in the State. May the future protect us from the favours of despotism; but may it preserve us from the unhappy consequences and stultifications of indoctrinated, or State Socialism. . . . Nothing living and human can prosper without freedom, and a form of Socialism which would do away with freedom, or which would not recognize it as the sole creative principle and basis, would lead us directly into slavery and bestiality."

Fifty years after Proudhon's letter to Marx, Peter Kropotkin summed up his idea of Socialism in the statement that the fullest development of individuality "will combine with the highest development of voluntary association in all its aspects, in all possible degrees, and for all possible purposes; an association that is always changing, that bears in itself the elements of its own duration, that takes on the forms which best correspond at any given moment to the manifold strivings of all." Kropotkin, like many of his socialist predecessors stressed the inherent tendencies for co-operation and mutual help present in man and in the animal kingdom.

Following the humanistic and ethical thought of Kropotkin was one of the last great representatives of anarchist thought, Gustav

[1] Letter to Jules Michelet, (January 1860) quoted in E. Dolleans, *loc. cit.*, p 7 (Italics mine, E.F.)

Landauer. Referring to Proudhon, he said that social revolution bears no resemblance at all to political revolution; that "although it cannot come alive and remain living without a good deal of the latter, it is nevertheless a peaceful structure, an organizing of new spirit *for* new spirit, and nothing else." He defined as the task of the socialists and their movement: "to loosen the hardening of hearts so that what lies buried may rise to the surface: so that what truly lives yet now seems dead may emerge and grow light." [1] [2]

The discussion of the theories of Marx and Engels requires more space than that of the other socialist thinkers mentioned above: partly because their theories are more complex, covering a wider range, and are not without contradictions, partly because the Marxian school of Socialism has become the dominant form which socialist thought has assumed in the world.

As with all other socialists, Marx's basic concern is man. "To be radical," he once wrote, "means to go to the root, and the root —is man himself." [3] The history of the world is nothing but the creation of man, is the history of the birth of man.[3] But all history is also the history of man's alienation from himself, from his own human powers; "the consolidation of our own product to an objective force above us, outgrowing our control, defeating our expectations, annihilating our calculations is one of the main factors in all previous historical development." Man has been the *object* of circumstances, he must become the *subject*, so that "man be-

---

[1] Quoted from M. Buber, *Paths in Utopia*, The Macmillan Company, New York, 1950, p. 48.

[2] The Socialist Revolutionary party in Russia adhered to a concept of Socialism which contained many elements to be found in the aforementioned socialist schools, rather than in those of Marxism. cf. I. N. Steinberg, *In the Workshop of the Revolution*, Rinehart & Company, Inc., New York, 1953.

[3] cf. "Nationalökonomie und Philosophie," published by S. Landshut, A. Kröner Verlag, Stuttgart, 1953, in Karl Marx, *Die Frühschriften*, p. 247. (My translation, E.F.)

comes the highest being for man." Freedom, for Marx, is not only freedom from political oppressors, but the freedom from the domination of man by things and circumstances. The free man is the rich man, but not the man rich in an economic sense, but rich in the human sense. The wealthy man, for Marx, is the man who *is* much, and not the one who *has* much.[1]

The analysis of society and of the historical process must begin with man, not with an abstraction, but with the real, concrete man, in his physiological and psychological qualities. It must begin with a concept of the essence of man, and the study of economics and of society serves only the purpose of understanding how circumstances have crippled man, how he has become alienated from himself and his powers. The nature of man cannot be deduced from the specific manifestation of human nature as it is engendered by the capitalist system. Our aim must be to know what is good for man. But, says Marx, "to know what is useful for a dog one must study dog nature. This nature itself is not to be deduced from the principle of utility. Applying this to man, he that would criticise all human acts, movements, relations, etc., by the principle of utility, must first deal with human nature in general, and then with human nature as modified in each historical epoch. Bentham makes short work of it. With the direst naïveté, he takes the modern shopkeeper, especially the English shopkeeper, as the normal man." [2]

The aim of the development of man, for Marx, is a new harmony between man and man, and between man and nature, a development in which man's relatedness to his fellow man will correspond to his most important human need. Socialism, for him, is "an association in which the free development of each is the condition

[1] *loc. cit., Die Frühschriften*, p. 243 ff.
[2] Karl Marx, *Capital*, translated from the third German edition, by S. Moore and E. Aveling, The Modern Library, Random House, Inc., New York, I, p. 688, footnote.

for the free development of all," a society in which "the full and free development of each individual becomes the ruling principle." This aim he calls the realization of naturalism, and of humanism, and states that it is different "from idealism as well as from materialism, and yet combines the truth in both of them." [1]

How does Marx think this "emancipation of man" can be attained? His solution is based on the idea that in the capitalistic mode of production the process of self-alienation has reached its peak, because man's physical energy has become a commodity, hence man has become a thing. The working class, he says, is the most alienated class of the population, and for this very reason the one which will lead the fight for human emancipation. In the socialization of the means of production he sees the condition for the transformation of man into an active and responsible participant in the social and economic process, and for the overcoming of the split between the individual and the social nature of man. "Only when man has recognized and organized his 'forces propres' as social forces (it is therefore not necessary, as Rousseau thinks, to change man's nature, to deprive him of his 'forces propres,' and give him new ones of a social character) and, consequently, no longer cuts off his social power from himself in the form of political power (*i.e.*, no longer establishes the state as the sphere of organized rule), only then will the emancipation of mankind be achieved." [2]

Marx assumes that if the worker is not "employed" any more, the nature and character of his work process will change. Work will become a meaningful expression of human powers, rather than meaningless drudgery. How important this new concept of work was for Marx, becomes clear when we consider that he went so far as to criticize the proposal for complete abolishment of child

[1] *Ibid.*, p. 273.
[2] Karl Marx, *On the Jewish Question.*

labor in the Gotha Program of the German Socialist Party.[1] While he was, of course, against the exploitation of children, he opposed the principle that children should not work at all, but demanded that education should be combined with manual labor. "From the factory system budded," he writes, "as Robert Owen has shown us in detail, the germ of the education of the future, an education that will, in the education of every child over a given age, combine productive labour with instruction and humanistics, not only as one of the methods of adding to the efficiency of production, but as the only method of producing fully developed human beings." [2] To Marx, as to Fourier, work must become attractive and correspond to the needs and desires of man. For this reason, he suggests, as Fourier and others did, that nobody should become specialized in one particular kind of work, but should work in different occupations, corresponding to his different interests and potentialities.

Marx saw in the economic transformation of society from Capitalism to Socialism the decisive means for the liberation and emancipation of men, for a "true democracy." While in his later writings the discussion of economics plays a greater role than that of man and his human needs, the economic sphere became at no point an end in itself, and never ceased to be a *means* for satisfying human needs. This becomes particularly clear in his discussion of what he calls "vulgar Communism," by which he means a Communism in which the exclusive emphasis is on the abolition of private property in the means of production. "Physical, immediate property remains for it [vulgar Communism] the only purpose of life and existence; the quality of the work is not changed, but only extended to all human beings; . . . This Communism

---

[1] On this point, I am much indebted to G. Fuchs for his comments and suggestions.
[2] Karl Marx, *Capital*, translated from the third German edition by S. Moore and E. Aveling, New York, 1889, p. 489.

by negating the personality of man throughout is only the consequent expression of private property which is, exactly, the negation of man. . . . The vulgar communist is only the perfection of envy, and of the leveling process on the basis of an imagined minimum. . . . How little this abolition of private property is a real appropriation [of human powers] is proven by the abstract negation of the whole world of education and civilization; the return to the unnatural simplicity of the poor man is not a step *beyond* private property, but a stage which has not even arrived at private property." [1]

Much more complex, and in many ways contradictory, are the views of Marx and Engels on the question of the State. There is no doubt that Marx and Engels were of the opinion that the aim of Socialism was not only a classless society, but a stateless society, stateless at least in the sense, as Engels put it, that the State would have the function of the "administration of things," and not that of the "government of people." Engels said, in 1874, quite in line with the formulation Marx gave in the report of the commission to examine the activities of the Bakuninists in 1872 "that all socialists were agreed that the State would wither away as a result of victorious Socialism." These anti-state views of Marx and Engels, and their opposition to a centralized form of political authority found a particularly clear expression in Marx's statements on the Paris Commune. In his address to the General Council of the International on the civil war in France, Marx stressed the necessity of decentralization, in place of a centralized State power, the origins of which lie in the principle of the absolute monarchy. There would be a largely decentralized community. "The few, but important, functions still left over for a Central Government were to be transferred to communal, *i.e.*, strictly answerable officials. . . . The communal constitution would have rendered up

[1] *Ibid.*, p. 233, 234.

to the body social all the powers which have hitherto been devoured by the parasitic excrescence of the 'State,' which fattens on society and inhibits its free movement." He sees in the Commune "the finally discovered political form, in whose sign the economic liberation of labour can march forward." The Commune wanted "to make individual property a truth, by converting the means of production, land and capital into the mere tools of free and associated labour, and labour amalgamated in Producer Cooperatives at that." [1]

Eduard Bernstein pointed out the similarity between these concepts of Marx with the antistatist, and anticentralistic views of Proudhon, while Lenin claimed that Marx's comments in no way indicate his favoring of decentralization. It seems that both Bernstein and Lenin were right in their interpretation of the Marx-Engels position, and that the solution of the contradiction lies in the fact that Marx was for decentralization and the withering of the state as the aim for which Socialism should strive, and at which it would eventually arrive, but he thought that this could happen only *after* and not *before* the working class had seized political power and transformed the state. The seizure of the state was, for Marx, the means which was necessary to arrive at the end, its abolition.

Nevertheless, if one considers Marx's activities in the First International, his dogmatic and intolerant attitude to everybody who disagreed with him in the slightest, there can be little doubt that Lenin's centralist interpretation of Marx did no injustice to Marx, even though Marx's decentralist agreement with Proudhon was also a genuine part of his views and doctrines. In this very centralism of Marx lies the basis for the tragic development of the socialist idea in Russia. While Lenin may have at least hoped for the

[1] Quoted from M. Buber, *Paths in Utopia*, The Macmillan Company, New York, 1950, pp. 86, 87.

eventual achievement of decentralization, an idea which in fact was manifest in the concept of the Soviets, where the decision making was rooted in the smallest and most concrete level of decentralized groups, Stalinism developed one side of the contradiction, the principle of centralization, into the practice of the most ruthless State organization the modern world has known, surpassing even the centralization principle which Fascism and Nazism followed.

The contradiction in Marx goes deeper than is apparent in the contradiction between the principles of centralization and decentralization. On the one hand Marx, like all other socialists, was convinced that the emancipation of man was not primarily a political, but an economic and social question; that the answer to freedom was not to be found in the change of the political form of the state, but in the economic and social transformation of society. On the other hand, and in spite of their own theories, Marx and Engels were in many ways caught in the traditional concept of the dominance of the political over the socio-economic spheres. They could not free themselves from the traditional view of the importance of the state and political power, from the idea of the primary significance of mere political change, an idea which had been the guiding principle of the great middle-class revolutions of the seventeenth and eighteenth centuries. In this respect Marx and Engels were much more "bourgeois" thinkers than were men like Proudhon, Bakunin, Kropotkin and Landauer. Paradoxical as it sounds, the Leninist development of Socialism represents a regression to the bourgeois concepts of the state and of political power, rather than the new socialist concept as it was expressed so much more clearly by Owen, Proudhon and others. This paradox in Marx's thinking has been clearly expressed by Buber: "Marx," he writes, "accepted these essential components of the commune-idea but without weighing them up against his own centralism and deciding between them. That he apparently did not see the profound problem that this opens up is due to the hegemony of the political point of view; a hegemony which persisted everywhere for him as far as it concerned the revolution, its preparation and its effects. Of the three modes of thinking in public matters—the economic, the social and the political—Marx exercised the first with methodical mastery, devoted himself with passion to the third, but—absurd as it may sound in the ears of the unqualified Marxist—only very seldom did he come into more intimate contact with the second, and it never became a deciding factor for him." [1]

Closely related to Marx's centralism is his attitude toward revolutionary action. While it is true that Marx and Engels admitted that socialist control of the state must not be necessarily acquired by force and revolution (as for instance, in England and the United States), it is equally true that on the whole they believed that the working class, in order to obtain their aims, had to seize power by a revolution. In fact, they were in favor of universal military service, and sometimes of international wars, as means which would facilitate the revolutionary seizure of power. Our generation has witnessed the tragic results of force and dictatorship in Russia; we have seen that the application of force within society is as destructive of human welfare as its application in international relations in the form of war. But when today Marx is accused primarily for his advocation of force and revolution, this is a twisting of facts. The idea of political revolution is not a specifically Marxist, or socialist idea, but it is the traditional idea of the middle class, bourgeois society in the last three hundred years. Because of the fact that the middle class believed that abolition of the political power vested in a monarchy, and the seizure of political power by the people was the solution

[1] Buber, *loc. cit.*, pp. 95, 96.

of the social problem, political revolution was seen as a means to the achievement of freedom. Our modern democracy is a result of force and revolution, the Kerensky revolution of 1917 and the German revolution of 1918 were warmly greeted in the Western democratic countries. It is the tragic mistake of Marx, a mistake which contributed to the development of Stalinism, that he had not freed himself from the traditional overevaluation of political power and force; but these ideas were part of the previous heritage, and not of the new socialist concept.

Even a brief discussion of Marx would be incomplete without a reference to his theory of historical materialism. In the history of thought this theory is probably the most lasting and important contribution of Marx to the understanding of the laws governing society. His premise is that before man can engage in any kind of cultural activity, he must produce the means for his physical subsistence. The ways in which he produces and consumes are determined by a number of objective conditions: his own physiological constitution, the productive powers which he has at his disposal and which, in turn, are conditioned by the fertility of the soil, natural resources, communications and the techniques which he develops. Marx postulated that the material conditions of man determine his mode of production and consumption, and that these in turn, determine his socio-political organization, his practice of life, and eventually his mode of thought and feeling. The widespread misunderstanding of this theory was to interpret it as if Marx had meant that the *striving for gain* was the main motive in man. Actually, this is the dominant view expressed in capitalistic thinking, a view which has stressed again and again that the main incentive for man's work is his interest in monetary rewards. Marx's concept of the significance of the economic factor was not a *psychological* one, namely, an economic motivation in a *subjective* sense; it was a *sociological* one, in which the economic development was the *objective* condition for the cultural development.[1] His main criticism of Capitalism was exactly that it had crippled man by the preponderance of economic interests, and Socialism for him was a society in which man would be freed from this domination by a more rational and hence productive form of economic organization. Marx's materialism was essentially different from the materialism which was prevalent in the nineteenth century. In the latter type of materialism one understood spiritual phenomena as being *caused* by material phenomena. Thus, for instance, the extreme representatives of this kind of materialism believed that thought was a product of brain activity, just "as urine is a product of kidney activity." Marx's view, on the other hand was, that the mental and spiritual phenomenon must be understood as an outcome of the whole practice of life, as the result of the kind of relatedness of the individual to his fellow men and to nature. Marx, in his dialectic method, overcame the materialism of the nineteenth century and developed a truly dynamic and holistic theory based on man's *activity*, rather than on his *physiology*.

The theory of historical materialism offers important scientific concepts for the understanding of the laws of history; it would have become more fruitful had the followers of Marx developed it further rather than permitting it to become bogged down in a sterile dogmatism. The point of development would have been to recognize that Marx and Engels had only made a first step, that of seeing the correlation between the development of economy and culture. Marx had underestimated the complexity of human passions. He had not sufficiently recognized that human nature has itself needs and laws which are in constant interaction with the

[1] cf. to this point my discussion in *Zur Aufgabe einer Analytischen Sozialpsychologie* in Ztsch. f. Sozialforschung, Leipzig, 1932, and J. A. Schumpeter's discussion of Marxism in *Capitalism, Socialism and Democracy*, Harper and Brothers, New York, 1947, pp. 11, 12.

economic conditions which shape historical development; [1] lacking in satisfactory psychological insights, he did not have a sufficient concept of human character, and was not aware of the fact that while man was shaped by the form of social and economic organization, he in turn also molded it. He did not sufficiently see the passions and strivings which are rooted in man's nature, and in the conditions of his existence, and which are in themselves the most powerful driving force for human development. But these deficiencies are limitations of one-sidedness, as we find them in every productive scientific concept, and Marx and Engels themselves were aware of these limitations. Engels expressed this awareness in a well-known letter, in which he said that because of the newness of their discovery, Marx and he had not paid sufficient attention to the fact that history was not only determined by economic conditions, but that cultural factors in turn also influenced the economic basis of society.

Marx's own preoccupation became more and more that with the purely economic analysis of Capitalism. The significance of his economic theory is not altered by the fact that his basic assumptions and predictions were only partly right and to a considerable extent mistaken, the latter especially as far as his assumption of the necessity of the (relative) deterioration of the working class is concerned. He was also wrong in his romantic idealization of the working class, which was a result of a purely theoretical scheme rather than of an observation of the human reality of the working class. But whatever its defects, his economic theory and penetrating analysis of the economic structure of Capitalism constitutes a definite progress over all other socialist theories from a scientific viewpoint.

However, this strength was at the same time its weakness. While

---

[1] cf. my analysis of this interaction in *Escape from Freedom*, Rinehart & Company, New York, 1941.

Marx started his economic analysis with the intention of discovering the conditions for the alienation of man, and while he believed that this would require only a relatively short study, he spent the greater part of his scientific work almost exclusively with economic analysis, and while he never lost sight of the aim —the emancipation of man—both the criticism of Capitalism and the socialist aim in *human terms* became more and more overgrown by economic considerations. He did not recognize the irrational forces in man which make him afraid of freedom, and which produce his lust for power and his destructiveness. On the contrary, underlying his concept of man was the implicit assumption of man's natural goodness, which would assert itself as soon as the crippling economic shackles were released. The famous statement at the end of the Communist Manifesto that the workers "have nothing to lose but their chains," contains a profound psychological error. With their chains they have also to lose all those irrational needs and satisfactions which were originated while they were wearing the chains. In this respect, Marx and Engels never transcended the naïve optimism of the eighteenth century.

This underestimation of the complexity of human passions led to the three most dangerous errors in Marx's thinking. First of all, to his neglect of the *moral* factor in man. Just because he assumed that the goodness of man would assert itself automatically when the economic changes had been achieved, he did not see that a better society could not be brought into life by people who had not undergone a moral change within themselves. He paid no attention, at least not explicitly, to the necessity of a new moral orientation, without which all political and economic changes are futile.

The second error, stemming from the same source, was Marx's grotesque misjudgment of the chances for the realization of Socialism. In contrast to men like Proudhon and Bakunin (and later on, Jack London in his "Iron Heel"), who foresaw the darkness which would envelop the Western world before new light would shine, Marx and Engels believed in the immediate advent of the "good society," and were only dimly aware of the possibility of a new barbarism in the form of communist and fascist authoritarianism and wars of unheard of destructiveness. This unrealistic misapprehension was responsible for many of the theoretical and political errors in Marx's and Engels's thinking, and it was the basis for the destruction of Socialism which began with Lenin.

The third error was Marx's concept that the socialization of the means of production was not only the *necessary*, but also the *sufficient* condition for the transformation of the capitalist into a socialist co-operative society. At the bottom of this error is again his oversimplified, overoptimistic, rationalistic picture of man. Just as Freud believed that freeing man from unnatural and overstrict sexual taboos would lead to mental health, Marx believed that the emancipation from exploitation would automatically produce free and co-operative beings. He was as optimistic about the immediate effect of changes in environmental factors as the encyclopedists of the eighteenth century had been, and had little appreciation for the power of irrational and destructive passions which were not transformed from one day to another by economic changes. Freud, after the experience of the First World War, came to see this strength of destructiveness, and changed his whole system drastically by accepting the drive for destruction as being equally strong and as ineradicable as Eros. Marx never came to such an awareness, and never changed his simple formula of socialization of the means of production as a straight way to the socialist aim.

The other source for this error was his overevaluation of political and economic arrangements to which I have pointed above. He was curiously unrealistic in ignoring the fact that it makes very little difference to the personality of the worker whether the enterprise is owned by the "people"—the State—a Government bureaucracy, or by the private bureaucracy hired by the stockholders. He did not see, quite in contrast to his own theoretical thought, that the only things that matter are the actual and realistic conditions of work, the relation of the worker to his work, to his fellow workers, and to those directing the enterprise.

In the later years of his life, Marx seems to have been ready to make certain changes in his theory. The most important one probably under the influence of Bachofen's and Morgan's work, led him to believe that the primitive agrarian community based on co-operation and common property in the land was a potent form of social organization, which could lead directly into higher forms of socialization without having to go through the phase of capitalistic production. He expressed this belief in his answer to Vera Zazulich, who asked him about his attitude toward the "mir," the old forms of agricultural community in Russia. G. Fuchs has pointed out [1] the great significance of this change in Marx's theory, and also the fact that Marx, in the last eight years of his life, was disappointed and discouraged, sensing the failure of his revolutionary hopes. Engels recognized, as I have mentioned above, the failure to pay enough attention to the power of ideas in their theory of historical materialism, but it was not given to Marx or to Engels to make the necessary drastic revisions in their system.

For us in the middle of the twentieth century, it is very easy to recognize Marx's fallacy. We have seen the tragic illustration of this fallacy occurring in Russia. While Stalinism proved that a socialist economy can operate successfully from an economic viewpoint, it also proved that it is in itself by no means bound to create a spirit of equality and co-operation; it showed that the owner-

[1] In personal communications.

ship of the means of production by "the people" can become the ideological cloak for the exploitation of the people by an industrial, military and political bureaucracy. The socialization of certain industries in England, undertaken by the Labour Government tends to show that to the British miner or worker in the steel or chemical industries it makes very little difference who appoints the managers of his enterprise, since the actual and realistic conditions of his work remain the same.

Summing up, it can be said that the ultimate aims of Marxist Socialism were essentially the same as those of the other socialist schools: emancipating man from domination and exploitation by man, freeing him from the preponderance of the economic realm, restoring him as the supreme aim of social life, creating a new unity between man and man, and man and nature. The errors of Marx and Engels, their overestimation of political and legal factors, their naïve optimism, their centralistic orientation, were due to the fact that they were much more rooted in the middle-class tradition of the eighteenth and nineteenth centuries, both psychologically and intellectually than men like Fourier, Owen, Proudhon and Kropotkin.

Marx's errors were to become important historically because the Marxist concept of Socialism became victorious in the European Continental labor movement. The successors of Marx and Engels in the European Labour Movement were so much under the influence of Marx's authority, that they did not develop the theory further, but largely repeated the old formulae with an ever-increasing sterility.

After the first World War, the Marxist labor movement became strictly divided into hostile camps. Its Social Democratic wing, after the moral collapse during the first World War, became more and more a party representing the purely economic interests of the working class, together with the trade unions from whom it, in turn, depended. It carried on the Marxist formula of "the socialization of the means of production," like a ritual to be pronounced by the party priests on the proper occasions. The Communist wing took a jump of despair, trying to build a socialist society on nothing except seizure of power, and socialization of the means of production; the results of this jump led to more frightful results than did the loss of faith in the Social Democratic parties.

Contradictory as the development of these two wings of Marxist Socialism is, they have certain elements in common. First, the deep disillusionment and despondency with regard to the over-optimistic hopes which were inherent in the earlier phase of Marxism. In the Right Wing, this disillusionment often led to the acceptance of nationalism, to the abandonment of a genuine socialist vision, and of any radical criticism of capitalistic society. The same disillusionment led the Communist Wing, under Lenin, to an act of despair, to a concentration of all efforts into political and purely economic realms, an emphasis which by its neglect of the social sphere was the complete contradiction of the very essence of socialist theory.

The other point which both wings of the Marxist movement have in common is their (in the case of Russia) complete neglect of man. The criticism of Capitalism became entirely a criticism from an economic standpoint. In the nineteenth century, when the working class suffered from ruthless exploitation and lived below the standard of dignified existence, this criticism was justified. With the development of Capitalism in the twentieth century, it became more and more obsolete, yet it is only a logical consequence of this attitude that the Stalinist bureaucracy in Russia is still feeding the population with the nonsense that workers in capitalistic countries are terribly impoverished and lacking any decent basis for subsistence. The concept of Socialism deteriorated more and more; in Russia, into the formula that Socialism meant state ownership of the means of production. In the Western countries, Socialism tended more and more to mean higher wages for the workers, and to lose its messianic pathos, its appeal to the deepest longings and needs of man. I say intentionally that it "tended" to because Socialism has by no means completely lost its humanistic and religious pathos. It has, even after 1914, been the rallying moral idea for millions of European workers and intellectuals, an expression of their hope for the liberation of man, for the establishment of new moral values, for the realization of human solidarity. The sharp criticism voiced in the foregoing pages was meant primarily to accentuate the necessity that Democratic Socialism must return to, and concentrate on the *human* aspects of the social problem; must criticize Capitalism from the standpoint of what it does to the human qualities of man, to his soul and his spirit, and must consider any vision of Socialism in human terms, asking in what way a socialist society will contribute toward ending the alienation of man, the idolatry of economy and of the state.

· 8 ·

ROADS TO SANITY

GENERAL CONSIDERATIONS

In the various critical analyses of Capitalism we find remarkable agreement. While it is true that the Capitalism of the nineteenth century was criticized for its neglect of the material welfare of the workers, this was never the main criticism. What Owen and Proudhon, Tolstoy and Bakunin, Durkheim and Marx, Einstein and Schweitzer talk about is *man,* and what happens to him in our industrial system. Although they express it in different concepts, they all find that man has lost his central place, that he has been made an instrument for the purposes of economic aims, that he has been estranged from, and has lost the concrete relatedness to, his fellow men and to nature, that he has ceased to have a meaningful life. I have tried to express the same idea by elaborating on the concept of alienation and by showing psychologically what the psychological results of alienation are; that man regresses to a receptive and marketing orientation and ceases to be productive; that he loses his sense of self, becomes dependent on approval, hence tends to conform and yet to feel insecure; he is dissatisfied, bored, and anxious, and spends most of his energy in the attempt to

270

compensate for or just to cover up this anxiety. His intelligence is excellent, his reason deteriorates and in view of his technical powers he is seriously endangering the existence of civilization, and even of the human race.

If we turn to views about the *causes* for this development, we find less agreement than in the diagnosis of the illness itself. While the early nineteenth century was still prone to see the causes of all evil in the lack of *political* freedom, and especially of universal suffrage, the socialists, and especially the Marxists stressed the significance of economic factors. They believed that the alienation of man resulted from his role as an object of exploitation and use. Thinkers like Tolstoy and Burckhardt on the other hand, stressed the spiritual and moral impoverishment as the cause of Western man's decay; Freud believed that modern man's trouble was the over-repression of his instinctual drives and the resulting neurotic manifestations. But any explanation which analyzes one sector to the exclusion of others is unbalanced, and thus wrong. The socio-economic, spiritual and psychological explanations look at the same phenomenon from different aspects, and the very task of a theoretical analysis is to see how these different aspects are inter-related, and how they interact.

What holds true for the causes holds, of course, true for the remedies by which modern man's defect can be cured. If I believe that "the" cause of the illness is economic, *or* spiritual, *or* psychological, I necessarily believe that remedying "the" cause leads to sanity. On the other hand, if I see how the various aspects are interrelated, I shall arrive at the conclusion that sanity and mental health can be attained only by simultaneous changes in the sphere of industrial and political organization, of spiritual and philosophical orientation, of character structure, and of cultural activities. The concentration of effort in any of these spheres, to the exclusion or neglect of others, is destructive of *all* change. In fact, here seems to lie one of the most important obstacles to the progress of mankind. Christianity has preached spiritual renewal, neglecting the changes in the social order without which spiritual renewal must remain ineffective for the majority of people. The age of enlightenment has postulated as the highest norms independent judgment and reason; it preached political equality without seeing that political equality could not lead to the realization of the brotherhood of man if it was not accompanied by a fundamental change in the social-economic organization. Socialism, and especially Marxism, has stressed the necessity for social and economic changes, and neglected the necessity of the inner change in human beings, without which economic change can never lead to the "good society." Each of these great reform movements of the last two thousand years has emphasized one sector of life to the exclusion of the others; their proposals for reform and renewal were radical—but their results were almost complete failure. The preaching of the Gospel led to the establishment of the Catholic Church; the teachings of the rationalists of the eighteenth century to Robespierre and Napoleon; the doctrines of Marx to Stalin. The results could hardly have been different. Man is a unit; his thinking, feeling, and his practice of life are inseparably connected. He cannot be free in his thought when he is not free emotionally; and he cannot be free emotionally if he is dependent and unfree in his practice of life, in his economic and social relations. Trying to advance radically in one sector to the exclusion of others must necessarily lead to the result to which it did lead, namely, that the radical demands in one sphere are fulfilled only by a few individuals, while for the majority they become formulae and rituals, serving to cover up the fact that in other spheres nothing has changed. Undoubtedly *one* step of integrated progress in all spheres of life will have more far-reaching and more lasting results for the progress of the human race than a hundred steps preached —and even for a short while lived—in only one isolated sphere.

Several thousands of years of failure in "isolated progress" should be a rather convincing lesson.

Closely related to this problem is that of *radicalism* and *reform*, which seems to form such a dividing line between various political solutions. Yet, a closer analysis can show that this differentiation as it is usually conceived of is deceptive. There is reform and reform; reform can be *radical*, that is, going to the roots, or it can be superficial, trying to patch up symptoms without touching the causes. Reform which is not radical, in this sense, never accomplishes its ends and eventually ends up in the opposite direction. So-called "radicalism" on the other hand, which believes that we can solve problems by force, when observation, patience and continuous activity is required, is as unrealistic and fictitious as reform. Historically speaking, they both often lead to the same result. The revolution of the Bolsheviks led to Stalinism, the reform of the right wing Social Democrats in Germany, led to Hitler. The true criterion of reform is not its tempo but its realism, its true "radicalism"; it is the question whether it goes to the roots and attempts to change causes—or whether it remains on the surface and attempts to deal only with symptoms.

If this chapter is to discuss roads to sanity, that is, methods of cure, we had better pause here for a moment and ask ourselves what we know about the nature of cure in cases of individual mental diseases. The cure of social pathology must follow the same principle, since it is the pathology of so many human beings, and not of an entity beyond or apart from individuals.

The conditions for the cure of individual pathology are mainly the following:

1.) A development must have occurred which is contrary to the proper functioning of the psyche. In Freud's theory this means that the libido has failed to develop normally and that as a result, symptoms are produced. In the frame of reference of humanistic psychoanalysis, the causes of pathology lie in the failure to develop a productive orientation, a failure which results in the development of irrational passions, especially of incestuous, destructive and exploitative strivings. The *fact* of suffering, whether it is conscious or unconscious, resulting from the failure of normal development, produces a dynamic *striving to overcome the suffering*, that is, *for change in the direction of health*. This striving for health in our physical as well as in our mental organism is the basis for any cure of sickness, and it is absent only in the most severe pathology.

2.) The first step necessary to permit this tendency for health to operate is the *awareness* of the suffering and of that which is shut out and disassociated from our conscious personality. In Freud's doctrine, repression refers mainly to *sexual* strivings. In our frame of reference, it refers to the repressed irrational passions, to the repressed feeling of aloneness and futility, and to the longing for love and productivity, which is also repressed.

3.) Increasing self-awareness can become fully effective only if a next step is taken, that of changing a practice of life which was built on the basis of the neurotic structure, and which reproduces it constantly. A patient, for instance, whose neurotic character makes him want to submit to parental authorities has usually constructed a life where he has chosen dominating or sadistic father images as bosses, teachers, and so on. He will be cured only if he changes his realistic life situation in such a way that it does not constantly reproduce the submissive tendencies he wants to give up. Furthermore, he must change his systems of values, norms and ideals, so that they further rather than block his striving for health and maturity.

The same conditions—*conflict* with the requirements of human nature and resulting suffering, *awareness* of what is shut out, and *change* of the realistic situation and of values and norms—are also necessary for a cure of *social* pathology.

To show the conflict between human needs and our social structure, and to further the awareness of our conflicts and of that which is dissociated, was the purpose of the previous chapter of this book. To discuss the various possibilities of practical changes in our economic, political and cultural organization is the intention of this chapter.

However, before we start discussing the practical questions, let us consider once more what, on the basis of the premises developed in the beginning of this book, constitutes mental sanity, and what type of culture could be assumed to be conducive to mental health.

The mentally healthy person is the productive and unalienated person; the person who relates himself to the world lovingly, and who uses his reason to grasp reality objectively; who experiences himself as a unique individual entity, and at the same time feels one with his fellow man; who is not subject to irrational authority, and accepts willingly the rational authority of conscience and reason; who is in the process of being born as long as he is alive, and considers the gift of life the most precious chance he has.

Let us also remember that these goals of mental health are not ideals which have to be forced upon the person, or which man can attain only if he overcomes his "nature," and sacrifices his "innate selfishness." On the contrary, the striving for mental health, for happiness, harmony, love, productiveness, is inherent in every human being who is not born as a mental or moral idiot. Given a chance, these strivings assert themselves forcefully, as can be seen in countless situations. It takes powerful constellations and circumstances to pervert and stifle this innate striving for sanity; and indeed, throughout the greater part of known history, the use of man by man has produced such perversion. To believe that this perversion is inherent in man is like throwing seeds in the soil of the desert and claiming they were not meant to grow.

What society corresponds to this aim of mental health, and what would be the structure of a sane society? First of all, a society in which no man is a means toward another's ends, but always and without exception an end in himself; hence, where nobody is used, nor uses himself, for purposes which are not those of the unfolding of his own human powers; where man is the center, and where all economic and political activities are subordinated to the aim of his growth. A sane society is one in which qualities like greed, exploitativeness, possessiveness, narcissism, have no chance to be used for greater material gain or for the enhancement of one's personal prestige. Where acting according to one's conscience is looked upon as a fundamental and necessary quality and where opportunism and lack of principles is deemed to be asocial; where the individual is concerned with social matters so that they become personal matters, where his relation to his fellow man is not separated from his relationship in the private sphere. A sane society, furthermore, is one which permits man to operate within manageable and observable dimensions, and to be an active and responsible participant in the life of society, as well as the master of his own life. It is one which furthers human solidarity and not only permits, but stimulates, its members to relate themselves to each other lovingly; a sane society furthers the productive activity of everybody in his work, stimulates the unfolding of reason and enables man to give expression to his inner needs in collective art and rituals.

Economic Transformation

A. SOCIALISM AS A PROBLEM

We have discussed in the previous chapter the three answers to the problem of present-day insanity, those of Totalitarianism, Super-Capitalism and Socialism. The totalitarian solution, be it of the Fascist or Stalinist type, quite obviously leads only to increased insanity and dehumanization; the solution of Super-Capitalism only deepens the pathology which is inherent in Capitalism; it increases man's alienation, his automatization, and completes the process of making him a servant to the idol of production. The only constructive solution is that of Socialism, which aims at a fundamental reorganization of our economic and social system in the direction of freeing man from being used as a means for purposes outside of himself, of creating a social order in which human solidarity, reason and productiveness are furthered rather than hobbled. Yet there can be no doubt that the results of Socialism, where it has been practiced so far, have been at least disappointing. What are the reasons for this failure? What are the aims and goals of social and economic reconstruction which can avoid this failure and lead to a sane society?

According to Marxist Socialism, a socialist society was built on two premises: the socialization of the means of production and distribution, and a centralized and planned economy. Marx and the early socialists had no doubt that if these aims could be accomplished, the human emancipation of all men from alienation, and a classless society of brotherliness and justice, would follow almost automatically. All that was necessary for the human transformation was, as they saw it, that the working class gained political control, either by force or by ballot, socialized industry, and instituted a planned economy. The question whether they were right in their assumption is not an academic question any more; Russia has done what the Marxist socialists thought was necessary to do in the economic sphere. While the Russian system showed that economically a socialized and planned economy can work efficiently, it proved that it is in no way a sufficient condition to create a free, brotherly and unalienated society. On the contrary, it showed that centralized planning can even create a greater degree of regimentation and authoritarianism than is to be found in Capitalism or in Fascism. The fact, however, that a socialized and planned economy has been realized in Russia does not mean that the Russian system is the realization of Socialism as Marx and Engels understood it. It means that Marx and Engels were mistaken in thinking that legal change in ownership and a planned economy were sufficient to bring about the social and human changes desired by them.

While socialization of the means of production in combination with a planned economy were the most central demands of Marxist Socialism, there were some others which have completely failed to materialize in Russia. Marx did not postulate complete equality of income, but nevertheless had in mind a sharp reduction of inequality as it exists in Capitalism. The fact is that inequality of income is much greater in Russia than in the United States or Britain. Another Marxist idea was that Socialism would lead to the withering of the state, and to the gradual disappearance of social classes. The fact is that the power of the state, and the distinction between social classes are greater in Russia than in any capitalist country. Eventually, the center of Marx's concept of Socialism was the idea that man, his emotional and intellectual powers, are the aim and goal of culture, that things (= capital) must serve life (labor) and that life must not be subordinated to that which is dead. Here again, the disregard for the individual and his human qualities is greater in Russia than in any of the capitalist countries.

But Russia was not the only country which tried to apply the economic concepts of Marxist Socialism. The other country was Great Britain. Paradoxically enough, the Labour Party, which is not based on Marxist theory, in its practical measures followed exactly the path of Marxist doctrine, that the realization of Socialism is based on the socialization of industry. The difference to Russia is clear enough. The British Labour Party always relied on peaceful means for the realization of its aims; its policy was not based on an all-or-nothing demand, but made it possible to socialize medicine, banking, steel, mining, railroads and the chemical industry, without nationalizing the rest of British industry. But while it introduced an economy in which socialist elements were blended with Capitalism, nevertheless the main idea for attaining Socialism was that of socialization of the means of production.

However, the British experiment, while less drastic in its failures, was also discouraging. On the one hand it created a good deal of regimentation and bureaucratization which did not endear it to anyone concerned with increase in human freedom and independence. On the other hand, it did not accomplish any of the basic expectations of Socialism. It became quite clear that it made very little or no difference to a worker in the British mining or steel industry whether the owner of the industry were a few thousand, or even hundred thousand individuals as in a public corporation, or the state. His wages, rights, and most important of all, his conditions of work, his role in the process of work remained essentially the same. There are few advantages brought about by nationalization which the worker could not have attained through his unions in a purely capitalist economy. On the other hand, while the main aim of Socialism has not been fulfilled by the measures of the Labour government, it would be shortsighted to ignore the fact that British Socialism has brought about favorable changes of the utmost importance in the life of the British people. One is the extension of the social security system to health. That no person in Great Britain has to be afraid of illness as of a catastrophe which may completely disorganize his life (not to speak of the possibility of losing it for lack of proper medical care), may sound little to a member of the middle or upper classes in the United States, who has no trouble paying the doctor's bill and hospitalization. But it is indeed a fundamental improvement to be compared to the progress made by the introduction of public education. It is furthermore true that the nationalization of industry, even to the limited degree that it was introduced in Britain (about ⅕ of the whole industry), permitted the state to regulate the total economy to a certain extent, a regulation from which the whole of the British economy profited.

But with all respect and appreciation for the achievements of the Labour government, their measures were not conducive to the realization of Socialism, if we take it in a human rather than in a purely economic sense. And if one were to argue that the Labour Party only began with the realization of its program, and that it would have introduced Socialism if it had been in power long enough to complete its work, such argument is not very convincing. Even visualizing the socialization of the whole of British heavy industry, one can see greater security, greater prosperity, and one need not be afraid that the new bureaucracy would be more dangerous to freedom than the bureaucracy of General Motors or General Electric. But in spite of all that could be said about its advantages, such socialization and planning would not be Socialism, if we mean by it a new form of life, a society of solidarity and faith, in which the individual has found himself and has emerged from the alienation inherent in the capitalistic system.

The terrifying result of Soviet Communism on the one hand, the disappointing results of Labour Party Socialism on the other, has led to a mood of resignation and hopelessness among many democratic socialists. Some still go on believing in Socialism, but more out of pride or stubbornness than out of real conviction. Others, busy with smaller or bigger tasks in one of the socialist parties, do not reflect too much and find themselves satisfied with the practical activities at hand; still others, who have lost faith in a renewal of society, consider it their main task to lead the crusade against Russian Communism; while they reiterate the charges against Communism, well-known and accepted by anybody who is not a Stalinist, they refrain from any radical criticism of Capitalism, and from any new proposals for the functioning of Democratic Socialism. They give the impression that everything is all right with the world, if only it can be saved from the Communist threat; they act like disappointed lovers who have lost all faith in love.

As one symptomatic expression of the general discouragement among democratic socialists, I quote from an article by R. H. S. Crossman, one of the most thoughtful and active leaders of the left wing of the Labour Party. "Living in an age not of steady progress towards a world welfare capitalism," Crossman writes, "but of world revolution, it is folly for us to assume that the socialist's task is to assist in the gradual improvement of the material lot of the human race and the gradual enlargement of the area of human freedom. The forces of history are all pressing toward totalitarianism: in the Russian bloc, owing to the conscious policy of the Kremlin; in the free world, owing to the growth of the managerial society, the effects of total rearmament, and the repression of colonial aspirations. The task of socialism is neither to accelerate this Political Revolution, nor to oppose it (this would be as futile as opposition to the Industrial revolution a hundred years ago), but to civilise it." [1]

It appears to me that Crossman's pessimism leads to two errors. One is the assumption that managerial or Stalinist totalitarianism can be "civilized." If by civilized is meant a less cruel system than that of Stalinist dictatorship, Crossman may be right. But the version of the Brave New World which rests entirely on suggestion and conditioning is as inhuman and as insane as Orwell's version

[1] *New Fabian Essays*, ed. by R. H. S. Crossman, Turnstile Press, London, 1953, p. 31.

of "1984." Neither version of a completely alienated society can be humanized. The other error lies in Crossman's pessimism itself. Socialism, in its genuine human and moral aspirations is still a potent aim of many millions all over the world, and the objective conditions for humanistic democratic socialism are more given today than in the nineteenth century. The reasons for this assumption are implicit in the following attempt to outline some of the proposals for a socialist transformation in the economic, political and cultural spheres. Before I go on, however, I should like to state, although it is hardly necessary, that my proposals are neither new nor are they meant to be exhaustive, or necessarily correct in detail. They are made in the belief that it is necessary to turn from a general discussion of principles to practical problems of how these principles can be realized. Long before political democracy was realized, the thinkers of the eighteenth century discussed blueprints of constitutional principles which were to show that—and how—the democratic organization of the state was possible. The problem in the twentieth century is to discuss ways and means to implement political democracy and to transform it into a truly human society. The objections which are made are largely based on pessimism and on a profound lack of faith. It is claimed that the advance of managerial society and the implied manipulation of man cannot be checked unless we regress to the spinning wheel, because modern industry needs managers and automatons. Other objections are due to a lack of imagination. Still others, to the deep-seated fear of being freed from commands and given full freedom to live. Yet it is quite beyond doubt that the problems of social transformation are not as difficult to solve —theoretically and practically—as the technical problems our chemists and physicists have solved. And it can also not be doubted that we are more in need of a human renaissance than we are in need of airplanes and television. Even a fraction of the reason and practical sense used in the natural sciences, applied to human problems, will permit the continuation of the task our ancestors of the eighteenth century were so proud of.

B. THE PRINCIPLE OF COMMUNITARIAN SOCIALISM

The Marxist emphasis on socialization of the means of production was influenced in itself by nineteenth-century Capitalism. Ownership and property rights were the central categories of capitalist economy, and Marx remained within this frame of reference when he defined Socialism by reversing the capitalist property system, demanding the "expropriation of the expropriators." Here, as in his orientation of political versus social factors, Marx and Engels were more influenced by the bourgeois spirit than other socialist schools of thought, which were concerned with the function of the worker in the work process, with his social relatedness to others in the factory, with the effect of the method of work on the character of the worker.

The failure—as perhaps also the popularity—of Marxist Socialism lies precisely in this bourgeois overestimation of property rights and purely economic factors. But other socialist schools of thought have been much more aware of the pitfalls inherent in Marxism, and have formulated the aim of Socialism much more adequately. Owenists, syndicalists, anarchists and guild socialists agreed in their main concern, which was the social and human situation of the worker in his work and the kind of relatedness to his fellow workers. (By "worker" I mean here and in the following pages everybody who lives from his own work, without additional profits from the employment of others.) The aim of all these various forms of Socialism, which we may call "communitarian Socialism," was an industrial organization in which *every working person would be an active and responsible participant, where work would be attractive and meaningful, where*

capital would not employ labor, but labor would employ capital.
They stressed the organization of work and the social relations
between men, not primarily the question of ownership. As I shall
show later, there is a remarkable return to this attitude by socialists
all over the world, who some decades ago considered the pure form
of Marxist doctrine to be *the* solution of all problems. In order to
give the reader a general idea of the principles of this type of
communitarian socialist thought, which in spite of considerable
differences is common to syndicalists, anarchists, guild socialists,
and increasingly so to Marxist Socialists, I quote the following
formulations by Cole:

He writes: "Fundamentally the old insistence on liberty is right;
it was swept away because it thought of liberty in terms of political
self-government alone. The new conception of liberty must be
wider. It must include the idea of man not only as a citizen in a
free state, but as a partner in an industrial commonwealth. The
bureaucratic reformer, by laying all the stress upon the purely
material side of life, has come to believe in a society made up of
well-fed, well-housed, well-clothed machines, working for a
greater machine, the state; the individualist has offered to men
the alternative of starvation and slavery under the guise of liberty
of action. The real liberty, which is the goal of the new Socialism,
will assure freedom of action and immunity from economic stress
by treating man as a human being, and not as a problem or a god.

"Political liberty by itself is, in fact, always illusory. A man
who lives in economic subjection six days, if not seven, a week,
does not become free merely by making a cross on a ballot-paper
once in five years. If freedom is to mean anything to the average
man it must include industrial freedom. Until men at their work
can know themselves members of a self-governing community of
workers, they will remain essentially servile, whatever the political
system under which they live. It is not enough to sweep away the

degrading relation in which the wage-slave stands to an individual employer. State Socialism, too, leaves the worker in bondage to a tyranny that is no less galling because it is impersonal. Self-government in industry is not merely the supplement, but the precursor of political liberty.

"Man is everywhere in chains, and his chains will not be broken till he feels that it is degrading to be a bondsman, whether to an individual or to a State. The disease of civilization is not so much the material poverty of the many as the decay of the spirit of freedom and self-confidence. The revolt that will change the world will spring, not from the benevolence that breeds "reform," but from the will to be free. Men will act together in the full consciousness of their mutual dependence; but they will act for themselves. Their liberty will not be given them from above; they will take it on their own behalf.

"Socialists, then, must put their appeal to the workers not in the question, 'Is it not unpleasant to be poor, and will you not help to raise the poor?' but in this form: 'Poverty is but the sign of man's enslavement: to cure it *you* must cease to labour for others and must believe in yourself.' Wage-slavery will exist as long as there is a man or an institution that is the master of men: it will be ended when the workers learn to set freedom before comfort. The average man will become a socialist not in order to secure a 'minimum standard of civilized life,' but because he feels ashamed of the slavery that blinds him and his fellows, and because he is resolved to end the industrial system that makes them slaves." [1]

"First, then, what is the nature of the ideal at which Labour must aim? What is meant by that 'control of industry' which the workers are to demand? It can be summed up in two words—

[1] G. D. H. Cole and W. Mellor, *The Meaning of Industrial Freedom*, Geo. Allen and Unwin, Ltd., London, 1918, pp. 3, 4.

direct management. The task of actually conducting the business must be handed over to the workers engaged in it. To them it must belong to order production, distribution, and exchange. They must win industrial self-government, with the right to elect their own officers; they must understand and control all the complicated mechanism of industry and trade; they must become the accredited agents of the community in the economic sphere." [1]

C. SOCIO-PSYCHOLOGICAL OBJECTIONS

Before discussing practical suggestions for the realization of communitarian Socialism in an industrial society, we had better stop and discuss some of the main objections to such possibilities; the first type of objection being based on the idea of the nature of industrial work, the other on the nature of man and the psychological motivations for work.

It is precisely with regard to any change in the work situation itself, that the most drastic objections to the ideas of communitarian Socialism are made by many thoughtful and well-meaning observers. Modern industrial work, so the argument runs, is by its very nature mechanical, uninteresting and alienated. It is based on an extreme degree of division of labor, and it can never occupy the interest and attention of the whole man. All ideas to make work interesting and meaningful again are really romantic dreams —and followed up with more consequence and realism they would logically result in the demand to give up our system of industrial production and to return to the pre-industrial mode of handicraft production. On the contrary, so the argument goes on, the aim must be to make work *more* meaningless and *more* mechanized. We have witnessed a tremendous reduction of working hours within the last hundred years, and a working day of four, or even two hours does not seem to be a fantastic expectation for the

[1] *Ibid.*, p. 22.

future. We are witnessing right now a drastic change in work methods. The work process is divided into so many small components, that each worker's task becomes automatic and does not require his active attention; thus, he can indulge in daydreams and reveries. Besides, we are using increasingly automatized machines, working with their own "brains" in clean, well-lit, healthy factories, and the "worker" does nothing but watch some instrument and pull some lever from time to time. Indeed, say the adherents of this point of view, *the complete automatization of work is what we hope for;* man will work a few hours; it will not be uncomfortable, nor require much attention; it will be an almost unconscious routine like brushing one's teeth, and the center of gravity will be the leisure hours in everybody's life.

This argument sounds convincing and who can say that the completely automatized factory and the disappearance of all dirty and uncomfortable work is not the goal which our industrial evolution is approaching? But there are several considerations to prevent us from making the automatization of work our main hope for a sane society.

First of all it is, at the least, doubtful whether the mechanization of work will have the results which are assumed in the foregoing argument. There is a good deal of evidence pointing to the contrary. Thus, for instance, a very thoughtful recent study among automobile workers shows that they disliked the job to the degree to which it embodied mass-production characteristics like repetitiveness, mechanical pacing, or related characteristics. While the vast majority liked the job for economic reasons (147 to 7), an even greater majority (96 to 1) disliked it for reasons of the immediate job content.[1] The same reaction was also expressed in the behavior of the workers. "Workers whose jobs had 'high mass

[1] Ch. R. Walker and R. H. Guest, *The Man on the Assembly Line,* Harvard University Press, Cambridge, Mass., 1952, pp. 142, 143.

production scores'—that is, exhibited mass production characteristics in an extreme form—were absent more often from their
jobs than workers on jobs with low mass production scores. More
workers quit jobs with high mass production scores than quit
jobs with low ones." [1] It must also be questioned whether the
freedom for daydreaming and reverie which mechanized work
gives is as positive and healthy a factor as most industrial psychologists assume. Actually, daydreaming is a symptom of lacking
relatedness to reality. It is not refreshing or relaxing—it is essentially an escape with all the negative results that go with
escape. What the industrial psychologists describe in such bright
colors is essentially the same lack of concentration which is so
characteristic of modern man in general. You do three things
at once because you do not do anything in a concentrated fashion.
It is a great mistake to believe that doing something in a nonconcentrated form is refreshing. On the contrary, any concentrated activity, whether it is work, play or rest (rest, too, is an
activity), is invigorating—any nonconcentrated activity is tiring.
Anybody can find out the truth of this statement by a few simple
self-observations.

But aside from all this, it will still be many generations before
such a point of automatization and reduction of working time is
reached, especially if we think not only of Europe and America
but of Asia and Africa, which still have hardly started their industrial revolution. Is man, during the next few hundred years,
to continue spending most of his energy on meaningless work,
waiting for the time when work will hardly require any expenditure of energy? What will become of him in the meantime?

---

[1] *Ibid.*, p. 144. The experiences with job enlargement made by I.B.M. point to
similar considerations. When one worker performed several operations which were
subdivided before among several workers, so that the worker could have a sense of
accomplishment and be related to the product of work, production rose and fatigue
decreased.

Will he not become more and more alienated and this just as much in his leisure hours as in his working time? Is the hope for effortless work not a daydream based on the fantasy of laziness and push-button power, and a rather unhealthy fantasy at that? Is not work such a fundamental part of man's existence that it cannot and should never be reduced to almost complete insignificance? Is not the mode of work in itself an essential element in forming a person's character? Does completely automatized work not lead to a completely automatized life?

While all these questions are so many doubts concerning the idealization of completely automatized work, we must now deal with those views which deny the possibility that work could be attractive and meaningful, hence that it could be truly humanized. The argument runs like this: modern factory work is by its very nature not conducive to interest and satisfaction; furthermore, there is necessary work to be done, which is positively unpleasant or repelling. Active participation of the worker in management is incompatible with the requirements of modern industry, and would lead to chaos. In order to function properly in this system, man must obey, adjust himself to a routinized organization. By nature man is lazy, and not prone to be responsible; he therefore must be conditioned to function smoothly and without too much initiative and spontaneity.

To deal with these arguments properly we must indulge in some speculations on the problem of *laziness* and on that of the various *motivations for work*.

It is surprising that the view of man's natural laziness can still be held by psychologists and laymen alike, when so many observable facts contradict it. *Laziness, far from being normal, is a symptom of mental pathology.* In fact, one of the worst forms of mental suffering is boredom, not knowing what to do with oneself and one's life. Even if man had no monetary, or any other reward, he would be eager to spend his energy in some meaningful way because he could not stand the boredom which inactivity produces.

Let us look at children: they are never lazy; given the slightest encouragement, or even without it, they are busy playing, asking questions, inventing stories, without any incentive except the pleasure in the activity itself. In the field of psycho-pathology we find that the person who has no interest in doing anything is seriously sick and is far from exhibiting the normal state of human nature. There is plenty of material about workers during periods of unemployment, who suffer as much, or more, from the enforced "rest," as from the material deprivations. There is just as much material to show that for many people over sixty-five the necessity to stop working leads to profound unhappiness, and in many instances to physical deterioration and illness.

Nevertheless, there are good reasons for the widespread belief in man's innate laziness. The main reason lies in the fact that alienated work is boring and unsatisfactory; that a great deal of tension and hostility is engendered, which leads to an aversion against the work one is doing and everything connected with it. As a result, we find a longing for laziness and for "doing nothing" to be the ideal of many people. Thus, people feel that their laziness is the "natural" state of mind, rather than the symptom of a pathological condition of life, the result of meaningless and alienated work. Examining the current views on work motivation, it becomes evident that they are based on the concept of alienated work and hence that their conclusions do not apply to non-alienated, attractive work.

The conventional and most common theory is that *money* is the main incentive for work. This answer can have two different meanings: first, that fear of starvation is the main incentive for work; in this case the argument is undoubtedly true. Many types of work would never be accepted on the basis of wages or other work conditions were the worker not confronted with the alternative of accepting these conditions or of starvation. The unpleasant, lowly work in our society is done not voluntarily, but because the need to make a living forces so many people to do it.

More often the concept of money incentive refers to the wish to earn *more* money as the motivation to greater effort in working. If man were not lured by the hope of greater monetary reward, this argument says, he would not work at all, or at least, would work without interest.

This conviction still exists among the majority of industrialists, as well as among many union leaders. Thus, for instance, fifty manufacturing executives replied to the question as to what is of importance in increasing worker's productivity as follows:

"Money alone is the answer" 44%

"Money is by far the chief thing but some importance is to be attached to less tangible things" 28%

"Money is important but beyond a certain point it will not produce results" 28%

100% [1]

Actually, employers throughout the world are in favor of wage-incentive plans as the only means which would lead to higher productivity of the individual worker, to higher earnings for the workers and employers and thus, indirectly, to reduced absenteeism, easier supervision, and so on. Reports and surveys from industry and government bureaus "generally attest to the effectiveness of wage-incentive plans in increasing productivity and achieving other objectives." [2] It seems that workers also believe

---

[1] cf. Survey reported in the Public Opinion Index for Industry in 1947, quoted from M. S. Viteles, *Motivation and Morale in Industry*, W. W. Norton & Company, New York, 1953.

[2] *Ibid.*, p. 27.

that incentive pay gets the most output per man. In a survey conducted by the Opinion Research Corporation in 1949, involving 1,021 manual workers comprising a national sample of employees of manufacturing companies, 65 per cent said that incentive pay increases output, and only 22 per cent that hourly pay makes for higher production. However, as to the question of which method of pay *they prefer*, 65 per cent answered hourly pay, and only 29 per cent were in favor of incentive pay. (The ratio of preference for hourly pay was 74 to 20 in the case of hourly workers, but even in the case of workers already on incentive pay, 59 per cent were in favor of hourly pay as against 36 per cent in favor of incentive pay.)

The latter findings are interpreted by Viteles as showing that "as useful as incentive pay is in raising output, it does not in itself solve the problem of obtaining workers' cooperation. In some circumstances it may intensify that problem." [1] This opinion is shared increasingly by industrial psychologists and even some industrialists.

However, the discussion about money incentives would be incomplete if we did not consider the fact that the wish for more money is constantly fostered by the same industry which relies on money as the main incentive for work. By advertising, installment plan systems, and many other devices, the individual's greed to buy more and newer things is stimulated to the point that he can rarely have enough money to satisfy these *"needs."* Thus, being artificially stimulated by industry, the monetary incentive plays a greater role than it otherwise would. Furthermore, it goes without saying that the monetary incentive must play a paramount role as long as it is the *only* incentive because the work process in itself is unsatisfactory and boring. There are many examples of

[1] *Ibid.*, pp. 49, 50.

cases in which people choose work with less monetary reward if the work itself is more interesting.

Aside from money, *prestige, status* and the *power* that goes with it are assumed to be the main incentives for work. There is no need to prove that the craving for prestige and power constitutes the most powerful incentive for work today among the middle and upper classes; in fact, the importance of money is largely that of representing prestige, at least as much as security and comfort. But the role which the need for prestige plays also among workers, clerks and the lower echelons of the industrial and business bureaucracy is often ignored. The name-plate of the Pullman porter, the bank teller, etcetera, are significant psychological boosts to his sense of importance; as are the personal telephone, larger office space for the higher ranks. These prestige factors play a role also among industrial workers.[1]

Money, prestige and power are the main incentives today for the largest sector of our population—that which is employed. But there are other motivations: the satisfaction in building an *independent economic existence,* and the performance of *skilled work,* both of which made work much more meaningful and attractive than it is under the motivation of money and power. But while economic independence and skill were important satisfactions for the independent businessman, artisan, and the highly skilled worker in the nineteenth, and beginning of the twentieth century, the role of these motivations is now rapidly decreasing.

As to the increase of employed, in contrast to independents, we note that in the beginning of the nineteenth century more or less four fifths of the occupied population were self-employed entrepreneurs; around 1870 only one third belonged to this group,

---

[1] cf. W. Williams, *Mainsprings of Men,* Charles Scribner's Sons, New York, 1925, p. 56, quoted in M. S. Viteles, *loc. cit.,* p. 65 ff.

and by 1940 this old middle class comprises only one fifth of the occupied population.

This shift from independents to employees is in itself conducive to decreasing work satisfaction for the reasons which have already been discussed. The employed person, more than the independent one, works in an alienated position. Whether he is paid a lower or a higher salary, he is an accessory to the organization rather than a human being doing something for himself.

There is one factor, however, which could mitigate the alienation of work, and that is the skill required in its performance. But here too, development moves in the direction of decreasing skill requirements, and hence increasing alienation.

Among the office workers there is a certain amount of skill required, but the factor of a "pleasant personality," able to sell himself, becomes of ever-increasing importance. Among industrial workers the old type of all-around skilled worker loses ever more in importance compared with the semi-skilled worker. At Ford, at the end of 1948, the number of workers who could be trained in less than two weeks was 75 to 80 per cent of the whole working personnel of the plant. From a professional school with an apprentice program at Ford, only three hundred men graduated each year, of which half entered other factories. In a factory making batteries in Chicago, there are, among one hundred mechanics who are considered as highly qualified, only fifteen who have a thorough all-round technical knowledge; forty-five others are "skilled" only in the use of one particular machine. At one of the Western Electric plants in Chicago, the average training of the workers takes from three to four weeks, and up to six months for the most delicate and difficult tasks. The total personnel of 6,400 employees was composed in 1948 of about 1,000 white collar workers, 5,000 industrial workers, and only 400 workers who could be considered skilled. In other words, less than 10 per cent of the total personnel is technically qualified. In a big candy factory in Chicago, 90 per cent of the workers require a training "on the job" which is not longer than 48 hours.[1]

Even an industry like the Swiss-watch industry, which was based on the work of highly qualified and skilled men, has changed drastically in this respect. While there are still a number of factories producing according to the traditional principle of craftsmanship, the great watch factories established in the Canton of Solothurn have only a small percentage of genuinely skilled workers.[2]

To sum up, the vast majority of the population work as employees with little skill required, and with almost no chance to develop any particular talents, or to show any outstanding achievements. While the managerial or professional groups have at least considerable interest in achieving something more or less personal, the vast majority sell their physical, or an exceedingly small part of their intellectual capacity to an employer to be used for purposes of profit in which they have no share, for things in which they have no interest, with the only purpose of making a living, and for some chance to satisfy their consumer's greed.

Dissatisfaction, apathy, boredom, lack of joy and happiness, a sense of futility and a vague feeling that life is meaningless, are the unavoidable results of this situation. This socially patterned syndrome of pathology may not be in the awareness of people; it may be covered by a frantic flight into escape activities, or by a craving for more money, power, prestige. But the weight of the latter motivations is so great only because the alienated person cannot help seeking for such compensations for his inner vacuity, not because these desires are the "natural" or most important incentives for work.

[1] These figures are quoted from G. Friedmann, *loc. cit.*, p. 152 ff.
[2] cf. G. Friedmann, *loc. cit.*, pp. 319, 320.

Is there any empirical evidence that most people today are not satisfied with their work?

In an attempt to answer this question we must differentiate between what people *consciously think* about their satisfaction, and what they *feel unconsciously*. It is evident from psychoanalytic experience that the sense of unhappiness and dissatisfaction can be deeply repressed; a person may consciously feel satisfied and only his dreams, psychosomatic illness, insomnia, and many other symptoms may be expressive of the underlying unhappiness. The tendency to repress dissatisfaction and unhappiness is strongly supported by the widespread feeling that not to be satisfied means to be "a failure," queer, unsuccessful, etcetera. (Thus, for instance, the number of people who consciously think they are happily married, and express this belief sincerely in answer to a questionnaire is by far greater than the number of those who are really happy in their marriage.)

But even the data on *conscious* job satisfaction are rather telling.

In a study about job satisfaction on a national scale, satisfaction with and enjoyment of their job was expressed by 85 per cent of the professionals and executives, by 64 per cent of white-collar people, and by 41 per cent of the factory workers. In another study, we find a similar picture: 86 per cent of the professionals, 74 per cent of the managerial, 42 per cent of the commercial employees, 56 per cent of the skilled, and 48 per cent of the semi-skilled workers expressed satisfaction.[1]

We find in these figures a significant discrepancy between professionals and executives on the one hand, workers and clerks on the other. Among the former only a minority is dissatisfied— among the latter, more than half. Regarding the total population, this means, roughly, that over half of the total employed population is consciously dissatisfied with their work, and do not enjoy

[1] cf. C. W. Mills, *White Collar*, Oxford University Press, New York, 1951, p. 229.

it. If we consider the unconscious dissatisfaction, the percentage would be considerably higher. Taking the 85 per cent of "satisfied" professionals and executives, we would have to examine how many of them suffer from psychologically determined high blood pressure, ulcers, insomnia, nervous tension and fatigue. Although there are no exact data on this, there can be no doubt that, considering these symptoms, the number of really satisfied persons who enjoy their work would be much smaller than the above figures indicate.

As far as factory workers and office clerks are concerned, even the percentage of *consciously* dissatisfied people is remarkably high. Undoubtedly the number of unconsciously dissatisfied workers and clerks is much higher. This is indicated by several studies which show that neurosis and psychogenic illnesses are the main reasons for absenteeism (the estimates for the presence of neurotic symptoms among factory workers go up to about 50 per cent). Fatigue and high labor turnover are other symptoms of dissatisfaction and resentment.

The most important symptom from the economic standpoint, hence the best studied one, is the widespread tendency of factory workers, not to give their best to the work, or "work restriction" as it is often called. In a poll conducted by the Opinion Research Corporation in 1945, 49 per cent of all the manual workers questioned answered that "when a man takes a job in a factory he should turn out *as much as he can*," but 41 per cent answered that he should *not do his best*, but only "turn out the average amount." [1] [2]

[1] M. S. Viteles, *loc. cit.*, p. 61.

[2] Under the heading "The Decline of 'Economic' Man," Viteles comes to this conclusion: "In general, studies of the type cited above give continuing support to the conclusions reached by Mathewson, as a result of plant observations and interviews with management representatives, that

"1. Restrictions is a widespread institution, deeply intrenched in the working habits of American laboring people.

"2. Scientific management has failed to develop that spirit of confidence between

We see that there is a great deal of conscious, and even more unconscious dissatisfaction with the kind of work which our industrial society offers most of its members. One tries to counteract their dissatisfaction by a mixture of monetary and prestige incentives, and undoubtedly these incentives produce considerable eagerness to work, especially in the middle and higher echelons of the business hierarchy. But it is one thing that these incentives make people work, and it is quite another thing whether the mode of this work is conducive to mental health and happiness. The discussion on motivation of work usually considers only the first problem, namely whether this or that incentive increases the *economic* productivity of the worker, but not the second, that of his *human* productivity. One ignores the fact that there are many incentives which can make a person do something, but which at the same time are detrimental to his personality. A person can work hard out of fear, or out of an inner sense of guilt; psychopathology gives us many examples of neurotic motives leading to overactivity as well as to inactivity.

Most of us assume that the kind of work current in our society, namely, alienated work, is the only kind there is, hence that aversion to work is natural, hence that money and prestige and power are the only incentives for work. If we would use our imagination

---

the parties to labor contracts which has been so potent in developing good-will between the parties to a sales contract.

"3. Underwork and restriction are greater problems than over-speeding and over-work. The efforts of managers to speed up working people have been offset by the ingenuity of the workers in developing restrictive practices.

"4. Managers have been so content with the over-all results of man-hour output that only superficial attention has been given to the workers' contribution or lack of contribution to the increased yield. Attempts to secure increased output have been marked by traditional and unscientific methods, while the workers have held to the time-honored practices of self-protection which antedate time study, bonus plans, and other devices to encourage capacity production.

"5. Regardless of how much the individual may or may not desire to contribute a full day's work, his actual experiences often turn him away from good working habits." (M. S. Viteles, *loc. cit.*, pp. 58, 59).

just a little bit, we could collect a good deal of evidence from our own lives, from observing children, from a number of situations which we can hardly fail to encounter, to convince us that we long to spend our energy on something meaningful, that we feel refreshed if we can do so, and that we are quite willing to accept rational authority if what we are doing makes sense.

But even if this is true, most people object, what help is this truth to us? Industrial, mechanized work cannot, by its very nature, be meaningful; it cannot give any pleasure or satisfaction —there are no ways of changing these facts, unless we want to give up our technical achievements. In order to answer this objection and proceed to discuss some ideas on how modern work could be meaningful, I want to point out two different aspects of work which it is very important to discern for our problem: the difference *between the technical and the social aspects of work.*

D.   INTEREST AND PARTICIPATION AS MOTIVATION

If we consider separately the technical and the social aspects of the work situation, we find that many types of work would be attractive as far as the technical aspect is concerned, provided the social aspect were satisfactory; on the other hand, there are types of work where the technical aspect can by its very nature not be interesting, and yet where the social aspect of the work situation could make it meaningful and attractive.

Starting with the discussion of the first instance, we find that there are many men who would, for example, take keen pleasure in being railroad engineers. But although railroad engineering is one of the highest paid and most respected positions in the working class, it is, nevertheless, not the fulfillment of the ambition of those who could "do better." No doubt, many a business executive would find more pleasure in being a railroad engineer than in his own work if the social context of the job were different.

Let us take another example: that of a waiter in a restaurant. This job could be an exceedingly attractive one for many people, provided its social prestige were different. It permits of constant interpersonal intercourse, and to people who like food, it gives pleasure to advise others about it, to serve it pleasantly, and so on. Many a man would find much more pleasure in working as a waiter than in sitting in his office over meaningless figures were it not for the low social rating and low income of this job. Again, many others would love the job of a cab driver were it not for its negative social and economic aspects.

It is often said that there are certain types of work which nobody would want to perform unless forced to do so by economic necessity; the work of a miner is often given as an example. But considering the diversity of people, and of their conscious and unconscious fantasies, it seems that there would be a considerable number of people for whom working within the earth, and extracting its riches would have a great attraction were it not for the social and financial disadvantages of this type of work. There is hardly any kind of work which would not attract certain types of personalities, provided it were freed from the negative aspects, socially and economically.

But even granted that the foregoing considerations are correct, it is undoubtedly true that much of the highly routinized work which is required by mechanized industry cannot in itself be a source of pleasure or satisfaction. Here again the differentiation between the technical and the social aspect of the work proves to be important. While the technical aspect may indeed be uninteresting, the total work situation may offer a good deal of satisfaction.

Here are some examples which serve to illustrate this point. Let us compare a housewife who takes care of the house and does the cooking, with a maid who is paid for doing exactly the same work. Both for the housewife and the maid, the work in its technical aspects is the same, and it is not particularly interesting. Yet it will have an entirely different meaning and satisfaction for the two, provided we think of a woman with a happy relationship to husband and children, and of an average maid, who has no sentimental attachment to her employer. To the former, the work will not be drudgery, while to the latter it will be exactly that, and the only reason for doing it is that she needs the money paid for it. The reason for this difference is obvious: while the work is the same in its technical aspects, the work situation is entirely different. For the housewife it is part of her total relationship to her husband and children, and in this sense her work is meaningful. The maid does not participate in the satisfaction of this social aspect of the work.

Let us take another example: a Mexican Indian selling his goods on the market. The technical aspect of the work, that of waiting the whole day for customers and performing from time to time the transaction of answering questions as to price, etcetera, would be as boring and disagreeable as is the work of a salesgirl in a five-and-ten-cent store. There is, however, one essential difference. For the Mexican Indian the market situation is one of a rich and stimulating human intercourse. He responds with pleasure to his customers, is interested in talking with them, and would feel very frustrated if he had sold all his wares in the early morning and had no further occasion for this satisfaction in human relations. For the salesgirl in the five-and-ten-cent store the situation is radically different. While she does not have to smile as much as a higher-paid salesgirl at a more fashionable store, her alienation from the customer is exactly the same. There is no genuine human intercourse. She operates as part of the sales' machine, is afraid of being fired, and eager to make good. The work situation as a social situation is inhuman, empty and deprived of any kind of satisfaction. It is true, of course that the Indian sells his own product, and reaps his own profit, but even a small independent shopkeeper will also be bored unless he transforms the social aspect of the work situation into a human one.

Turning now to recent studies in the field of industrial psychology, we find a good deal of evidence for the significance of the differentiation between the technical and the social aspect of the work situation, and furthermore for the enlivening and stimulating effect of the active and responsible participation of the worker in his job.

One of the most striking examples of the fact that technically monotonous work can be interesting, if the work situation as a whole permits of interest and active participation, is the by now classic experiment carried out by Elton Mayo [1] at the Chicago Hawthorne Works of the Western Electric Company. The operation selected was that of assembling telephone coils, work which ranks as a repetitive performance, and is usually performed by women. A standard assembly bench with the appropriate equipment, and with places for five women workers was put into a room, which was separated by a partition from the main assembly room; altogether six operatives worked in this room, five working at the bench, and one distributing parts to those engaged in the assembly. All of the women were experienced workers. Two of them dropped out within the first year, and their places were taken by two other workers of equal skill. Altogether, the experiment lasted for five years, and was divided into various experimental periods, in which certain changes were made in the conditions of work. Without going into the details of these changes, it suffices to state that rest pauses were adopted in the morning

[1] cf. Elton Mayo, *The Human Problems of an Industrial Civilization*, The Macmillan Company, 2nd ed., New York, 1946. cf. also F. J. Roethlisberger and W. J. Dickson, *Management and the Worker*, Harvard University Press, Cambridge, 10th ed. 1950.

and afternoon, refreshments offered during these rest pauses, and the hours of work cut by half an hour. Throughout these changes, the output of each worker rose considerably. So far, so good; nothing was more plausible than the assumption that increased rest periods and some attempt to make the worker "feel better" were the cause for an increased efficiency. But a new arrangement in the twelfth experimental period disappointed this expectation and showed rather dramatic results: by arrangement with the workers, the group returned to the conditions of work as they had existed in the beginning of the experiment. Rest periods, special refreshments, and other improvements were all abolished for approximately three months. To everybody's amazement this did not result in a *decrease* of output but, on the contrary, the daily and weekly output rose to a higher point than at any time before. In the next period, the old concessions were introduced again, with the only exception that the girls provided their own food, while the company continued to supply coffee for the midmorning lunch. The output still continued to rise. And not only the output. What is equally important is the fact that the rate of sickness among the workers in this experiment fell by about 80 per cent in comparison with the general rate, and that a new social friendly intercourse developed among the working women participating in the experiment.

How can we explain the surprising result that "the steady increase seemed to ignore the experimental changes in its upward development"? [1] If it was not the rest pauses, the tea, the shortened working time, what was it that made the workers produce more, be more healthy and more friendly among themselves? The answer is obvious: while the *technical* aspect of monotonous, uninteresting work remained the same, and while even certain improvements like rest pauses were not decisive, the *social* aspect of the total

[1] E. Mayo, *loc. cit.*, p. 63.

work situation had changed, and caused a change in the attitude of the workers. They were informed of the experiment, and of the several steps in it; their suggestions were listened to and often followed, and what is perhaps the most important point, they were aware of participating in a meaningful and interesting experiment, which was important not only to themselves, but to the workers of the whole factory. While they were at first "shy and uneasy, silent and perhaps somewhat suspicious of the company's intentions," later their attitude was marked "by confidence and candour." The group developed a sense of participation in the work, because they knew what they were doing, they had an aim and purpose, and they could influence the whole procedure by their suggestions.

The startling results of Mayo's experiment show that sickness, fatigue and a resulting low output are not caused primarily by the monotonous *technical* aspect of the work, but by the alienation of the worker from the total work situation in its social aspects. As soon as this alienation was decreased to a certain extent by having the worker participate in something that was meaningful to him, and in which he had a voice, his whole psychological reaction to the work changed, although technically he was still doing the same kind of work.

Mayo's Hawthorne experiment was followed by a number of research projects which tend to prove that the social aspect of the work situation has a decisive influence on the attitude of the worker, even though the work process in its technical aspect remains the same. Thus, for instance, Wyatt and his associates ". . . provided clues as to other characteristics of the work situation which affect the *will to work*. These showed that variation in the rate of work in different individuals was dependent upon the prevailing group or *social atmosphere, i.e.,* on a collective influence which formed an intangible background and determined the general nature of the reactions to the conditions of work." [1] It is to the same point that in a smaller-sized working group, subjective satisfaction and output are higher than in larger working groups, although in the factories compared, the nature of the work process was almost identical, and physical conditions and welfare amenities were of a high order and much alike.[2] The relationship between group size and morale have also been noted in a study by Hewitt and Parfit, conducted in a British textile plant.[3] Here, the nonsickness "absence rate" was found to be significantly greater among workers in large-sized rooms than among those in smaller rooms accommodating fewer employees." [4] An earlier study in the aircraft industry, conducted during World War II by Mayo and Lombard,[5] arrives at very similar results.

The social aspect of the work situation as against the purely technical one has been given special emphasis by G. Friedmann. As one example of the difference between these two aspects, he describes the "Psychological climate" which often develops among the men working together on a conveyor belt. Personal bonds and interests develop among the working team, and the work situation in its total aspect is much less monotonous than it would appear to the outsider who takes into account only the technical aspect.[6]

[1] Survey reported in the Public Opinion Index for Industry in 1947, quoted from M. S. Viteles, *Motivation and Morale in Industry*, W. W. Norton & Company, New York, 1953, p. 134.

[2] M. S. Viteles, *loc. cit.*, p. 138.

[3] D. Hewitt and J. Parfit on *Working Morale and Size of Group Occupational Psychology*, 1953.

[4] M. S. Viteles, *loc. cit.*, p. 139.

[5] E. Mayo and G. F. F. Lombard, "Team Work and Labour Turnover in the Aircraft Industry of Southern California," Harvard Graduate School of Business, *Business Research Series No. 32*, 1944.

[6] G. Friedmann, *Où va le Travail Humain?*, Gallimard, Paris, 1950, p. 139. cf. also his *Machine et Humanisme*, Gallimard, Paris, 1946, pp. 329, 330 and 370 ff.

While the previous examples from research in industrial psychology [1] show us the results of even a small degree of active participation within the framework of modern industrial organization, we arrive at insights which are much more convincing from the standpoint of the possibilities of the transformation of our industrial organization by turning to the reports on the *communitarian movement,* one of the most significant and interesting movements in Europe today.

There are around one hundred Communities of Work in Europe, mainly in France, but also some in Belgium, Switzerland and Holland. Some of them are industrial, and some of them are agricultural. They differ among themselves in various aspects; nevertheless the basic principles are sufficiently similar so that the description of one gives an adequate picture of the essential features of all. [2]

Boimondau is a watch-case factory. In fact, it has become one of the seven largest such factories in France. It was founded by Marcel Barbu. He had to work hard in order to save enough to

---

[1] In the same direction are the experiments with "job enlargement" made by I.B.M. the main point of which is to show that the worker feels more satisfied if the extreme division of labor and the ensuing senselessness of his work is changed for an operation which combines several thus far separated operations in one more meaningful one. Furthermore, the experience reported by Walker and Guest, who found that automobile workers preferred a method of work in which they could at least *see* the parts they had finished ("banking"). In an experiment conducted in a Harwood Manufacturing Co. plant, democratic methods and decision making by the workers in an experimental group, led to an increase of output of 14 per cent within this group. (cf. Viteles, *loc. cit.*, pp. 164–167.) A study by P. French Jr. on sewing machine operators reports a rise of output of 18 per cent as a result of increased participation of workers in planning of the work and decision making. (J. R. P. French, "Field Experiments," in J. G. Miller, [ed.] *Experiments in Social Process,* The McGraw-Hill Book Co., New York, 1950, pp. 83–88). The same principle was applied in England during the war, when pilots came to visit factories to explain to the workers how their products were actually used in combat.

[2] I follow here a description of the Work Communities given in *All Things Common,* by Claire Huchet Bishop, Harper and Brothers, New York, 1950. I consider this penetrating and thoughtful work one of the most enlightening ones dealing with the psychological problems of industrial organization and the possibilities for the future.

have a factory of his own, where he introduced a factory council and a wage rating approved by all, including sharing in the profits. But this enlightened paternalism was not what Barbu was aiming at. After the French defeat in 1940, Barbu wanted to make a real start toward the liberation he had in mind. Since he could not find mechanics in Valence, he went out into the streets, and found a barber, a sausagemaker, a waiter—practically anyone except specialized industrial workers. "The men were all under thirty. He offered to teach them watch-case making, provided they would agree to *search* with him for a setup in which the 'distinction between employer and employee would be abolished.' The point was the search." . . . "The first and epoch-making discovery was that each worker should be free to tell the other off. . . . At once, this complete freedom of speech between themselves and their employer created a buoyant atmosphere of confidence.

"It soon became evident, however, that 'telling each other off' led to discussions and a waste of time on the job. So they unanimously set apart a time every week for an informal meeting to iron out differences and conflicts.

"But as they were not out just for a better economic setup but a new way of living together, discussions were bound to lead to the disclosure of basic attitudes. 'Very soon,' says Barbu, 'we saw the necessity of a common basis, or what we called, from then on, our common ethics.'

"Unless there was a common ethical basis, there was no point to start from together and therefore no possibility of building anything. To find a common ethical basis was not easy, because the two dozen workers now engaged were all different: Catholics, Protestants, materialists, Humanists, atheists, Communists. They all examined their own individual ethics, that is, not what they had been taught by rote, or what was conventionally accepted, but what they, out of their own experiences and thoughts, found necessary.

"They discovered that their individual ethics had certain points in common. They took those points and made them the common minimum on which they agreed unanimously. It was not a theoretical, vague declaration. In their foreword they declared:

" 'There is no danger that our common ethical minimum should be an arbitrary convention, for, in order to determine the points we rely on life experiences. All our moral principles have been tried in real life, everyday life, everybody's life. . . .'

"What they had rediscovered, all by themselves and step by step, was natural ethics, the Decalogue,[1] which they expressed in their own words as follows:

"Thou wilt love thy neighbor.
"Thou shalt not kill.
"Thou shalt not take thy neighbor's good.
"Thou shalt not lie.
"Thou wilt be faithful to thy promise.
"Thou shalt earn thy bread by the sweat of thy brow.
"Thou shalt respect thy neighbor, his person, his liberty.
"Thou shalt respect thyself.
"Thou shalt fight first against thyself, all vices which debase man, all the passions which hold man in slavery and are detrimental to social life: pride, avarice, lust, covetousness, gluttony, anger, laziness.
"Thou shalt hold that there are goods higher than life itself: liberty, human dignity, truth, justice. . . ."

"The men pledged themselves to do their best to practice their common ethical minimum in their everyday life. They pledged themselves to each other. Those who had more exacting private ethics pledged themselves to try to live what they believed, but recognized that they had absolutely no right to infringe on the

---

[1] Minus the first commandment, which bears on man's destiny and not on ethics.

liberties of others. In fact, they all agreed to respect fully the others' convictions or absence of convictions to the extent of never laughing at them or making jokes about it." [1]

The second discovery the group made was that they craved to educate themselves. They figured out that the time they saved on production could be used for education. Within three months, the productivity of their work grew so much, that they could save nine hours on a forty-eight-hour week. What did they do? They used these nine hours for education and were paid for it as for regular work hours. First they wanted to sing well together, then to polish their French grammar, then to learn how to read business accounts. From there, other courses developed, all given at the factory by the best instructors they could find. The instructors were paid the regular rates. There were courses in engineering, physics, literature, Marxism, Christianity, dancing, singing and basket ball.

Their principle is: "We do not start from the plant, from the technical activity of man, but from man himself. . . . In a Community of Work accent is not on *acquiring* together, but on *working together* for a collective and personal fulfillment." [2] The aim is not increased productivity, or higher wages, but a new style of life which "far from relinquishing the advantages of the industrial revolution, is adapted to them." [3] These are the principles on which this and other Communities of Work are built:

"1. In order to live a man's life one has to enjoy the whole fruit of one's labor.

"2. One has to be able to educate oneself.

1 C. H. Bishop, *loc. cit.*, pp. 5, 6, 7.
2 *Ibid.*, p. 12. (Italics mine, E.F.)
3 *Ibid.*, p. 13.

"3. One has to pursue a common endeavor within a professional group proportioned to the stature of man (100 families maximum).

"4. One has to be actively related to the whole world.

"When these requisites are examined one discovers that they amount to a shifting of the center of the problem of living—from making and acquiring 'things,' to discovering, fostering and developing human relationships. From a civilization of objects to a civilization of persons; better even—a civilization of movement between persons." [1]

As to payment, it corresponds to the achievement of the single worker, but it takes into account not only professional work, but also "any human activity which had value for the group: A first-class mechanic who can play the violin, who is jolly and a good mixer, etc., has more value to the Community than another mechanic, equally capable professionally, but who is a sourpuss, a bachelor, etc." [2] On an average all workers earn between 10 and 20 per cent more than they would with union wages, not counting all the special advantages.

The Community of Work acquired a farm of 235 acres, on which everybody, including the wives, work three periods of ten days each year. As everybody has a month's vacation, it means that people work only ten months a year at the factory. The idea behind it is not only the characteristic love of the Frenchman for the country, but also the conviction that no man should be entirely divorced from the soil.

Most interesting is the solution they have found for a blend between centralization and decentralization which avoids the danger of chaos, and at the same time makes every member of the community an active and responsible participant in the life

[1] *Ibid.*, p. 13.
[2] *Ibid.*, p. 14.

of the factory and of the community. We see here how the same kind of thought and observation which led to the formulation of the theories underlying the modern democratic state in the eighteenth and nineteenth centuries, (division of powers, system of checks and balances, etcetera) was applied to the organization of an industrial enterprise.

"Ultimate power rests on the *General Assembly*, which meets twice a year. Only unanimous decisions bind the Companions (members).

"The General Assembly elects a *Chief of Community*. Unanimous vote only. The Chief is not only the most qualified technically, as a manager should be, he is also 'the man who is an example, who educates, who loves, who is selfless, who serves. To obey a so-called Chief without those qualities would be cowardice.'

"The Chief has all executive power for three years. At the end of this period he may find himself back at the machines.

"The Chief has the right of veto against the General Assembly. If the General Assembly does not want to yield, a vote of confidence has to be taken. If confidence is not granted unanimously, the Chief has the choice either to rally to the General Assembly's opinion or to resign.

"The General Assembly elects the members of the *General Council*. The General Council's task is to counsel the Chief of Community. Members are elected for one year. The General Council meets at least every four months. There are seven members plus the Heads of Departments. All decisions have to be taken unanimously.

"Within the General Council, section managers and eight members (including two wives) and the Chief of Community form the *Council of Direction*, which meets weekly.

"All responsible positions in the Community, including section managers and foremen, are secured only through 'double trust' appointment, that is, the person is proposed by one level and unanimously accepted by the other level. Usually, but not always, candidates are proposed by the higher level and accepted or rejected by the lower. This, say the members, prevents both demagogy and authoritarianism.

"All members meet once a week in an *Assembly of Contact*, which, as the name indicates, aims at keeping everybody abreast of what is happening in the Community and also of keeping in touch with each other." [1]

A particularly important feature of the whole Community are the *Neighbor Groups,* which meet periodically. "A Neighbor Group is the smallest organism of the Community. Five or six families which do not live too far from each other get together in the evening after supper under the guidance of a Chief of Neighbor Groups chosen according to the principle mentioned above.

"In a sense, the Neighbor Group is the most important unit in the Community. It is 'leaven' and 'lever.' It is required to meet at one of the families' home and at no other place. There, while drinking coffee, all the issues are thrashed out together. Minutes of the meeting are taken down and sent to the Chief of Community, who sums up the minutes of all the Neighbor Groups. Answers to their questions are then given by those who are in charge of the different departments. In that way Neighbor Groups not only ask questions but voice discontent or make suggestions. It is also of course in the Neighbor Groups that people come to know each other best and help each other." [2]

Another feature of the Community is the *Court.* It is elected

[1] *Ibid.*, pp. 17, 18.
[2] *Ibid.*, pp. 18, 19.

by the General Assembly, and its function is to decide on conflicts which arise between two departments, or between a department and a member; if the Chief of the Community cannot iron it out, the eight members of the Court (unanimous votes, as usual), do so. There is no set of laws, and the verdict is based on, and directed by the constitution of the Community, the common ethic minimum and common sense.

At Boimondau there are two main sectors: the social and the industrial sector. The latter has the following structure:

"Men—maximum 10—form technical teams.

"Several teams form a section, a shop.

"Several sections form a service.

"Members of teams are responsible all together toward the section, several sections toward the service." [1]

The social department deals with all activities other than technical ones. "All members, including wives, are expected to carry on their spiritual, intellectual, artistic and physical development. In that respect reading the monthly review of Boimondau, *Le Lien*, is enlightening. Reports and commentaries on everything: football matches (competing with outside teams), photographic displays, visits to art exhibits, cooking recipes, ecumenical gatherings, reviews of musical performances such as Loewenguth Quartet, appreciation of films, lectures on Marxism, basketball scores, discussion on conscientious objectors, accounts of days at the farm, reports on what America has to teach, passages from St. Thomas of Aquinas regarding money, reviews of books such as Louis Bromfield's *Pleasant Valley* and Sartre's *Dirty Hands*, etcetera. A resilient spirit of good will permeates it all. *Le Lien* is a candid picture of people who have said 'yes' to life, and this with a maximum of consciousness.

[1] *Ibid.*, p. 23.

"There are 28 social sections, but new ones are constantly added:

" (Teams listed according to numerical importance).

"1. Spiritual Section:
   Catholic team
   Humanist team
   Materialist team
   Protestant team

"2. Intellectual Section:
   General Knowledge team
   Civic Instruction team
   Library team

"3. Artistic Section:
   Theater team
   Singing team
   Interior Decorating team
   Photo team

"4. Communitarian Life Section:
   Cooperative team
   Festivals and Gatherings team
   Movie team
   Countereffort team

"5. Mutual Aid Section:
   Solidarity team
   Household Maintenance team
   Bookbinding team

"6. Family Section:
   Child Care team
   Education team
   Social Life team

"7. Health Section:
   2 registered nurses

   1 practical nurse for general information
   3 visiting nurses
"8. Sports Section:
   Basketball team (men)
   Basketball team (women)
   Cross-country team
   Football team
   Volleyball team
   Physical Culture team (men)
   Physical Culture team (women)
"9. Newspaper Team" [1]

Perhaps better than any definition, some statements of members of the Community can give an idea of the spirit and practice of the Community of Work:

"A union member writes:

"I was shop delegate in 1936, arrested in 1940 and sent to Buchenwald. For twenty years I have known many capitalist firms. . . . In the Community of Work production is not the aim for living, but the means. . . . I did not dare hope such large and complete results during my generation.

"A Communist writes:

"As a member of the French Communist Party, and in order to avoid misunderstanding, I declare that I am entirely satisfied with my work and my communitarian life; my political opinions are respected, my complete liberty and my previous life ideal have become a reality.

"A materialist writes:

"As an atheist and a materialist, I consider that one of the most beautiful human values is tolerance and the respect of religious and philosophical opinions. For that reason I feel particularly at home in our Community of Work. Not only is my

[1] *Ibid.*, p. 35.

315

freedom of thought and expression left intact, but I find in the Community the material means and the time necessary to a deeper study of my philosophical conviction.

"A Catholic writes:

"I have been in the Community for four years. I belong to the Catholic group. Like all Christians I am trying to build a society in which the liberty and the dignity of the human being will be respected. . . . I declare, in the name of the whole Catholic group, that the Community of Work is the type of society that a Christian can wish for. There, every man is free, respected, and everything inclines him to do better and to search for Truth. If outwardly that society cannot be called Christian, it is Christian in fact. Christ gave us the sign through which it is possible to recognize his own: And we do love one another.

"A Protestant writes:

"We, Protestants in the Community, declare that this revolution of society is the solution that enables every man, freely to find his fulfillment in the way he has chosen. This without any conflict with his materialist or Catholic companions. . . . The Community composed of men who love one another fulfills our wishes to see men living in harmony together and knowing why they want to live.

"A Humanist writes:

"I was 15 years old when I left school, I left the church at 11, after my first communion. I had gone a little ahead in my schooling, but the spiritual problem was gone out of my mind. I was like the great majority: 'I did not give a d——' At 22 I entered the Community. At once I found there an atmosphere of study and work like in no other place. First I was attracted by the social side of the Community, and it was only later that I understood what the human value could be. Then I rediscovered that spiritual and moral side which is in man and which I had lost at the age of 11. . . . I belong to the humanist group, because I do not see the problem like the Christians or the materialists do. I love our Community because through it all the deep aspirations which are in each of us can be awakened, met and developed, so that we may be transformed from individuals into men." [1]

The principles of other communities whether they are agricultural or industrial, resemble those of Boimondau. Here are some statements from the Rule of the R. G. Workshops, a Community of Work which manufactures picture frames, quoted by the author of *All Things Common:*

"Our Community of Work is not a new form of enterprise nor a reform in order to harmonize the relation capital-labor.

"It is a new mode of living in which man should find his fulfillment, and in which all problems are solved in relation to the whole man. Thereby it is in opposition to present-day society, where solutions for the one or for the few are the usual concern.

". . . the consequence of bourgeois morality and capitalist system is a specialization of the activities of man to such a degree that man lives in moral misery, physical misery, intellectual misery or material misery.

"Often, in the working class, men suffer these four kinds of misery all together, and, under such conditions, it is a lie to speak of liberty, equality, fraternity.

"The aim of the Community of Work is to make possible the full development of man.

"Companions of R. G. declare that this is possible only within an atmosphere of liberty, equality, fraternity.

"But it should be acknowledged that, very often, those three words bring nothing to our mind except the picture on currency or the inscriptions on front doors of public buildings.

[1] *Ibid.,* pp. 35–37.

"LIBERTY

"A Man is really free only under three conditions:

"Economic freedom

"Intellectual freedom

"Moral freedom

"Economic Freedom. Man has an inalienable right to work. He has to have absolute right to the fruit of his work from which he should not part except freely.

"This conception is opposed to private property of collective means of production and to the reproducing of money by money which makes possible the exploitation of man by man.

"We also declare that by 'Work' should be understood everything of value man brings to society.

"Intellectual Freedom. A man is free only if he can choose. He can choose only if he knows enough to compare.

"Moral Freedom. A man cannot be really free if he is enslaved by his passions. He can be free only if he has an ideal and a philosophical attitude which makes it possible for him to have a coherent activity in life.

"He cannot, under pretext of hastening his economic or intellectual liberation, use means contrary to the ethics of the Community.

"Last, moral freedom does not mean license. It would be easy to demonstrate that moral freedom is to be found only within strict observance of the group ethics freely accepted.

"FRATERNITY

"Man can blossom only in society. Selfishness is a dangerous and non-lasting way of helping oneself. Man cannot separate his true interests from those of society. He can help himself only by helping society.

"He should become conscious that his own inclination makes him find an increase of joy with others.

"Solidarity is not only a task, it is a satisfaction and the best guarantee of security.

"Fraternity leads to mutual tolerance and to the determination never to separate. This makes it possible to take all decisions unanimously on a common minimum.

"EQUALITY

"We condemn those who declare demagogically that all men are equal. We can see that men are not equal in value.

"For us equality of rights means to put at the disposal of everyone the means to fulfill oneself completely.

Thereby we substitute a hierarchy of personal value for the conventional or hereditary hierarchy." [1]

Summing up the most remarkable points in the principles of these Communities, I want to mention the following:

1. The Communities of Work do make use of all modern industrial techniques, and avoid the tendency of going back to handicraft production.

2. They have devised a scheme in which active participation of everyone does not contradict a sufficiently centralized leadership; irrational authority has been replaced by rational authority.

3. The emphasis on the practice of life as against ideological differences. This emphasis enables men of the most varied and contradictory convictions to live together in brotherliness and tolerance without any danger of having to follow the "right opinion" proclaimed by the community.

4. The integration of work, social and cultural activities. Inasmuch as the work is not attractive technically, it is meaningful and attractive in its social aspect. Activity in the arts and sciences is an integral part of the total situation.

5. The situation of alienation is overcome, work has become a

[1] *Ibid.*, pp. 134–137.

meaningful expression of human energy, human solidarity is established without restriction of freedom—or the danger of conformity.

While many of the arrangements and principles of the Communities can be questioned and argued about, it seems nevertheless that we have here one of the most convincing empirical examples of a productive life, and of possibilities which are generally looked upon as fantastic from the standpoint of our present-day life in Capitalism.[1]

The communities described so far are, of course not the only examples for the possibility of communitarian life. Whether we take Owen's communities, or those of the Mennonites or Hutterites,[2] or the agricultural settlements in the State of Israel, they all contribute to our knowledge of the possibilities of a new style of life. They also show that most of these communitarian experiments are executed by men with a shrewd intelligence, and an immensely practical sense. They are by no means the dreamers our so-called realists believe them to be; on the contrary, they are mostly more realistic and imaginative than our conventional business leaders appear to be. Undoubtedly there have been many shortcomings in the principles and practice of these experiments,

[1] Mention must be made of the efforts of A. Olivetti in Italy to create a communitarian movement there. As head of the greatest typewriter factory in Italy, he has not only organized his factory in terms of the most enlightened practices to be found anywhere, but he has also worked out a whole scheme for an organization of society in a federation of communities based on principles which have Christian and socialist concerns (cf. his *L'Ordine Politico delle Communitá*, Roma, 1946). Olivetti has also made a certain beginning by founding community centers in various Italian cities; nevertheless the main difference from the communities mentioned so far is that on the one hand his own factory has not been transformed into a Community of Work, and apparently cannot be because Olivetti is not the sole owner, and also the fact that Olivetti has made specific plans for the organization of the whole society, thus giving more emphasis to a specific picture of the social and political structure than the communities in the communitarian movement have done.

[2] Cf. the article by C. Kratu, J. W. Fretz, R. Kreider, "Altruism in Mennonite Life" in *Form and Techniques of Altruistic and Spiritual Growth*, ed. by P. A. Sorokin, The Beacon Press, Boston, 1954.

which must be recognized in order to be avoided. Undoubtedly also, the nineteenth century with its unshakable belief in the wholesome effect of industrial competitiveness was less conducive to the success of these colonies than the second half of the twentieth century will be. But the glib condescension implying the futility and lack of realism of all these experiments is not any more reasonable than was the first popular reaction to the possibilities of railroad and later of aeroplane travel. It is essentially a symptom of the laziness of the mind and the inherent conviction that what has not been cannot be and will not be.

E. PRACTICAL SUGGESTIONS

The question is whether conditions similar to those created by the communitarians can be created for the whole of our society. The aim then would be to create a work situation in which man gives his lifetime and energy to something which has meaning for him, in which he knows what he is doing, has an influence on what is being done, and feels united with, rather than separated from, his fellow man. This implies that the work situation is made concrete again; that the workers are organized into sufficiently small groups to enable the individual to relate himself to the group as real, concrete human beings, even though the factory as a whole may have many thousands of workers. It means that methods of blending centralization and decentralization are found which permit active participation and responsibility for everybody, and at the same time create a unified leadership as far as it is necessary.

How can this be done?

The first condition for an active participation of the worker is that he is well informed not only about his own work, but about the performance of the whole enterprise. Such knowledge is, for one thing, technical knowledge of the work process.

A worker may have to make only a specific move on the conveyor belt, and it may be sufficient for his performance if he is trained on the job for two days, or two weeks, but his whole attitude toward his work would be different if he had a wider knowledge of all the technical problems involved in the production of the whole product. Such technical knowledge can be acquired in the first place by attendance at an industrial school, simultaneously with his first years of work in a factory. Furthermore, they can be acquired continuously by participating in technical and scientific courses given to all the workers of the factory, even at the expense of time taken from the job.[1] If the technical process employed in the factory is an object of interest and knowledge to the worker, if his own thinking process is stimulated by such knowledge, even the otherwise monotonous technical work he has to perform will assume a different aspect. Aside from technical knowledge about the industrial process, another knowledge is necessary: that of the economic function of the enterprise he is working for, and its relationship to the economic needs and problems of the community as a whole. Again, by schooling during the first years of his work, and by constant information given to him about the economic processes involved in his enterprise, the worker can acquire real knowledge of its function within the national and world economy.

However important, technically and economically, this knowledge of the work process and the functioning of the whole enterprise is, it is not enough. Theoretical knowledge and interest stagnate if there is no way of translating them into action. The worker can become an active, interested and responsible partici-

---

[1] This is already being done as a first step in this direction by some of the great industrial enterprises. The Communitarians have shown that not only technical, but also many other kinds of instruction can be given during working time.

pant only if he can have influence on the decisions which bear upon his individual work situation and the whole enterprise. His alienation from work can be overcome only if he is not employed by capital, if he is not the object of command, but if he becomes a responsible *subject who employs capital.* The principal point here is not *ownership of the means of production,* but *participation in management and decision making.* As in the political sphere, the problem here is to avoid the danger of an anarchic state of affairs in which central planning and leadership would be lacking; but the alternative between centralized authoritarian management and planless, unco-ordinated workers' management is not a necessary one. The answer lies in a blending of centralization and decentralization, in a synthesis between decision making flowing from above to below, and from below to above.

The principle of co-management and workers' participation can be worked out in such a way that the responsibility for management is divided between the central leadership and the rank and file. Well-informed small groups discuss matters of their own work situation and of the whole enterprise; their decisions would be channelled to the management and form the basis for a real co-management. As a third participant, the consumer would have to participate in the decision making and planning in some form. Once we accept the principle that the primary purpose of any work is to serve people, and not to make a profit, those who are served must have a say in the operation of those

---

[1] cf. the ideas expressed by G. G. Friedmann in his wise and stimulating study *Machine et Humanisme,* Gallimard, Paris, 1946, especially p. 371 ff. One of the great masters of sociology, and one of the great personalities of our time, Alfred Weber, in his profound *Der Drittee oder der Vierte Mensch,* Piper Co., München, 1953, arrives at conclusions similar to the ones expressed here. He emphasizes the need for co-management of workers and employees, and the reduction of big enterprises into smaller units of optimal size coupled with the abolition of the profit motive, and introduction of a socialist form of competition. However, no external change will suffice; "we need a new human cristallization." (*loc. cit.,* p. 91 ff.)

who serve them. Again, as in the case of political decentralization, it is not easy to find such forms, but certainly it is not an unsurmountable problem, provided the general principle of co-management is accepted. In constitutional law we have solved similar problems with regard to the respective rights of various branches of government, and in the laws concerning corporations we have solved the same problem with regard to the right of various types of stockholders, management, etc.

The principle of co-management and co-determination means a serious restriction of property rights. The owner or owners of an enterprise would be entitled to a reasonable rate of interest on their capital investment, but not to the unrestricted command over men whom this capital can hire. They would have at least to share this right with those who work in the enterprise. In fact, as far as the big corporations are concerned, the stockholders do not really exercise their property rights by making decisions; if the workers shared the right to make decisions with the management, the factual role of the stockholders would not be fundamentally different. A law introducing co-management would be a restriction of property rights, but by no means any revolutionary change in such rights. Even an industrialist as conservative as the protagonist of profit sharing in industry, J. F. Lincoln, proposes, as we have seen, that the dividends should not exceed a relatively fixed and constant amount, and that the profit exceeding this amount should be divided among the workers. There are possibilities for workers co-management and control even on the basis of present-day conditions. B. F. Fairless, for instance, the chairman of the Board of the United States Steel Corporation said in a recent address, (published in a condensed form in the *Reader's Digest*, November 15, 1953, p. 17) that the three hundred thousand employees of United States Steel could buy all the common stock of the corporation by purchasing

87 shares apiece, at a total cost of $3,500. "By investing $10 (per week) apiece—which is about what our steel workers gained in the recent wage increase—the employees of U.S. Steel could buy all of the outstanding common stock in less than seven years." Actually, they would not even have to purchase that much, but only part of it in order to have enough of the stock to give them a voting majority.

Another proposal has been made by F. Tannenbaum in his *A Philosophy of Labor.* He suggests that the unions could buy sufficient shares of the enterprises whose workers they represent to control the management of these enterprises.[1] Whatever the method employed is, it is an evolutionary one, only continuing trends in property relations which already exist, and they are means to an end—and only means—to make it possible that men work for a meaningful aim in a meaningful way, and are not bearers of a commodity—physical energy and skill—which is bought and sold like any other commodity.

In discussing workers' participation one important point must be stressed, the danger namely, that such participation could develop in the direction of the profit sharing concepts of the super-capitalist type. If the workers and employees of an enterprise were exclusively concerned with *their* enterprise, the alienation between man and his social forces would remain unchanged. The egotistical, alienated attitude would only have been extended from one individual to the "team." It is therefore not an incidental but an essential part of workers' participation that they look beyond their own enterprise, that they be interested in and connected with consumers as well as with other workers in the same industry, and with the working population as a whole. The development of a kind of local patriotism for the firm, of an "esprit de corps" similar to that of college and uni-

[1] F. Tannenbaum, *A Philosophy of Labor,* loc. cit.

versity students, as recommended by Wyatt and other British social psychologists, would only reinforce the asocial and egotistical attitude which is the essence of alienation. All such suggestions in favor of "team" enthusiasm ignore the fact that there is only one truly social orientation, namely the one of solidarity with mankind. Social cohesion within the group, combined with antagonism to the outsider, is not social feeling but extended egotism.

Concluding these remarks on workers' participation, I want to stress again, even at the risk of being repetitious, that all suggestions in the direction of the humanization of work do not have the aim of increasing economic output nor is their goal a greater satisfaction with work *per se*. They make sense only in a totally different social structure, in which economic activity is a part—and a subordinate part—of social life. One cannot separate work activity from political activity, from the use of leisure time and from personal life. If work were to become interesting without the other spheres of life becoming human, no real change would occur. In fact, it could not become interesting. It is the very evil of present-day culture that it separates and compartmentalizes the various spheres of living. The way to sanity lies in overcoming this split and in arriving at a new unification and integration within society and within the individual human being.

I have spoken before of the discouragement among many socialists with the results of applied Socialism. But there is a growing awareness that the fault was not with the basic aim of Socialism, an unalienated society in which every working person participates actively and responsibly in industry and in politics, but with the wrong emphasis on private versus communal property and the neglect of the human and properly social factors. There is, correspondingly, a growing insight into the necessity for a socialist vision which is centered around the idea of workers' participation and co-management, on decentralization, and on the concrete function of man in the working process, rather than on the abstract concept of property. The ideas of Owen, Fourier, Kropotkin, Landauer, of religious and secular communitarians, become fused with those of Marx and Engels; one becomes skeptical of purely ideological formulations of the "final aims," and more concerned with the concrete person, with the here and now. There is hope that there may be also growing awareness among democratic and humanist socialists that Socialism begins at home, that is to say, with the *socialization of the socialist parties*. Socialism is meant here, of course, not in terms of property rights, but in terms of responsible participation of each member. As long as the socialist parties do not realize the principle of Socialism within their own ranks, they cannot expect to convince others; their representatives would, if they had political power, execute their ideas in the spirit of Capitalism, regardless of the socialist labels they used. The same holds true for trade unions; inasmuch as their aim is industrial democracy, they must introduce the principle of democracy in their own organizations, rather than run them as any other big business is run in Capitalism—or sometimes even worse.

The influence of this communitarian emphasis on the concrete situation of the worker in his work process was quite powerful in the past among Spanish and French anarchists and syndicalists, and among the Russian Social Revolutionaries. Although the importance of these ideas had been receding in most countries for some time, it seems that they are slowly gaining ground again in less ideological and dogmatic and hence more real and concrete forms.

In one of the most interesting recent publications on the problems of Socialism, the *New Fabian Essays,* one can detect this growing emphasis on the functional and human aspect of Socialism. C. A. R. Crosland writes in his essay on "The Transition from Capitalism": "Socialism requires that this hostility in industry should give way to a feeling of participation in a joint endeavour. How is this to be achieved? The most direct and easily exploitable line of advance is in the direction of joint consultation. Much fruitful work has been done in this sphere, and it is now clear that something more is needed than joint production committees on the present model—some more radical effort to give the worker a sense of participation in the making of decisions. A few progressive firms have already made bold advances, and the results are encouraging." [1] He suggests three measures: large-scale extension of nationalization, statutory dividend limitation or: "A third possibility is so to alter the legal structure of company ownership as to substitute for shareholders' sole control a constitution which explicitly defines the responsibilities of the firm to worker, consumer and community; workers would become members of the company, and have their representatives on the board of directors." [2]

R. Jenkins in his paper on "Equality" sees as the issue of the future, ". . . in the first place, whether the capitalists, having surrendered or had taken from them so much of their power, and therefore of their functions, should be allowed to retain the quite substantial portion of their privileges which still remain to them; and, in the second place, whether the society which is growing out of capitalism is to be a participant, democratic socialist society, or whether it is to be a managerial society, controlled by a privileged elite enjoying a standard of living substantially different from that of the mass of the population." [3] Jenkins

[1] cf. C. A. R. Crosland, "The Transition from Capitalism," in the *New Fabian Essays*, ed. by R. H. S. Crossman, Turnstile Press, Ltd., London, 1953, p. 66.
[2] *loc. cit.*, p. 67.
[3] *Ibid.*, p. 72.

came to the conclusion that "a participant, democratic socialist society" requires that the "ownership of enterprises, when it passes from wealthy individuals, should go, not to the state, but to less remote public bodies," and should permit greater diffusion of power and "encourage people of all sorts to play a more active part in the work and control of public and voluntary organizations."

A. Albu in "The Organisation of Industry" states: "However successful the nationalisation of basic industries has been in technical and economic terms, it has not satisfied the desire for a wider and more democratic distribution of authority nor built up any real measure of participation, by those engaged in them, in managerial decisions and their execution. This has been a disappointment to many socialists who never wished for a great concentration of state power, but who had none but the most hazy and Utopian ideas of any alternatives. The lessons of totalitarianism abroad and the growth of the managerial revolution at home have underlined their anxiety; all the more so as full employment in a society which remains democratic is seen to create problems which need for their solution the widest possible popular sanction based on information and consultation. Consultation is the less successful the further it recedes from face-to-face discussion on the job; and the size and structure of industrial units and the degree to which they can exercise independent initiative are therefore seen as matters of supreme importance." [1] "What is finally required," says Albu, "is a consultative system which will provide sanction for policy decisions and for an executive authority willingly accepted by all the members of an industry. How to reconcile this conception of industrial democracy with the more primitive desire for self-government which activated the syndicalists, and which underlies so much current discussion

[1] *New Fabian Essays*, p. 121, 122.

on joint consultation, is a matter on which much research needs still to be done. It would seem, however, that there must exist some process by which all those employed in an industry are enabled to participate in policy decisions; either through directly elected representatives on the board or through a hierarchical system of joint consultation with considerable powers. In either case there must also be an increasing participation in the process of interpreting policy and of making decisions at subordinate levels.

"The creation of a feeling of common purpose in the activities of industry still remains, therefore, one of the outstanding un-attained objectives of socialist industrial policy." [1]

John Strachey, who is the most optimistic and perhaps the most satisfied with the result of the Labour government among the writers in the *New Fabian Essays,* agrees with Albu's emphasis on the necessity of workers participation. "After all," Strachey writes in *Tasks and Achievement of British Labour,* "what is the matter with the joint stock company is the irre-sponsible dictatorship exercised over it, nominally by its share-holders, actually in many cases by one or two self-appointing and self-perpetuating directors. Make public companies directly re-sponsible both to the community and to the whole body of those engaged in their activities, and they would become institutions of a very different kind." [2]

I have quoted the voices of some of the British Labour leaders because their views are the result of a good deal of practical experience with the socialization measures of the Labour Govern-ment, and of a thoughtful criticism of these accomplishments. But also Continental socialists have paid more and more atten-tion to workers' participation in industry than ever before. In France and Germany after the war, laws were adopted which

[1] *Ibid.,* p. 129, 130.
[2] *Ibid.,* p. 198.

provided for workers' participation in the management of enterprises. Even though the results of these new provisions were far from satisfactory (the reasons being the halfheartedness of the measures and the fact that in Germany union representatives were transformed into "managers" rather than that the workers of the factory themselves participated), it is nevertheless clear that there is a growing insight among socialists into the fact that the transfer of property rights from the private capitalist to society or the state has, in itself, only a negligible effect on the situation of the worker, and that the central problem of Socialism lies in the change of the work situation. Even in the rather weak and confused declarations of the newly formed Socialist International in Frankfurt (1951) emphasis is put on the necessity of decentralizing economic power, wherever this is compatible with the aims of planning.[1] Among scientific observers of the industrial scene, it is especially Friedmann, and to some extent Gillespie, who arrive at conclusions similar to my own, concerning the transformation of work.

Emphasizing the necessity for co-management rather than centering plans for communitarian transformation on the change of property rights does not mean that a certain degree of direct state intervention and socialization are not necessary. The most important problem, aside from co-management, lies in the fact that our whole industry is built upon the existence of an ever-widening inner market. Each enterprise wants to sell more and more in order to conquer an ever-widening share of the market. The result of this economic situation is that industry uses all means within its power to whet the buying appetite of the population, to create and reinforce the receptive orientation which is so detrimental to mental sanity. As we have seen, this means

---

[1] cf. A. Albu "The Organization of Industry," in the *New Fabian Essays, loc. cit.,* p. 121, and also A. Sturmthal "Nationalization and Workers Control in Britain and France," *The Journal of Pol. Economy,* Vol. 61, I, 1953.

that there is a craving for new but unnecessary things, a constant wish to buy more, even though from the standpoint of human, unalienated use, there is no need for the new product. (The automobile industry, for instance, spent some billion dollars on the changes for the new 1955 models, Chevrolet alone some hundred million dollars to compete with Ford. Without doubt, the older Chevrolet was a good car, and the fight between Ford and General Motors has not primarily the effect of giving the public a better car, but of making them buy a new car when the old one would have done for another few years.)[1] Another aspect of the same phenomenon is the tendency to waste, which is furthered by the economic need for increasing mass production. Aside from the economic loss implied in this waste, it has also an important psychological effect: it makes the consumer lose respect for work and human effort; it makes him forget the needs of people within his own and in poorer lands, for whom the product he wastes could be a most valuable possession; in short, our habits of waste show a childish disregard for the realities of human life, for the economic struggle for existence which nobody can evade.

It is quite obvious that in the long run no amount of spiritual influence can be successful if our economic system is organized in such a way that a crisis threatens when people do not want to buy more and more newer and better things. Hence if our aim is to change alienated into human consumption, changes are necessary in those economic processes which produce alienated consumption.[2] It is the task of economists to devise such measures.

[1] R. Moley expressed the point very lucidly: when writing in *Newsweek* on the expenses for the new 1955 car models, he stated that Capitalism wants to make people feel unhappy with what they have, so that they want to buy something new, while Socialism would want to do the opposite.

[2] cf. Clark's statement in *Condition of Economic Progress:* "The same amount of income comparatively equally distributed will create a greater relative demand for manufacture than if it is unequally distributed" (quoted from N. N. Foote and

Generally speaking, it means to direct production into fields where existing real needs have not yet been satisfied, rather than where needs must be created artificially. This can be done by means of credits through state-owned banks, by the socialization of certain enterprises, and by drastic laws which accomplish a transformation of advertising.

Closely related to this problem is that of economic help from the industrialized societies to the economically less developed part of the world. It is quite clear that the time of colonial exploitation is over, that the various parts of the world have been brought together as closely as one continent was a hundred years ago, and that peace for the wealthier part of the world is dependent on the economic advancement of the poorer part. Peace and liberty in the Western World cannot, in the long run, coexist with hunger and sickness in Africa and China. Reduction of unnecessary consumption in the industrialized countries is a must if they want to help the nonindustrialized countries, and they must want to help them, if they want peace. Let us consider a few facts: according to H. Brown, a world development program covering fifty years would increase agricultural production to the point where all persons would receive adequate nutrition and would lead to an industrialization of the now undeveloped areas similar to the prewar level of Japan.[1] The yearly outlay for the United States for such a program would be between four and five billion dollars each year for the first thirty years, and afterwards less. "When we compare this to our national income," says the author, "to our present federal budget, to the

---

P. K. Hatt, "Social Mobility and Economic Advancement," *The American Econ. Rev.*, XLII, May, 1953).

[1] cf. Harrison Brown, *The Challenge of Man's Future*, The Viking Press, New York, 1954, pp. 245 ff. I know few books which present so clearly the alternative between sanity and insanity, progress and destruction for modern society, based on compelling reasoning and indisputable facts.

funds required for armament, and to the cost of waging war, the amount required does not appear to be excessive. When we compare it to the potential gains that can result from a successful program, it appears even smaller. And when we compare the cost with that of inaction and to the consequences of maintaining the status quo, it is indeed insignificant." [1]

The foregoing problem is only part of the more general problem as to what extent the interests of profitable capital investment may be permitted to manipulate the public needs in a detrimental and unhealthy way. The most obvious examples are our movie industry, the comic-book industry and the crime pages of our newspapers. In order to make the highest profit, the lowest instincts are artificially stimulated and the mind of the public is poisoned. The Food and Drug Act has regulated the unrestricted production and advertising of harmful food and drugs; the same can be done with regard to all other vital necessities. If such laws should prove to be ineffective, certain industries, such as the film industry, must be socialized, or at least competing industries must be created, financed with public funds. In a society in which the only aim is the development of man, and in which material needs are subordinated to spiritual needs, it will not be difficult to find legal and economic means to insure the necessary changes.

As far as the economic situation of the individual citizen is concerned, the idea of equality of income has never been a socialist demand and is for many reasons neither practical nor even desirable. What is necessary is an income which will be the basis for a dignified human existence. As far as inequalities of income are concerned, it seems that they must not transcend the point where differences in income lead to differences in the experience

[1] *Ibid.*, p. 147, 148.

of life. The man with an income of millions, who can satisfy any whim without even thinking about it, experiences life in a different way from the man who to satisfy one costly wish has to sacrifice another. The man who can never travel beyond his town, who can never afford any luxury (that is to say, something that is not necessary), again has a different life experience from his neighbor who can do so. But even within certain differences of income the basic experience of life can remain the same, provided the income difference does not exceed a certain margin. What matters is not so much the greater or lesser income as such, but the point where quantitative differences of income are transformed into a qualitative difference of life experience.

Needless to say, the system of social security, as it exists now in Great Britain for instance, must be retained. But this is not enough. The existing social-security system must be extended to a *universal subsistence guarantee.*

Each individual can act as a free and responsible agent only if one of the main reasons for present-day un-freedom is abolished: the economic threat of starvation which forces people to accept working conditions which they would otherwise not accept. There will be no freedom as long as the owner of capital can enforce his will on the man who owns "only" his life, because the latter, being without capital, has no work except what the capitalist offers him.

A hundred years ago it was a widely accepted belief that no one had the responsibility for his neighbor. It was assumed—and scientifically "proved" by economists—that the laws of society made it necessary to have a vast army of poor and jobless people in order to keep the economy going. Today, hardly anybody would dare to voice this principle any longer. It is generally accepted that nobody should be excluded from the wealth of the nation, either by the laws of nature, or by those of society. The rationalizations which were current a hundred years ago, that the poor owed their condition to their ignorance, lack of responsibility —briefly, to their "sins"—are outdated. In all Western industrialized countries a system of insurance has been introduced which guarantees everyone a minimum for subsistence in case of unemployment, sickness and old age. It is only one step further to postulate that, even if these conditions are not present, everyone has a right to receive the means to subsist. Practically speaking, that would mean that every citizen can claim a sum, enough for the minimum of subsistence even though he is not unemployed, sick, or aged. He can demand this sum if he has quit his job voluntarily, if he wants to prepare himself for another type of work, or for any personal reason which prevents him from earning money, without falling under one of the categories of the existing insurance benefits; shortly, he can claim this subsistence minimum without having to have any "reason." It should be limited to a definite time period, let us say two years, so as to avoid the fostering of a neurotic attitude which refuses any kind of social obligation.

This may sound like a fantastic proposal,[1] but so would our insurance system have sounded to people a hundred years ago. The main objection to such a scheme would be that if each person were entitled to receive minimum support, people would not work. This assumption rests upon the fallacy of the inherent laziness in human nature; actually, aside from neurotically lazy people, there would be very few who would not want to earn more than the minimum, and who would prefer to do nothing rather than to work.

---

[1] Dr. Meyer Shapiro called my attention to the fact that Bertrand Russell made the same suggestion in *Proposed Roads to Freedom*, Blue Ribbon Books, New York, p. 86 ff.

However, the suspicions against a system of guaranteed subsistence minimum are not unfounded from the standpoint of those who want to use ownership of capital for the purpose of forcing others to accept the work conditions they offer. If nobody were forced any more to accept work in order not to starve, work would have to be sufficiently interesting and attractive to induce one to accept it. Freedom of contract is possible only if both parties are free to accept and reject it; in the present capitalist system this is not the case.

But such a system would be not only the beginning of real freedom of contract between employers and employees; it would also enhance tremendously the sphere of freedom in interpersonal relationships between person and person in daily life.

Let us look at some examples. A person who is employed today, and dislikes his job, is often forced to continue in it because he does not have the means to risk unemployment even for one or two months, and naturally if he quits the job, he has no right to unemployment benefits. But actually the psychological effects of this situation go much deeper; the very fact that he cannot risk being fired, tends to make him afraid of his boss or whomever he is dependent on. He will be inhibited in answering back; he will try to please and to submit, because of the constantly present fear that the boss could fire him if he asserted himself. Or let us take the man who at the age of forty decides that he wants an entirely different kind of job, for which it will take one or two years to prepare himself. Since under the conditions of a guaranteed existence minimum this decision would imply having to live with a minimum of comfort, it would require great enthusiasm for and interest in his newly chosen field, and thus only those who were gifted and really interested would make the choice. Or let us take a woman living in an unhappy marriage,

337

whose only reason for not leaving her husband is the inability to support herself even for the time necessary to be trained for a job. Or let us think of an adolescent living in severe conflicts with a neurotic or destructive father, whose mental health would be saved if he were free to leave his family. Briefly, the most fundamental coercion on economic grounds in business and private relations would be removed and the freedom to act would be restored to everybody.

What about costs? Since we already have adopted the principle for the unemployed, the sick and the aged, there would only be a marginal group of additional people who would make use of this privilege, the ones who are particularly gifted, those who find themselves in a temporary conflict, and the neurotic ones who have no sense of responsibility, or interest in work. Considering all factors involved, it would seem that the number of people using this privilege would not be extraordinarily high, and by careful research an approximate estimate could even be made today. But it must be emphasized that this proposal is to be taken together with the other social changes suggested here, and that in a society in which the individual citizen actively participates in his work, the number of people not interested in work would only be a fraction of what it is under present-day conditions. Whatever their number, it seems that the cost for such a scheme would hardly be more than what big states have spent for the maintenance of armies in the last decades, not taking into consideration the cost of armaments. It should also not be forgotten that in a system which restores interest in life and in work to everybody, the productivity of the individual worker would be far above that reported today as a result of even a few favorable changes in the work situation; in addition, our expenses due to criminality, neurotic or psychosomatic illness would be considerably less.

POLITICAL TRANSFORMATION

I have tried to show in a previous chapter that democracy cannot work in an alienated society, and that the way our democracy is organized contributes to the general process of alienation. If democracy means that the individual expresses his conviction and asserts his will, the premise is that he has a conviction, and that he has a will. The facts, however, are that the modern, alienated individual has opinions and prejudices but no convictions, has likes and dislikes, but no will. His opinions and prejudices, likes and dislikes, are manipulated in the same way as his taste is, by powerful propaganda machines—which might not be effective were he not already conditioned to such influences by advertising and by his whole alienated way of life.

The average voter is poorly informed too. While he reads his newspaper regularly, the whole world is so alienated from him that nothing makes real sense or carries real meaning. He reads of billions of dollars being spent, of millions of people being killed; figures, abstractions, which are in no way interpreted in a concrete, meaningful picture of the world. The science fiction he reads is little different from the science news. Everything is unreal, unlimited, impersonal. Facts are so many lists of memory items, like puzzles in a game, not elements on which his life and that of his children depends. It is indeed a sign of resilience and basic sanity of the average human being, that in spite of these conditions, political choices today are not entirely irrational, but that to some extent sober judgment finds expression in the process of voting.

In addition to all this, one must not forget that the very idea of majority vote lends itself to the process of abstractification and alienation. Originally, majority rule was an alternative to minority rule, the rule by the king or feudal lords. It did not mean that the majority was *right;* it meant that it is better for the majority to be wrong than for a minority to impose its will on the majority. But in our age of conformity the democratic method has more and more assumed the meaning that a majority decision is necessarily right, and morally superior to that of the minority, and hence has the moral right to impose *its* will on the minority. Just as a nationally advertised product claims, "Ten million Americans can't be wrong," so the majority decision is taken as an argument for its rightness. This is obviously an error; in fact, historically speaking, all "right" ideas in politics as well as in philosophy, religion or science, were originally the ideas of minorities. If one had decided the value of an idea on the basis of numbers, we would still be dwelling in caves.

As Schumpeter has pointed out, the voter simply expresses preferences between two candidates competing for his vote. He is confronted with various political machines, with a political bureaucracy which is torn between good will for the best for the country, and the professional interest of keeping in office, or getting back into it. This political bureaucracy, needing votes is, of course, forced to pay attention to the will of the voter to some extent. Any signs of great dissatisfaction force the political parties to change their course in order to obtain votes, and any sign of a very popular course of action will induce them to continue it. In this respect even the nondemocratic authoritarian regime is to some extent dependent on the popular will, except that by its coercive methods it can afford for a much longer time to pursue an unpopular course. But aside from the restricting or furthering influence which the electorate has on the decisions of the political bureaucracy, and which is more an indirect than a direct influence, there is little the individual citizen can do to participate in the decision making. Once he has cast his vote, he has abdicated his political will to his representative, who exercises it according to the mixture of responsibility and egotistical professional interest which is characteristic of him, and the individual citizen can do little except vote at the next election, which gives him a chance to continue his representative in office or "to throw the rascals out." The voting process in the great democracies has more and more the character of a plebiscite, in which the voter cannot do much more than register agreement or disagreement with powerful political machines, to one of which he surrenders his political will.

The progress of the democratic process from the middle of the nineteenth to the middle of the twentieth centuries is one of the enlargement of franchise, which has by now led to the general acceptance of unrestricted and universal suffrage. But even the fullest franchise is not enough. The further progress of the democratic system must take a new step. In the first place, it must be recognized that true decisions cannot be made in an atmosphere of mass voting, but only in the relatively small groups corresponding perhaps to the old Town Meeting, and comprising not more than let us say five hundred people. In such small groups the issues at stake can be discussed thoroughly, each member can express his ideas, can listen to, and discuss reasonably other arguments. People have personal contact with each other, which makes it more difficult for demagogic and irrational influences to work on their minds. Secondly, the individual citizen must be in the possession of vital facts which enables him to make a reasonable decision. Thirdly, whatever he, as a member of such a small and face-to-face group decides, must have a direct influence on the decision making exercised by a centrally elected parliamentary executive. If this were not so, the citizen would remain as politically stupid as he is today.

The question arises whether such a system of combining a centralized form of democracy, as it exists today, with a high degree of decentralization is possible; whether we can reintroduce the principle of the Town Meeting into modern industrialized society.

I do not see any insoluble difficulty in this. One possibility is to organize the whole population into small groups of say five hundred people, according to local residence, or place of work, and as far as possible these groups should have a certain diversification in their social composition. These groups would meet regularly, let us say once a month, and choose their officials and committees, which would have to change every year. Their program would be the discussion of the main political issues, both of local and of national concern. According to the principle mentioned above, any such discussion, if it is to be reasonable, will require a certain amount of factual information. How can this be given? It seems perfectly feasible that a cultural agency, which is politically independent, can exercise the function of preparing and publishing factual data to be used as material in these discussions. This is only what we do in our school system, where our children are given information which is relatively objective and free from the influence of fluctuating governments. One could imagine arrangements, for instance, by which personalities from the fields of art, sciences, religion, business, politics, whose outstanding achievements and moral integrity are beyond doubt, could be chosen to form a nonpolitical cultural agency. They would differ in their political views, but it can be assumed that they could agree reasonably on what is to be considered objective information about facts. In the case of disagreement, different sets of facts could be presented to the citizens, explaining the basis for the difference. After the small face-to-face groups have received information and have discussed matters, they will vote; with the help of the technical devices we have today, it would be very easy to register the over-all result of these votes in a short time, and then the problem would be how decisions arrived at in this way could be channeled into the level of the central government and made effective in the field of decision making. There is no reason why forms for this process could not be found. In the parliamentary tradition we have usually two parliamentary houses, both participating in the decision making, but elected according to different principles. The decision of the face-to-face groups would constitute the true "House of Commons," which would share power with the house of universally elected representatives and a universally elected executive. In this way, decision making would constantly flow, not only from above to below, but from below to above, and it would be based on an active and responsible thinking of the individual citizen. Through the discussion and voting in small face-to-face groups, a good deal of the irrational and abstract character of decision making would disappear, and political problems would become in reality a concern for the citizen. The process of alienation in which the individual citizen surrenders his political will by the ritual of voting to powers beyond him would be reversed, and each individual would take back into himself his role as a participant in the life of the community.[1]

CULTURAL TRANSFORMATION

No social or political arrangement can do more than further or hinder the realization of certain values and ideals. The ideals of the Judaeo-Christian tradition cannot possibly become realities in a materialistic civilization whose structure is centered around production, consumption and success on the market. On the other hand, no socialist society could fulfill the goal of brotherliness, justice and individualism unless its ideas are capable of filling the hearts of man with a new spirit.

We do not need new ideals or new spiritual goals. The great

[1] cf. to the problem of face-to-face groups, Robert A. Nisbet, *The Quest for Community*, Oxford University Press, New York, 1953.

teachers of the human race have postulated the norms for sane living. To be sure, they have spoken in different languages, have emphasized different aspects and have had different views on certain subjects. But, altogether, these differences were small; the fact that the great religions and ethical systems have so often fought against each other, and emphasized their mutual differences rather than their basic similarities, was due to the influence of those who built churches, hierarchies, political organizations upon the simple foundations of truth laid down by the men of the spirit. Since the human race made the decisive turn away from rootedness in nature and animal existence, to find a new home in conscience and brotherly solidarity, since it conceived first the idea of the unity of the human race and its destiny to become fully born—the ideas and ideals have been the same. In every center of culture, and largely without any mutual influence, the same insights were discovered, the same ideals were preached. We, today, who have easy access to all these ideas, who are still the immediate heirs to the great humanistic teachings, we are not in need of new knowledge of how to live sanely—but in bitter need of taking seriously what we believe, what we preach and teach. The revolution of our hearts does not require new wisdom—but new seriousness and dedication.

The task of impressing on people the guiding ideals and norms of our civilization is, first of all, that of education. But how woefully inadequate is our educational system for this task. Its aim is primarily to give the individual the knowledge he needs in order to function in an industrialized civilization, and to form his character into the mold which is needed: ambitious and competitive, yet co-operative within certain limits; respectful of authority, yet "desirably independent," as some report cards have it; friendly, yet not deeply attached to anybody or anything. Our high schools and colleges continue with the task of providing their students with the knowledge they must have to fulfill their practical tasks in life, and with the character traits wanted on the personality market. Very little, indeed, do they succeed in imbuing them with the faculty of critical thought, or with character traits which correspond to the professed ideals of our civilization. Surely there is no need to elaborate on this point, and to repeat a criticism which has been made so competently by Robert Hutchins and others. There is only one point which I want to emphasize here: the necessity of doing away with the harmful separation between theoretical and practical knowledge. This very separation is part of the alienation of work and thought. It tends to separate theory from practice, and to make it more difficult, rather than easier, for the individual to participate meaningfully in the work he is doing. If work is to become an activity based on his knowledge and on the understanding of what he is doing, then indeed there must be a drastic change in our method of education, in the sense that from the very beginning theoretical instruction and practical work are combined; for the young people, practical work should be secondary to theoretical instruction; for the people beyond school age, it should be the reverse; but at no age of development would the two spheres be separated from each other. No youngster should graduate from school unless he had learned some kind of handicraft in a satisfactory and meaningful manner; no primary education would be considered finished before the student has a grasp of the fundamental technical processes of our industry. Certainly high school ought to combine practical work of a handicraft and of modern industrial technique with theoretical instruction.

The fact that we aim primarily at the usefulness of our citizens for the purposes of the social machine, and not at their human development is apparent in the fact that we consider education necessary only up to the age of fourteen, eighteen, or at most, the early twenties. Why should society feel responsible only for the education of children, and not for the education of all adults of every age? Actually, as Alvin Johnson has pointed out so convincingly, the age between six and eighteen is not by far as suitable for learning as is generally assumed. It is, of course, the best age to learn the three R's, and languages, but undoubtedly the understanding of history, philosophy, religion, literature, psychology, etcetera, is limited at this early age, and in fact, even around twenty, at which age these subjects are taught in college, is not ideal. In many instances to really understand the problems in these fields, a person must have had a great deal more experience in living than he has had at college age. For many people the age of thirty or forty is much more appropriate for learning—in the sense of understanding rather than of memorizing—than school or college age, and in many instances the general interest is also greater at the later age than at the stormy period of youth. It is around this age also at which a person should be free to change his occupation completely, and hence to have a chance to study again, the same chance which today we permit only our youngsters.

A sane society must provide possibilities for adult education, much as it provides today for the schooling of children. This principle finds expression today in the increasing number of adult-education courses, but all these private arrangements encompass only a small segment of the population, and the principle needs to be applied to the population as a whole.

Schooling, be it transmission of knowledge or formation of character, is only one part, and perhaps not the most important part of education; using "education" here in its literal and most fundamental sense of "e-ducere" = "to bring out," that which is within man. Even if man has knowledge, even if he performs his work well, if he is decent, honest, and has no worries with regard to his material needs—he is not and cannot be satisfied. Man, in order to feel at home in the world, must grasp it not only with his head, but with all his senses, his eyes, his ears, with all his body. He must act out with his body what he thinks out with his brain. Body and mind cannot be separated in this, or in any other aspect. If man grasps the world and thus unites himself with it by thought, he creates philosophy, theology, myth and science. If man expresses his grasp of the world by his senses, he creates art and ritual, he creates song, dance, drama, painting, sculpture. Using the word "art," we are influenced by its usage in the modern sense, as a separate area of life. We have, on the one hand, the artist, a specialized profession—and on the other hand the admirer and consumer of art. But this separation is a modern phenomenon. Not that there were not "artists" in all great civilizations. The creation of the great Egyptian, Greek or Italian sculptures were the work of extraordinarily gifted artists who specialized in their art; so were the creators of Greek drama or of music since the seventeenth century.

But what about a Gothic cathedral, a Catholic ritual, an Indian rain dance, a Japanese flower arrangement, a folk dance, community singing? Are they art? Popular art? We have no word for it, because art in a wide and general sense, as a part of everybody's life, has lost its place in our world. What word can we use then? In the discussion of alienation I used the term "ritual." The difficulty here is, of course, that it carries a religious meaning, which puts it again in a special and separate sphere. For lack of a better word, I shall use "collective art," meaning the same as ritual; it means *to respond to the world with our senses in a meaningful, skilled, productive, active, shared way.* In this description the "shared" is important, and differentiates the concept of "collective art" from that of art in the modern sense. The latter is individualistic, both in its production, and in its consumption.

"Collective art," is shared; it permits man to feel one with others in a meaningful, rich, productive way. It is not an individual "leisure time" occupation, *added* to life, it is an integral part of life. It corresponds to a basic human need, and if this need is not fulfilled, man remains as insecure and anxious as if the need for a meaningful thought picture of the world were unrealized. In order to grow out of the receptive into the productive orientation, he must relate himself to the world artistically and not only philosophically or scientifically. If a culture does not offer such a realization, the average person does not develop beyond his receptive or marketing orientation.

Where are *we?* Religious rituals have little importance any more, except for the Catholics. Secular rituals hardly exist. Aside from the attempts to imitate rituals in lodges, fraternities, etc., we have a few patriotic and sport rituals, appealing only to a most limited extent to the needs of the total personality. We are a culture of consumers. We "drink in" the movies, the crime reports, the liquor, the fun. There is no active productive participation, no common unifying experience, no meaningful acting out of significant answers to life. What do we expect from our young generation? What are they to do when they have no opportunity for meaningful, shared artistic activities? What else are they to do but to escape into drinking, movie-daydreaming, crime, neurosis and insanity? What help is it to have almost no illiteracy, and the most widespread higher education which has existed at any time—if we have no collective expression of our total personalities, no common art and ritual? Undoubtedly a relatively primitive village in which there are still real feasts, common artistic shared expressions, and no literacy at all—is more advanced culturally and more healthy mentally than our educated, newspaper-reading, radio-listening culture.

No sane society can be built upon the mixture of purely intellectual knowledge and almost complete absence of shared artistic experience, college plus football, crime stories plus Fourth of July celebrations, with Mothers' and Fathers' day and Christmas thrown in for good measure. In considering how we can build a sane society, we must recognize that the need for the creation of collective art and ritual on a nonclerical basis is at least as important as literacy and higher education. The transformation of an atomistic into a communitarian society depends on creating again the opportunity for people to sing together, walk together, dance together, admire together—together, and not, to use Riesman's succinct expression, as a member of a "lonely crowd."

A number of attempts have been made to revive collective art and ritual. The "Religion of Reason" with its new feast days and rituals, was the form created by the French Revolution. National feelings created some new rituals, but they never gained the importance which the lost religious ritual once had. Socialism created its ritual in the First of May celebration, in the use of the fraternal "comrade," etcetera, but the significance was never greater than that of the patriotic ritual. Perhaps the most original and profound expression of collective art and ritual was to be found in the German Youth movement, which flourished in the years before and after the first World War. But this movement remained rather esoteric and was drowned in the rising flood of Nationalism and Racism.

On the whole, our modern ritual is impoverished and does not fulfill man's need for collective art and ritual, even in the remotest sense, either as to quality or its quantitive significance in life.

What are we to do? Can we invent rituals? Can one artificially create collective art? Of course not! But once one recognizes the need for them, once one begins to cultivate them, seeds will grow, and gifted people will come forth who will add new forms to old ones, and new talents will appear which would have gone unnoticed without such new orientation.

Collective art will begin with the children's games in kindergarten, be continued in school, then in later life. We shall have common dances, choirs, plays, music, bands, not entirely replacing modern sport, but subordinating it to the role of one of the many nonprofit and nonpurpose activities.

Here again, as in industrial and political organization, the decisive factor is decentralization; concrete face-to-face groups, active responsible participation. In the factory, in the school, in the small political discussion groups, in the village, various forms of common artistic activities can be created; they can be stimulated as much as is necessary by the help and suggestion from central artistic bodies, but not "fed" by them. At the same time, modern radio and television techniques give marvelous possibilities to bring the best of music and literature to large audiences. Needless to say it cannot be left to business to provide for these opportunities, but that they must rank with our educational facilities which do not make a profit for anybody.

It might be argued that the idea of a large-scale revival of ritual and collective art is romantic; that it suits an age of handicrafts, and not an age of machine production. If this objection were true, we might as well resign ourselves to the fact that our way of life would destroy itself soon, because of its lack of balance, and sanity. But actually, the objection is not any more compelling than the objections made to the "possibility" of railroads and heavier-than-air flying machines. There is only one valid point in this objection. The way we *are*, atomized, alienated, without any genuine sense of community, we shall not be able to create new forms of collective art and ritual.

But this is just what I have been emphasizing all along. One cannot separate the change in our industrial and political organization from that of the structure of our educational and cultural life. No serious attempt for change and reconstruction will succeed if it is not undertaken in all those spheres simultaneously.

Can one speak of a spiritual transformation of society without mentioning *religion?* Undoubtedly, the teachings of the great monotheistic religions stress the humanistic aims which are the same as those which underlie the "productive orientation." The aims of Christianity and Judaism are those of the dignity of man as an aim and an end in himself, of brotherly love, of reason and of the supremacy of spiritual over material values. These ethical aims are related to certain concepts of God in which the believers of the various religions differ among themselves, and which are unacceptable to millions of others. However, it was an error of the nonbelievers to focus on attacking the idea of God; their real aim ought to be to challenge religionists to take their religion, and especially the concept of God, seriously; that would mean to practice the spirit of brotherly love, truth and justice, hence to become the most radical critics of present-day society.

On the other hand, even from a strictly monotheistic standpoint, discussions about God mean to use God's name in vain. But while we cannot say what God *is,* we can state what God is *not.* Is it not time to cease to argue about God, and instead to unite in the unmasking of contemporary forms of idolatry? Today it is not Baal and Astarte but the deification of the state and of power in authoritarian countries and the deification of the machine and of success in our own culture; it is the all-pervading alienation which threatens the spiritual qualities of man. Whether we are religionists or not, whether we believe in the necessity for a new religion or in the continuation of the Judaeo-Christian tradition, inasmuch as we are concerned with the essence and not with the shell, with the experience and not with the word, with man and not with the institution, we can unite in firm negation of idolatry and find perhaps more of a common faith in this negation than in any affirmative statements about God. Certainly we shall find more of humility and of brotherly love.

This statement remains true even if one believes, as I do, that the theistic concepts are bound to disappear in the future development of humanity. In fact, for those who see in the monotheistic religions only one of the stations in the evolution of the human race, it is not too far-fetched to believe that a new religion will develop within the next few hundred years, a religion which corresponds to the development of the human race; the most important feature of such a religion would be its universalistic character, corresponding to the unification of mankind which is taking place in this epoch; it would embrace the humanistic teachings common to all great religions of the East and of the West; its doctrines would not contradict the rational insight of mankind today, and its emphasis would be on the practice of life, rather than on doctrinal beliefs. Such a religion would create new rituals and artistic forms of expression, conducive to the spirit of reverence toward life and the solidarity of man. Religion can, of course, not be invented. It will come into existence with the appearance of a new great teacher, just as they have appeared in previous centuries when the time was ripe. In the meantime, those who believe in God should express their faith by *living* it; those who do not believe, by living the precepts of love and justice and— waiting.[1]

[1] The same suggestion for a new humanistic religion has been made by Julian Huxley in "Evolutionary Humanism," *The Humanist*, Vol. XII, 5, 1953, p. 201 ff.

▪ 9 ▪

SUMMARY—CONCLUSION

Man first emerged from the animal world as a freak of nature. Having lost most of the instinctive equipment which regulates the animal's activities, he was more helpless, less well equipped for the fight for survival, than most animals. Yet he had developed a capacity for thought, imagination and self-awareness, which was the basis for transforming nature and himself. For many thousands of generations man lived by food gathering and hunting. He was still tied to nature, and afraid of being cast out from her. He identified himself with animals and worshiped these representatives of nature as his gods. After a long period of slow development, man began to cultivate the soil, to create a new social and religious order based on agriculture and animal husbandry. During this period he worshiped goddesses as the bearers of natural fertility, experienced himself as the child dependent on the fertility of the earth, on the life-giving breast of Mother. At a time some four thousand years ago, a decisive turn in man's history took place. He took a new step in the long-drawn-out process of his emergence from nature. He severed the ties with nature and with Mother, and set himself a new goal, that of being fully born, of being fully awake, of being fully human; of being free.

Reason and conscience became the principles which were to guide him; his aim was a society bound by the bonds of brotherly love, justice and truth, a new and truly human home to take the place of the irretrievably lost home in nature.

And then again about five hundred years before Christ in the great religious systems of India, Greece, Palestine, Persia and China, the idea of the unity of mankind and of a unifying spiritual principle underlying all reality assumed new and more developed expressions. Lao-tse, Buddha, Isaiah, Heraclitus and Socrates, and later, on Palestinian soil, Jesus and the Apostles, on American soil, Quetzalcoatl, and later again, on Arabian soil, Mohammed, taught the ideas of the unity of man, of reason, love and justice as the goals man must strive for.

Northern Europe seemed to sleep for a long time. Greek and Christian ideas were transmitted to its soil, and it took a thousand years before Europe was saturated with them. Around 1500 A.D. a new period began. Man discovered nature and the individual, he laid the foundations for the natural sciences, which began to transform the face of the earth. The closed world of the Middle Ages collapsed, the unifying heaven broke up, man found a new unifying principle in science, and was searching for a new unity in the social and political unification of the earth and in the domination of nature. Moral conscience, the heritage of the Judaeo-Christian tradition, and intellectual conscience, the heritage of the Greek tradition, fused and brought about a flowering of human creation as man had hardly ever known it before.

Europe, the youngest child of humanity, culturally speaking, developed such wealth and such weapons that it became the master of the rest of the world for several hundred years. But again, in the middle of the twentieth century, a drastic change is occurring, a change as great as ever occurred in the past. The new techniques replace the use of the physical energy of animals and men by that of steam, oil and electricity; they create means of communication which transform the earth into the size of one continent, and the human race into one society where the fate of one group is the fate of all; they create marvels of devices which permit the best of art, literature and music to be brought to every member of society; they create productive forces which will permit everybody to have a dignified material existence, and reduces work to such dimensions that it will fill only a fraction of man's day.

Yet today, when man seems to have reached the beginning of a new, richer, happier human era, his existence and that of the generations to follow is more threatened than ever. How is this possible?

Man had won his freedom from clerical and secular authorities, he stood alone with his reason and his conscience as his only judges, but he was afraid of the newly won freedom; he had achieved "freedom from"—without yet having achieved "freedom to"—to be himself, to be productive, to be fully awake. Thus he tried to escape from freedom. His very achievement, the mastery over nature, opened up the avenues for his escape.

In building the new industrial machine, man became so absorbed in the new task that it became the paramount goal of his life. His energies, which once were devoted to the search for God and salvation, were now directed toward the domination of nature and ever-increasing material comfort. He ceased to use production as a means for a better life, but hypostatized it instead to an end in itself, an end to which life was subordinated. In the process of an ever-increasing division of labor, ever-increasing mechanization of work, and an ever-increasing size of social agglomerations, man himself became a part of the machine, rather than its master. He experienced himself as a commodity, as an investment; his aim became to be a success, that is, to sell himself as profitably as possible on the market. His value as a person lies in his salability, not in his human qualities of love, reason, or in his artistic capacities. Happiness becomes identical with consumption of newer and better commodities, the drinking in of music, screen plays, fun, sex, liquor and cigarettes. Not having a sense of self except the one which conformity with the majority can give, he is insecure, anxious, depending on approval. He is alienated from himself, worships the product of his own hands, the leaders of his own making, as if they were above him, rather than made by him. He is in a sense back where he was before the great human evolution began in the second millennium B.C.

He is incapable to love and to use his reason, to make decisions, in fact incapable to appreciate life and thus ready and even willing to destroy everything. The world is again fragmentalized, has lost its unity; he is again worshiping diversified things, with the only exception that now they are man-made, rather than part of nature.

The new era started with the idea of individual initiative. Indeed, the discoverers of new worlds and sea lanes in the sixteenth and seventeenth centuries, the pioneers of science, and the founders of new philosophies, the statesmen and philosophers of the great English, French and American revolutions, and eventually, the industrial pioneers, and even the robber barons showed marvelous individual initiative. But with the bureaucratization and managerialization of Capitalism, it is exactly the individual initiative that is disappearing. Bureaucracy has little initiative, that is its nature; nor have automatons. The cry for individual initiative as an argument for Capitalism is at best a nostalgic yearning, and at worst a deceitful slogan used against those plans for reform which are based on the idea of truly human individual initiative. Modern society has started out with the vision of creating a culture which would fulfil man's needs; it has as its ideal the harmony between the individual and social needs, the end of the conflict between human nature and the social order. One believed one would arrive at this goal in two ways; by the increased productive technique which permitted feeding everybody satisfactorily, and by a rational, objective picture of man and of his real needs. Putting it differently, the aim of the efforts of modern man was to create a sane society. More specifically, this meant a society whose members have developed their reason to that point of objectivity which permits them to see themselves, others, nature, in their true reality, and not distorted by infantile omniscience or paranoid hate. It meant a society, whose members have developed to a point of independence when they know the difference between good and evil, where they make their own choices, where they have convictions rather than opinions, faith rather than superstitions or nebulous hopes. It meant a society whose members have developed the capacity to love their children, their neighbors, all men, themselves, all of nature; who can feel one with all, yet retain their sense of individuality and integrity; who transcend nature by creating, not by destroying.

So far, we have failed. We have not bridged the gap between a minority which realized these goals and tried to live according to them, and the majority whose mentality is far back, in the Stone Age, in totemism, in idol worship, in feudalism. Will the majority be converted to sanity—or will it use the greatest discoveries of human reason for its own purposes of unreason and insanity? Will we be able to create a vision of the good, sane life, which will stir the life forces of those afraid of marching forward? This time, mankind is at one crossroad where the wrong step could be the last step.

In the middle of the twentieth century, two great social collosi have developed which, being afraid of each other, seek security in ever-increasing military rearmament. The United States and her allies are wealthier; their standard of living is higher, their interest in comfort and pleasure is greater than that of their rivals, the Soviet Union and her satellites, and China. Both rivals claim that their system promises final salvation for man, guarantees the paradise of the future. Both claim that the opponent represents the exact opposite to himself, and that his system must be eradicated—in the short or long run—if mankind is to be saved. Both rivals speak in terms of nineteenth-century ideals. The West in the name of the ideas of the French Revolution, of liberty, reason, individualism. The East in the name of the socialist ideas of solidarity, equality. They both succeed in capturing the imagination and the fanatical allegiance of hundreds of millions of people.

There is today a decisive difference between the two systems. In the Western world there is freedom to express ideas critical of the existing system. In the Soviet world criticism and expression of different ideas is suppressed by brutal force. Hence, the Western world carries within itself the possibility for peaceful progressive transformation, while in the Soviet world such possibilities are almost non-existent; in the Western world the life of the individual is free from the terror of imprisonment, torture or death, which confront any member of the Soviet society who has not become a well-functioning automaton. Indeed, life in the Western world has been, and is even now sometimes as rich and joyous as it has ever been anywhere in human history; life in the Soviet system can never be joyous, as indeed it can never be where the executioner watches behind the door.

But without ignoring the tremendous differences between free Capitalism and authoritarian Communism today, it is short-sighted not to see the similarities, especially as they will develop in the future. Both systems are based on industrialization, their goal is ever-increasing economic efficiency and wealth. They are societies run by a managerial class, and by professional politicians. They both are thoroughly materialistic in their outlook, regardless of Christian ideology in the West and secular messianism in the East. They organize man in a centralized system, in large factories, political mass parties. Everybody is a cog in the machine, and has to function smoothly. In the West, this is achieved by a method of psychological conditioning, mass suggestion, monetary rewards. In the East by all this, plus the use of terror. It is to be assumed that the more the Soviet system develops economically, the less severely will it have to exploit the majority of the population, hence the more can terror be replaced by methods of psychological manipulation. The West develops rapidly in the direction of Huxley's *Brave New World,* the East *is* today Orwell's "1984." But both systems tend to converge.

What, then, are the prospects for the future? The first, and perhaps most likely possibility, is that of atomic war. The most likely outcome of such a war is the destruction of industrial civilization, and the regression of the world to a primitive agrarian level. Or, if the destruction should not prove to be as thorough as many specialists in the field believe, the result will be the necessity for the victor to organize and dominate the whole world. This could only happen in a centralized state based on force—and it would make little difference whether Moscow or Washington were the seat of government. But, unfortunately, even the avoidance of war alone does not promise a bright future. In the development of both Capitalism and of Communism as we can visualize them in the next fifty or a hundred years, the process of automatization and alienation will proceed. Both systems are developing into managerial societies, their inhabitants well fed, well clad, having their wishes satisfied, and not having wishes which cannot be satisfied; automatons, who follow without force, who are guided without leaders, who make machines which act like men and produce men who act like machines; men, whose reason deteriorates while their intelligence rises, thus creating the dangerous situation of equipping man with the greatest material power without the wisdom to use it.

This alienation and automatization leads to an ever-increasing insanity. Life has no meaning, there is no joy, no faith, no reality. Everybody is "happy"—except that he does not feel, does not reason, does not love.

In the nineteenth century the problem was that *God is dead;* in the twentieth century the problem is that *man is dead.* In the nineteenth century inhumanity meant cruelty; in the twentieth century it means schizoid self-alienation. The danger of the past was that men became slaves. The danger of the future is that men may become robots. True enough, robots do not rebel. But given man's nature, robots cannot live and remain sane, they become "Golems," they will destroy their world and themselves because they cannot stand any longer the boredom of a meaningless life.

Our dangers are war and robotism. What is the alternative? To get out of the rut in which we are moving, and to take the next step in the birth and self-realization of humanity. The first condition is the abolishment of the war threat hanging over all of us now and paralyzing faith and initiative. We must take the responsibility for the life of all men, and develop on an international scale what all great countries have developed internally, a relative sharing of wealth and a new and more just division of economic resources. This must lead eventually to forms of international economic co-operation and planning, to forms of world government and to complete disarmament. We must retain the industrial method. But we must decentralize work and state so as to give it *human proportions,* and permit centralization only to an optimal point which is necessary because of the requirements of industry. In the economic sphere we need co-management of all who work in an enterprise, to permit their active and responsible participation. The new forms for such participation can be found. In the political sphere, return to the town meetings, by creating thousands of small face-to-face groups, which are well informed, which discuss, and whose decisions are integrated in a new "lower house." A cultural renaissance must combine work education for the young, adult education and a new system of popular art and secular ritual throughout the whole nation.

Our only alternative to the danger of robotism is humanistic communitarianism. The problem is not primarily the legal problem of property ownership, nor that of sharing *profits;* it is that of sharing *work,* sharing *experience.* Changes in ownership must be made to the extent to which they are necessary to create a community of work, and to prevent the profit motive from directing production into socially harmful directions. Income must be equalized to the extent of giving everybody the material basis for a dignified life, and thus preventing the economic differences from creating a fundamentally different experience of life for various social classes. Man must be restituted to his supreme place in society, never being a means, never a thing to be used by others or by himself. Man's use by man must end, and economy must become the servant for the development of man. Capital must serve labor, things must serve life. Instead of the exploitative and hoarding orientation, dominant in the nineteenth century, and the receptive and marketing orientation dominant today, the *productive orientation* must be the end which all social arrangements serve.

No change must be brought about by force, it must be a simultaneous one in the economic, political and cultural spheres. Changes restricted to *one* sphere are destructive of every change.

Just as primitive man was helpless before natural forces, modern man is helpless before the social and economic forces created by himself. He worships the works of his own hands, bowing to the new idols, yet swearing by the name of the God who commanded him to destroy all idols. Man can protect himself from the consequences of his own madness only by creating a sane society which conforms with the needs of man, needs which are rooted in the very conditions of his existence. A society in which man relates to man lovingly, in which he is rooted in bonds of brotherliness and solidarity, rather than in the ties of blood and soil; a society which gives him the possibility of transcending nature by creating rather than by destroying, in which everyone gains a sense of self by experiencing himself as the subject of his powers rather than by conformity, in which a system of orientation and devotion exists without man's needing to distort reality and to worship idols.

Building such a society means taking the next step; it means the end of "humanoid" history, the phase in which man had not become fully human. It does not mean the "end of days," the "completion," the state of perfect harmony in which no conflicts or problems confront men. On the contrary, it is man's fate that his existence is beset by contradictions, which he has to solve without ever solving them. When he has overcome the primitive state of human sacrifice, be it in the ritualistic form of the Aztecs or in the secular form of war, when he has been able to regulate his relationship with nature reasonably instead of blindly, when things have truly become his servants rather than his idols, he will be confronted with the truly human conflicts and problems; he will have to be adventuresome, courageous, imaginative, capable of suffering and of joy, but his powers will be in the service of life, and not in the service of death. The new phase of human history, if it comes to pass, will be a new beginning, not an end.

Man today is confronted with the most fundamental choice; not that between Capitalism or Communism, but that between *robotism* (of both the capitalist and the communist variety), or Humanistic Communitarian Socialism. Most facts seem to indicate that he is choosing robotism, and that means, in the long run, insanity and destruction. But all these facts are not strong enough to destroy faith in man's reason, good will and sanity. As long as we can think of other alternatives, we are not lost; as long as we can consult together and plan together, we can hope. But, indeed, the shadows are lengthening; the voices of insanity are becoming louder. We are in reach of achieving a state of humanity which corresponds to the vision of our great teachers; yet we are in danger of the destruction of all civilization, or of robotization. A small tribe was told thousands of years ago: "I put before you life and death, blessing and curse—and you chose life." This is our choice too.

INDEX

368